PAPA'S LAST WORDS

THEY
LIED
ABOUT
G☦D

PAPA'S LAST WORDS

THEY LIED ABOUT G✝D

When the inconsistencies in mainstream
Christianity no longer suffice...

R. H. BEN-SHALOM

ERAS Press

ERAS Press, LLC

Papa's Last Words: They Lied About God

Copyright © 2020 by R. H. Ben-Shalom

Scriptures marked NASB are taken from the NEW AMERICAN STANDARD BIBLE (NASB): Scripture taken from the NEW AMERICAN STANDARD BIBLE®, copyright© 1960, 1962, 1963, 1968, 1971, 1972, 1973, 1975, 1977, 1995 by The Lockman Foundation. Used by permission.

Scriptures marked CJB are taken from the COMPLETE JEWISH BIBLE (CJB): Scripture taken from the COMPLETE JEWISH BIBLE, copyright© 1998 by David H. Stern. Published by Jewish New Testament Publications, Inc. www.messianicjewish.net/ jntp. Distributed by Messianic Jewish Resources Int'l. www.messianicjewish.net. All rights reserved. Used by permission.

Scriptures marked YLT are taken from the 1898 YOUNG'S LITERAL TRANSLATION OF THE HOLY BIBLE (YLT): YOUNG'S LITERAL TRANSLATION OF THE HOLY BIBLE by J. N. Young, (Author of the Young's Analytical Concordance), public domain.

Edited by Tasche Laine from EditProof Services and Sky Rodio Nuttall
Cover design and formatting by Damonza.com

Library of Congress Control Number: 2020910484

ISBN: 978-1-952544-00-2 (hbk)
ISBN: 978-1-952544-01-9 (pbk)
ISBN: 978-1-952544-02-6 (ebk)

For information about special discounts on bulk purchases, or for information on bringing authors to your live event, please contact ERAS Press. All inquiries should be addressed to info@ERASpress.com.

HELP

I use a lot of uncommon names in this book, and many suggested that I include a visual aid.

As my thanks to you, my readers, I am offering this additional resource for free. Please go to www.eraspress.com/they-lied and subscribe. You will receive an email with a link to the PDF file. Print it in either color or grayscale, fold it in three, and it can double as a bookmark while reading. Lamination is also an option. The bookmark will have a list of the uncommon names linked with their more mainstream names (e.g. Y'hoshua = Jesus).

Other than the bookmark, the only time you should receive further emails is when the next book publishes. So, no more than once a year, and no more than a grand total of three.

Your email address WILL NOT be sold to any third parties. I hate that sort of thing too.

In memory of Nanay, my mother, who was the first to teach me the greatest matter of life—God. I love you and miss you deeply. I am now implementing everything you ever taught me, everything you thought I did not heed. I hope I made you proud, Mom. Until we see each other again in His Kingdom . . .

"And it will come about that whoever calls on the Name of YHVH will be saved; for on Mount Tziyon and in Yerushalayim there is an escape, as YHVH has said, and among the remnants whom YHVH is calling."

–Joel 2:32

ACKNOWLEDGMENTS

To Nanay, my mom, my earthly inspiration, an example of steadfast godliness, ferocious tenacity, and joyful grace, who exhorted me to seek and stand upon the Truth at all costs.

To my wife, who challenges me to defend my beliefs with clarity, constantly encourages me to obey God's calling, and supports my spiritual leadership of our household.

To my children, who inspire me to strive for higher standards, who inspire me to be as amazing a person and parent as my mom, who give me the drive to reach the goals that God sets for me, and whose care God has given to me as my purpose.

To Jeffrey Adam, with whom I sought the meaning of life and with whom I now walk in the meaning of life, and to Michael Allen, who taught me how to read the Scriptures.

To Rusty W. and Rod B., pastors from my past who let me know that I wasn't crazy and isolated in hearing the voice of God.

To John Michael, with whom I can test my beliefs against the Truth with care of keeping integrity to His written Word.

To Amy Nicole, who dedicated much time in pouring over my words and provided much needed and unbiased constructive criticism.

To Richard Mark, who mentors me in the Way but gives me the freedom of disagreement without condemnation, who enlightens me with pieces of the Truth and whose deep understanding of His written Word challenges me to plumb deeper into the Scriptures.

CONTENTS

INTRODUCTION

My Children,

WHY DID I write this book?

I have this urgency to leave behind a legacy for you . . . as if the Lord will take me home soon, home being wherever He is, whether that be the mainstream Gentile Christian idea of heaven, or the Hebrew perspective of paradise (Eden in Hebrew). I do not believe there is any way to be sure how the details of the afterlife work, despite the assurances of many. My only assurance is that home will be wherever He is, and that is sweet enough for me.

What kind of legacy do I leave for you?

Is it stashes of firearms for a violent revolution if the government becomes hostile, as some former military and military enthusiasts would encourage? Is it stashes of gold or cash or stocks to provide financial security that might spoil your spirit for eternity, as some financial gurus advise? Is it a house in the middle of nowhere, powered off the grid so you can hide away from all people, as some ultra-conservative American Christians rave? Is it political clout, fame, or status, with which the world seems to be spellbound?

The legacy I give to you, the dearest thing for me to give to you before I leave this temporal world, is my testimony—my testimony of my relationship with my God. He is the God of Avraham, Yitzchak (Isaac), and

Ya'akov (Jacob). When no one was with me and Nanay could not protect me, He walked me through the valleys of sexual abuse, physical abuse, attempted suicide, isolation, loneliness, betrayal, condemnation, loved ones in ICU, loss, and heartbreak. He was there with me when Nanay and others could not be. Some people would blame God for the evil that befell me, but He did not bring the painful circumstances. People brought the pain.

The Lord gives free will to us all, free will to do right, free will to harm others, free will to harm ourselves. . .because free will is necessary for love. Only if you have the freedom to choose to love does love become real. You could program a robot to "love" through a display of actions, but a program is not true love because it has no choice. Robots are incapable of true love because there is no choice for them to love or not to love.

Love is only real when you have a choice, and with that power of choice, people choose to either love God or love evil. They think they choose to love themselves, but loving the self voids a key definition of love: selflessness. To love the self is, in fact, to love evil. When people chose to bring evil upon me, He chose to love me in and through those dark seasons. He did not whisk me away like some genie because He desired for me to grow, to acquire strength, to acquire resolve, to choose . . . either evil or love.

I desire for you to know His great encompassing love, because I know firsthand that His love is greater than anyone else's love; it is greater than my love for you, greater even than Nanay's colossal love for me. He is love. He is YHVH, blessed be His Name.

If my testimony of relationship is what I give to you, why do I begin with this book? Why would I hold off on my testimony until two books later and instead begin with this book about the identity of God?

This idea of a legacy first began with Nanay's passing, and the legacy itself began with a book concerning the Good News of the Lord's gift of salvation. When I completed my study upon the matter of salvation in 2014, I came across an old letter that I wrote to you, my children, from October 31, 2012, concerning the identity of Yah, blessed be His Name.

I thought the letter was an apropos beginning to my study on salvation. After all, how could salvation and the covenants of salvation be of any import to you if you do not even know who offers us salvation? I explained in the study why we need salvation and *from what* we need salvation. The story of salvation, however, does not begin with us. The story of life begins with the Creator. If I write two books then, why not the traditional trilogy? Therefore, my testimony will have to wait until the third book. In this first book, I will tell you about my first love, the One who first loved me. Then in the next book, I will tell you how He demonstrated that love and how He opened a gateway for relationship. Finally, I will tell you about relationship with Him.

Adam embraced death, but life begins with the Creator. You must first know who the Creator is before anything else will matter, before you can begin to understand. When He revealed Himself to His people and to the Egyptians, many Israelites and Egyptians (yes, many Egyptians left with Moshe) chose to trust God, leave the comforts of civilization, and follow Him into the wilderness. You cannot know any different life outside slavery, to death and destruction, if you do not know the Holy One of Yisrael. Once you know Him, then you can begin to know everything else that He created and offers, and everything else defined by rebellion and separation from Him. Only then can you understand how everything comes together and interweaves.

As I delved into His identity and into His written Word, however, I found that I had more to share with you concerning the identity of Yah, blessed be His Name. I had more to say than could be captured in one introductory chapter in a book about salvation. One hundred pages into my study of His identity and I realized that I needed to write a separate book. Here is the result.

I cannot tell you enough how much I love you, how much I never want to be parted from you. Yah, blessed be His Name, loves you much, much more . . . beyond the capacity of words. I once heard an explanation that seemed trite, but it's nevertheless still accurate.

"I asked Jesus, 'How much do you love me?' And Jesus said, 'This much.' Then He stretched out His arms and died."

Pause and ponder those words for a moment. Imagine.

He never wants to be apart from you, which is why He died to make sure that eternity together with Him was available to you, to make sure that the spirit of death passed over you, skipped you. The Good News of His salvation is simply this: He died so that you could have relationship with Him, with Him who is Life.

At your young ages, I know you didn't realize the times Mama and I avoided going places where we couldn't take you with us because we treasured our time with you. We didn't want to leave you behind. I can't possibly tell you the number of parties and engagements we passed up because they didn't allow children. We preferred to be with you than go to those parties.

You didn't realize that we gave you the tenderest cuts of meat, the tastiest parts of the dessert, and the last bite of ice cream; you didn't realize that we shopped for you rather than us, that we saved for your future rather than satisfying our pleasures. I compile every act of love that we gave to you and I know that the Lord gives more. Just as you didn't realize the acts of love that we gave to you, so too you may not realize the acts of love the Lord gives to you.

Whether you realize it or not, He does love you. I would say, He loves you more than words can express, but He sent His Word to decrease in glory and be born in flesh to show you His love in action on the cross. He loves you . . . even more than I love you, and I love you more than I love myself. I beg you to know His love. The Creator of the universe desires the most intimate relationship with you.

I feel the need to share with you all that I know concerning Him because of His great love for you. Hopefully, you will take what I give to you and seek to know Him more, seek to know Him as only you can know Him, because all His followers have both a unique and shared knowledge of Him. Our knowledge of Him is shared because He reveals Himself to us through His written Word. Our knowledge of Him is also unique because we know Him through our walk and our experiences with Him, though that unique knowledge should always align with His written Word.

Any time knowledge of Him deviates from His written Word, such knowledge is, in fact, not knowledge, but rather lies, deception, and mis-judgment that a person chooses to embrace. The Lord never contradicts His Word, never goes back on His Word, never breaks His own com-mandments, and never fails to keep His covenant relationships.

Avraham was so sure of that fact that he was willing to kill his only son in obedience to God's command. He trusted that God Almighty would resurrect his son (Hebrews 11:17-19) from the dead to fulfill God's Word that Avraham would have many descendants through Yitzchak (Isaac).[1]

I tell you of God's faithfulness so that you can rest assured that, in Him, you will find the only unchanging element in life. You see. . .par-ents die. Children die. Spouses die—or leave. Family forsakes. Friends begrudge. Happiness is fleeting.

Tests and suffering, thank God, pass away too. Human institutions crumble. Societies and cultures change. Even dying itself will pass away (Revelation 20:14). Nothing is permanent except Yah, blessed be His Name. He is the Rock that does not change.

He was there in my joys and He was there in my suffering. He kept me from committing suicide, and He gave me purpose. His purpose ful-fills all who seek it, strive in it, and persevere in it until the end. He gave me understanding and wisdom. He gave me answers to mysteries and revelations to comfort me when He took Nanay. Life with Him is the only fulfilling life.

I have heard stories of some who have turned away from Him in bitterness. They experienced betrayal from congregations, encountered questions to which they could not find answers, or made unwise deci-sions based on their misaligned expectations from misinterpretations of the Scriptures.

Firstly, He is not the congregation of *talmidim* (disciples). His people, His followers, are still only people; while we strive to imitate the Anointed One (Christ), we are not Him and He is not us. His *talmidim* are capable of betrayal, just like the coward in the movie *Saving Private Ryan*. Cor-poral Upham cowered on the staircase while Private Mellish struggled against a Nazi soldier. Upham chose not to save his brother-in-arms. Do

---

1 Genesis 15:4-6; Genesis 21:12; Genesis 22:15-18

not mistake the congregation of *talmidim* for Yah, blessed be His Name. Priests, pastors, elders, and leaders are also not exempt from betrayal and sin.

Furthermore, I guarantee that you will encounter questions for which you will not find the answers, this side of life. Now, answers for some questions you will find. Some answers you will immediately obtain; some will take many years. Patience mixed with contentment will proactively destroy the poisons of bitterness and resentment that can develop from unanswered questions.

Know that you can stand upon the Word of Yah, blessed be His Name. Know all His Word and not just the select few brought to your attention. For example, do not give everything to God and serve His Kingdom and expect retirement money to be waiting for you if you did not save and invest. Do not take amputated pieces of His written Word as isolated nuggets and stand upon them. You must stand upon His entire Word.

If you take Matthew 6:19-20, 24-25, 33, Luke 12:33-34, and Luke 18:18-25 out of context, you will have a distorted and perverted understanding of the Scriptures. Know the fullness of the Scriptures. "Do not store up for yourselves wealth here on earth, where moth and rust destroy, and where thieves break in and steal. Instead, store up for yourselves treasures in heaven, where neither moth nor rust destroys, and where thieves do not break in and steal" (Matthew 6:19-20). Also take into account Deuteronomy 8:18, Proverbs 6:6-8, Proverbs 15:22, Proverbs 27:23-24, Ecclesiastes 11:1-2, Ecclesiastes 12:13, and 1 Timothy 5:8. "Moreover, anyone who does not provide for his own, especially for his household, has denied the faith and is worse than an unbeliever" (1 Timothy 5:8). Consider the fullness of His written Word, the complete Scriptures.

Mysteries and difficult topics and tragic circumstances in no way change who God is . . . in no way prove or disprove that He is. Time and life have proven Him to me, proven that He is who He says He is through His written Word. Time and life have proven to me that He is the only security, the only dependable hope in this world. Therefore, know the One who first loved you, even from the beginning of the world.

Before you read this book, allow me to clarify some possibly confusing elements, especially if I do not live long enough to teach you my idiosyncrasies.

Most, if not all, of my quotes from the Scriptures are taken from a cut-and-paste of several translations/interpretations: The New American Standard Bible (NASB), the Complete Jewish Bible (CJB), and the Young's Literal Translation (YLT). I also sometimes include the Orthodox Jewish Bible (OJB). I found that limiting oneself to only one translation leaves room for inaccuracy, and I want to be as close to the Truth as possible, not being able to read the original languages for myself. I believe that the three versions (NASB, CJB, YLT) I previously mentioned provide the best balance for the accurate representation of the original language.

I believe the best overall standalone translation is the NASB, bringing insight from and based upon the Masoretic text for the Instruction and Prophets (Old Testament) and the Alexandrian text for the Good News and Letters (New Testament). The CJB provides continuity between the Hebrew Instruction and Prophets, and the Greek Good News and Letters since almost all the individual books/scrolls were written by Hebrews with Hebrew thought patterns and Hebrew idioms and Hebrew style. The YLT provides word-for-word comparison, more accurate verb tenses, and insight from the Byzantine text to complement the Alexandrian text of both the NASB and the CJB. Sometimes I also like to include the Jewish Publication Society's version (JPS) of the Instruction and the Prophets to compare the Jewish and Christian biases upon the Instruction and the Prophets.

You will also notice that I use a different terminology than the mainstream use of words. First, I prefer to use a more direct transliteration of names rather than the traditional transliteration for a few reasons. I will herein provide three of those reasons:

1. I believe it is respectful to a person of a different culture to use their birth name rather than the name they adopt due to the lack of familiarity others may have with it. I encounter this often in the States, in which, for example, a Chinese person named Hua might use the name Catherine for the benefit of other Americans. I am not so tongue-tied nor lazy as to not even attempt to say a

person's birth name. Even if my attempt sounds poor, I find the other person typically receives my attempt as a gesture of respect.

2. I become confused when translators use James to transliterate Ya'akov and when they use Jacob to transliterate the same Hebrew name in the Instruction and the Prophets. Another example is Joshua and Jesus from Y'hoshua. I still cannot understand the purpose of using two different transliterations for the same name. Some people might say that the translators used the name Jesus to separate the name of the Master from others who bore the same name, but that argument doesn't stand in the face of Jesus the Just (Colossians 4:11). In other words, translators should never have used James or Jesus at all. They should have kept Jacob and Joshua consistent through the texts of the Scriptures.

3. You can see meanings that are inherent in names more easily when the original names are used. Seeing the links between the original names is also easier, such as Hoshea's name change to Y'hoshua (Joshua). I am speaking of Hoshea/Y'hoshua, son of Nun, who led Yisrael after Moshe (Moses). Hoshea means "salvation" while Y'hoshua means "Yah is salvation." Keeping the same name consistent then allows you to see the link between the Y'hoshua after Moshe and Y'hoshua the Anointed One (Jesus the Christ).

Someone once accused me of being an "academic snob" because I used unfamiliar terms when I started diving into the Hebrew Roots Movement (HRM). I could see the validity of the person's accusations. I live in the United States of America where most speak American English. So, I took this to heart, but upon a consistent basis. If I would no longer use Shabbat, then neither would I use Sabbath. If I would no longer use Mashiach, then neither would I use Christ. People who are unfamiliar with the Scriptures or Christianity, including many Christians themselves, do not know the meaning of faith, grace, justification, sanctification, and even the title Christ. Thus, I use more common terms, such as trust in place of faith, loving-kindness in place of grace, being-made-in-right-standing in place of justification, being-set-apart in place of sanctification, set-apart in place of holy, congregation in place of church, and the Anointed One in place of the Christ.

Even the word "anointed" is not so commonly understood, but it is the most basic word I can use without losing the inherent meaning in the title "Christ," which has a profound implication and impact. If I use the word "chosen" instead of "anointed," I lose the implication and impact of the word "anointed." Consider that a Jew inherently understands the significance of the word anointed because the Instruction (first five books of the Bible) commands the anointing of oil upon all kings, priests, and prophets. Those three layers of importance are the impact of the title—the Anointed One.

The Christ does not mean Savior, although Y'hoshua (Jesus) the unique begotten Son of God is most definitely the Savior. The title "Christ" points to kingship, priesthood, and the mouthpiece of God, but only if you know what the title "Christ" means. I had no idea what "Christ" meant for the longest time, even though I liberally used it. I thought it meant Savior. Therefore, I now use "Anointed One" instead of "Christ." I resolve to never use a word whose meaning is unknown to me or widely unknown by the masses.

I also use "congregation" or "assembly" instead of the word "church" since the word "church" etymologically comes from the Proto-Germanic *kirika*, which comes from the Greek phrase *kyriakon doma*, meaning the Lord's house. The word "church" is typically used to translate the Greek word *ekklesia* in the Apostolic Scriptures (New Testament). *Ekklesia* is also frequently used in the Septuagint, the Greek translation of the Instruction. Scholars translated that same Greek word *ekklesia* to "congregation" or "assembly" in the Instruction.

I don't know why they decided to use the word "church" in the Apostolic Scriptures. Perhaps they use it because some Christians have a bias that the congregation of the Apostolic Scriptures replaced Yisrael (Israel) as the people of God. Christians label that belief "replacement theology," and it is utterly wrong according to Romans 11. *Ekklesia* is best translated into English as congregation, assembly, or gathering. *Ekklesia* means the people of God; the people of God are Yisrael—both physical and spiritual—both the Jews and the followers of the Anointed One.

God's people are God's people, no matter how you examine it. In other words, Jews are God's people, no matter how much Christians would like to permanently and eternally disown them. Similarly, Christians are God's people, no matter how much Jews would like to rabidly denounce them as idolaters and heretics.

Speaking of Apostolic Scriptures, I prefer to use different labels than Old Testament and New Testament. I find a negative connotation imbued into the term "Old Testament," such as something that is old and not worthwhile. The word "old" has a negative connotation in American culture, where the elderly are ignored, disrespected, and often disdained.

Another incorrect connotation is that the new replaces the old. The covenants of God never replace a previous covenant, but rather build on the previous covenant like bricks to make a final structure. The capstone does not stand without the presence, active involvement, and use of the bottom bricks. The capstone does not replace the bricks. The capstone is not called new while the bricks are called old. The older covenants are still active in their uses, albeit now applied differently than when the Temple stood. Thus, I use the phrase "the Instruction and the Prophets" in reference to the "Old Testament," much like how the Master referred to them (Matthew 7:12). I use "the Apostolic Scriptures" in reference to the "New Testament," which I in turn further categorize as the Good News (gospels) and the Letters.

The word "apostle" means "sent-one, messenger, ambassador, or emissary." The closest Hebrew word to apostle in the Scriptures that I could find was *malak* (H4397), which means "messenger." It typically references the spiritual messengers of God Almighty, first referenced in Genesis 16:7-11 and Genesis 19:1. The word *malak* also first appears for human messengers in Genesis 32:3. I avoid making a link between the Hebrew *malak* and the Greek *apostolos* (Strong's G652), however, due to the common use of *malak* for spiritual beings sent by God. I nevertheless think that if the authors wrote the Apostolic Scriptures in Hebrew, they would have used the word *malak* for the apostles.

Some say that the word "apostle" is related to the Hebrew word *shalach* (Strong's H7971), which means "to send," or Shiloach (Strong's H7975), a proper noun meaning "sent." There is, however, no direct usage of Shiloach or *shalach* to denote "a person who is sent as a messenger" in the Scriptures. Therefore, I use the word apostle only because I can find no easy replacement for it that is fluid to use in speaking and writing. I am still seeking a proper replacement of the word since few people truly understand the word "apostle." The title apostle does not mean congregation-planter, but rather one who is directly sent out on a mission by the Anointed One.

Notice that the apostles, when selecting a replacement for Y'hudah (Judas) the betrayer, placed a requirement of direct involvement and discipleship under the Master (Acts 1:21-22). Thus, Sha'ul (Saul/Paulos/Paul) was the only one in a special position. He was sent on a mission directly by the Master . . . but after His ascension (Acts 9:15-19), and not sent before His resurrection like the other apostles (1 Corinthians 15:3-8). I did not know what apostle truly meant for many years. Many Christians still do not know what it means, and you will find examples of its misuse today with people donning the title for themselves. Label me rash, impetuous, or a fool, but I refuse to give regard to any person alive today who claims to be an apostle.

I use the Hebrew word *talmid* instead of "disciple" because I believe there is a significant reference to the Hebrew culture that is inherent in the word *talmid*. That reference is lost in the translated word "disciple." Disciple can mean student or follower, but the implication of the Hebrew *talmid* is imitation (2 Kings 2:1-14). Moreover, we are to imitate our Master, Y'hoshua the Anointed One (Romans 8:29), and be transformed into His image (2 Corinthians 3:18), not just study and follow His teachings. Y'hoshua, in Hebrew, became Yeshua in Aramaic, then Iesous in Greek (last "S" is silent) and Latin ("S" is pronounced), to Jesus in German ("J" pronounced as a "Y"), and finally Jesus as we know it in English. We are to be as He is and live as He lives. Jewish culture even goes so far as to encourage *talmidim* (disciples) to imitate even the mannerisms of their rabbi—their master.

I created a short list of words with references to the Strong's Concordance for your own studies and analysis in the glossary. I hope that you reference it for further understanding and interesting nuggets of revelation on the Jewish and Christian cultures, their similarities, differences, and application to the Scriptures.

I beg you not to use the knowledge that I impart to you as a tool for arrogance. Do not disdain others who follow different methods of worshiping Yah, blessed be His Name. He judges the heart, not the outward appearance (1 Samuel 16:7). Knowledge is vain if you lose humility, but especially vain if you lose love.[2] The purpose of this knowledge that I share with you is not for the purpose of arrogance, disdain, or condemnation, but to help you draw closer to the Lord in Truth[3]. I desired the Truth all my life (I still do), and I desire that you strive for Truth as well.

The purpose of this knowledge that I give to you is so that you do not have to start from ignorance as I did. So often I could not find adequate answers to my questions, even from elders. Here I give to you the answers that I received through wrestling with His written Word, living life with Him, and listening to His still small voice. I see dimly, just as Sha'ul (Saul/Paulos/Paul) said (1 Corinthians 13:12). I do not have all the answers. Even the answers I have may not be complete. Nevertheless, I give you the answers I have. They have served me well, and I hope they are a strong springboard for you to find your own answers with Him.

My daily prayer to Yah, blessed be His Name, is this:

Heavenly Father, you are the One who gives and takes away, blessed be the Name of YHVH. Thank you for another day of life, for my family and our health, for purpose, salvation, and relationship with You. Please have mercy on me and forgive me the things I have done wrong. Please fill me with Your loving-kindness and help me to obey Your will in all things and to forgive those who have wronged me. I bring my children to You. I beg You, please, bind them to Your eternal Kingdom, seal them for Your salvation, and keep them in close and constant relationship with You. Favor them and protect them. Enlighten them with Your presence

---

2 Leviticus 19:18; 1 Corinthians 13:1-3
3 Joshua 24:14; John 4:23-24

and fill them with your loving-kindness. Glorify Your presence in them and give them Your peace. Open their ears and speak to them so that they may know Your voice, even now. Reveal Yourself to them so that they may know You, trust You, fear You, and love You. Give them the years to become adults so that they may serve You. Give Mama and me many years with them, Your wisdom, and Your loving-kindness to raise them in Your Way. In every way that we fall short, please stand in the gap. Put a hedge of protection around us and keep us safe from all harm. Send Your *keruvim* (cherubim) to surround us and our home and protect us from all evil and all evil influence. I ask this, in Your Son, Y'hoshua's Name. So be it.

Love,

Papa

CHAPTER ONE

HASHEM

MY CHILDREN, THERE is only one God.

Many will use the word "God," but all it means is deity. For all you know, they might be referring to the Zoroastrian deity, or any one of numerous Hindu deities, or the Muslim deity, or any variety of others. They might even be referring to the same God as you . . . but are they? Do they know His Name? Do they attribute His Word, His character, and His actions to His Name?

He is referred in His written Word (the Instruction and the Prophets, the Good News, and the Apostolic Letters) by His Name more than any other title. Understand the significance of what I just said. He is referred in the Scriptures more frequently by His Name (6,510 times) than the titles of Great God/Elohim (2,346 times), Lord/Adonai (431 times), and God/El (213 times). There must be some significance to His Name and to knowing His Name. When you first meet a person, you may easily remember the person's face, but the best way to identify that person to others is by using that person's name.

In English	In Hebrew	Hebrew Transliteration	First Appearance	Frequency in Scripture
Great God	אֱלֹהִים	Elohim (H430)	Gen 1:1	2,346
Lord	אֲדֹנָי	Adonai (H136)	Gen 15:2	431
God	אֵל	El (H410)	Gen 14:18; 16:13	213
Almighty	שַׁדַּי	Shaddai (H7706)	Gen 17:1	48
Holy One	קָדוֹשׁ	Kaddosh	2 Kgs 19:22	39
Most High	עֶלְיוֹן	Elyon (H5945)	Gen 14:18	18
Father	אָב	Av (H1)	Is 63:16	?

The titles Almighty and Most High are normally preceded with God (e.g., God Almighty or God Most High). The title Holy One is normally depicted fully as Holy One of Yisrael (Israel). I have not done extensive research to find where in the Instruction and the Prophets that His title of Father is found, but I saw a few in the books of Yeshayah (Isaiah) and Yeremyah (Jeremiah).

Also, you will find two depictions of the word "Lord" in reference to the One True God—Lord and LORD. Lord is the accurately translated title for the Hebrew *Adonai*. The all capitalized L-O-R-D, however, represents His Name, YHVH, blessed be He eternally. Know His Name well, my children, because "at that time, whoever calls on the Name of YHVH is saved. For in Mount Tziyon and Yerushalayim there is an escape, as YHVH has said, among the survivors whom YHVH is calling."[4] Opposite to English, you read Hebrew from right to left. Thus, you would read His

---

4 Psalm 91:14; Isaiah 11:11; Isaiah 43:6-7; Isaiah 52:6; Jeremiah 12:14-17; Zechariah 13:9; Joel 3:5 (in CJB or JPS); Joel 2:32; Acts 2:17-21

Name, from right to left, as Yud-Heh-Vav-Heh, with the Hebrew character for *yud* appearing on the far right.

יְהֹוָה

Heh-Vav-Heh-Yud

The reason for the depiction of His Name as the all capitalized L-O-R-D instead of His actual Name is a human tradition started by the Jews due to their interpretation of Leviticus 24:16. One of the Jewish respected leaders in history, Moshe ben Maimon, otherwise known as Maimonides, best summarized his belief by saying:

It is not only a false oath that is forbidden.[5] Instead, it is forbidden even one of the names designated for G-d in vain, although one does not take an oath. For the verse commands us, saying, "To fear the glorious and awesome name" (Devarim [Deuteronomy] 28:58). Included in fearing it is not to mention it in vain.

Therefore, if because of a slip of the tongue, one mentions G-d's name in vain, he should immediately hurry to praise, glorify and venerate it, so that it will not have been mentioned in vain. What is implied? If he mentions G-d's name, he should say, "Blessed be He for all eternity," "He is great and exceedingly praiseworthy," or the like, so that it will not have been in vain (Mishneh Torah, Laws of Vows 12:11). (Ben Ya'ocov)

Despite this teaching, Jews still avoid saying His Name, rather than saying His Name followed by the appropriate "who is great and exceedingly praiseworthy." According to the website, Judaism 101, "Nothing in the Torah prohibits a person from pronouncing the Name of God. Indeed, it is evident from scripture that God's Name was pronounced routinely" (Rich). Furthermore, daily Temple service used His Name. The Mishnah confirmed that the Scriptures and ancient Israelite laws held no prohibition against saying His Name. Berakhot 9 of the Mishnah men-

---

5 Leviticus 19:12; Deuteronomy 18:20; Jeremiah 14:14-15; Jeremiah 29:9, 21-23

tions that the religious leaders "decreed that a person should greet his fellow in God's Name . . ." Only after the Mishnah did Jewish religious leaders condemn the use of His Name (Rich).

Though the pronunciation of His Name may not be fully known, still strive to use it. Say Yahveh, or Yehovah, or Yud-Heh-Vav-Heh, or the shortened Yah, blessed be He for all eternity, but use The Name that He gave to His people so that others know who your God is. Some Jews will argue that Ruth 2:4 is not an obvious example of the common usage of the Name of the Lord, but the Scriptures speak for themselves. In the ancient days of the judges of the Lord, before the kings of Yisrael, Israelites used His Name in their daily greetings to one another.

I believe that Leviticus 24:16 concerns the abstinence from using The Name of the Lord in an inappropriate and abusive manner. In Leviticus 24:16, the word "blasphemes" comes from the Hebrew verb *nakav* (H5344), which means "to pierce or perforate." A person can take The Name of the Lord in an inappropriate and abusive manner through more than just words, but also through deeds. For example, calling oneself a *talmid* (disciple) of the Anointed One, an elder of the congregation, or a lover of God while still continuing a willful or secret lifestyle of sin, disobedience, and rebellion is another way of abusing His Name.[6] His Name should be handled with great care, but that does not mean that you should be forbidden to speak it or avoid speaking it. By all means, speak His Name as He commands you to do,[7] but remember to set-apart His Name with the appropriate honorific.[8]

I find it interesting that devout Muslims will venerate the name of their prophet in much the same way as Maimonides advised venerating the Name of Yah, blessed be His Name. I also find it interesting that the same Muslims do not venerate the word God in Arabic, which is Allah, as they do the name of their prophet. In other words, Muslims will speak and say Allah. Yet, when they speak and mention the name of their prophet, they will normally say,

---

6 Exodus 20:7; Isaiah 48:1; Jeremiah 34:16; 1 John 4:20

7 Exodus 3:15; Exodus 9:16; Exodus 20:24; Numbers 6:27; Deuteronomy 6:13; Deuteronomy 10:20; Jeremiah 4:1-2

8 Isaiah 29:23; Isaiah 48:11; Malachi 2:2

"Peace be upon him." They will, in fact, say this about any whom they consider a prophet, including Y'hoshua the Anointed One (Jesus the Christ) and Miryam (Mary), His earthly mother. I bring attention to this Muslim practice to make a point—if Muslims can venerate the name of their prophet, we who follow the Anointed One can definitely venerate the Name of Yah, blessed be He for all eternity, and Y'hoshua His Anointed One, who is great and exceedingly praiseworthy. Instead, we have a disgraceful Western Christian culture in which many will use His titles as part of an expletive or byword. Notice the number of Christians who say, "Oh my G-d!"

His Name is the eleventh most frequently used word in the Scriptures and the first most frequently used proper noun. His Name is used a total of 6,510 times in the Instruction and the Prophets, which is almost three times the amount that Elohim is used. Elohim, meaning "magnified authority" or a "plural authority," is the most common title given to HaShem (literally "The Name") [9] in the Scriptures. Elohim is also used for figures of supernatural authority, including idols and evil spirits. Elohim is a unique word. It is a plural noun.

When used in reference to HaShem, however, the verb conjugation is more appropriate to a singular noun, similar to saying something along the lines of "We is." Eliyah (Elijah) also used this unique noun-verb relationship when he spoke of Baal to the prophets of Baal (I Kings 18:27), but this time he used it in disdainful sarcasm. He was by no means making Baal equal to the Holy One of Yisrael.

When Christianity began on the appointed time of Shavu'ot (Weeks, or Pentecost—Fiftieth day) following the death and resurrection of the Anointed One, it was, albeit a fairly new one, very obviously a sect of Judaism, along with the P'rushim (Pharisees—Separated Ones, Separatists), the Tzadikim (Sadducees—Righteous Ones), the Osey HaTorah (Essenes—Observers of The Instruction), Zealots, and even the Herodians. At AD 40, Second Temple Judaism had six major sects, with Christianity simply being one of them (Acts 24:14-15).

---

9 HaShem, a transliteration from the Hebrew, translates to English as "The Name" and is a way of referencing His Name without actually stating His Name and thus refraining from profaning it, from making something common that is meant to be set-apart.

Matthew . . . presents Jesus as a Torah teacher of supreme authority whose mission is only to Israel. Jesus teaches his apostles the
true interpretation of Torah, and after his death and resurrection
they bring this interpretation to all nations. The author was probably a Jewish Christian who did not conceive of Christianity as
a new religion. Rather, Christianity for him was the true Israel,
following the correct interpretation of Torah as taught by God's
own representative, Jesus. (Murphy, 405)

Study Acts and the Apostolic Letters. You will find that Christians
were never treated as though they were outside the umbrella of Second
Temple Judaism (Acts 24:5). If Christianity had been a new religion, the
Jewish leaders would have had no authority over them (Acts 23:1-5). The
Sanhedrin (Jewish Supreme Court) of P'rushim and Tzadikim pushed for
a manhunt on Christians led by Sha'ul (Acts 8:1-3). When Sha'ul joined
the Christian sect while still maintaining membership in the P'rushim
sect, however, he only escaped the judgment of the Sanhedrin because he
sought the judgment of the Romans as a Roman citizen.[10]

It is often thought that Christianity split from Judaism when
Christians claimed that Jesus was divine, a belief incompatible
with Jewish monotheism. But things were not so simple. J. D.
G. Dunn shows that the split did not happen all at once nor was
only one issue involved. Acts sees the initial tensions as resulting
from attitudes to Torah and temple, not from conflicts over the
divinity of Christ. Over time, Christianity did become a separate
religion from Judaism. But this can blind us to the fact that it
began as a group within Second Temple Judaism. (Murphy, 434)

Christians were mainly Jews at the onset, although Gentiles exponen-
tially flooded the Jewish sect as time progressed, creating many debates
and arguments that converged upon the issue of circumcision.

The issue of circumcision could be summarized by a question: Should
a Gentile become a Jew through circumcision before they could become

---

10 Acts 22: 28; Acts 23: 16-35

a *talmid* of the Anointed One? You can find the final conclusion of the apostles on the issue in Acts 15 and Sha'ul's letter to Galatia, which was: a Gentile did not need to become a Jew through circumcision in order to become a *talmid* (disciple) of the Anointed One and immerse into the New Covenant of Yah, blessed be His Name, to receive His forgiveness of sins and His salvation leading to eternal life. Sha'ul even went further to say that if a Gentile endured circumcision in order to become a Jew for the purpose of receiving the salvation of Yah, blessed be His Name, then that Gentile no longer trusted HaShem (The Name) for salvation. Such a one trusted his own physical status as a convert to Judaism through circumcision as his salvation, thereby proclaiming that the Lord's gift of salvation through His Anointed One was not sufficient. Sha'ul clearly stated that circumcision, if completed specifically for the purpose of salvation, annulled the gift of salvation that God offered through the death and resurrection of the Anointed One.

After the destruction of the Temple, the resulting Jewish tax by the Romans, the death of the last surviving apostle, and the Torah-departing teachings of believing Gentile elders,[11] the rift widened between the Christian sect and the rest of Second Temple Judaism. That rift came to a boil during the reign of the false anointed one, Shimon Ben Kosevah, when he removed Roman rule from Y'hudah. Jews still celebrate Ben Kosevah today, but under the more laudable name of Bar Kochba, meaning "son of the star," from the star prophecy in Numbers 24:17. Ben Kosevah's reign and Second Temple Judaism both came to an end at AD 135.

From the ashes of Second Temple Judaism, two religions were born. I call them Rabbinic Judaism, the legacy of the P'rushim (Pharisees), and Christian Judaism. The world, however, labels them Rabbinic Judaism and Proto-Orthodox Christianity. While Second Temple Judaism welcomed the variety of forms of worship and belief in YHVH, blessed be His Name, these two new religions immediately grew exclusive, quick to call other groups who were not in agreement with their tenets "heretics."

I encourage you to study the Ebionites, Elchasaites, and Nazarenes,

---

11 Deuteronomy 12:32; Deuteronomy 13:1-5 [Deuteronomy 13:1-6]; The Epistle of Ignatius to the Magnesians, chapter 8

all labeled as heretics by both Rabbinic and Christian Judaism. Take note also that the Tzadikim (Sadducees), Osey HaTorah (Essenes), and Zealots did not survive the end of Second Temple Judaism but were either absorbed or persecuted by Rabbinic Judaism. I truly believe that Yah, blessed be His Name, has a purpose for these events, but I am not yet privy to what that purpose might be. Perhaps God Almighty desired to maintain two very different paths (Ezekiel 37:15-22).

I give you this historical backstory only to make the point that Christianity began as a sect of Judaism. It only became a "new religion" after Jews became vehemently anti-Christ in order to maintain their identity and put an end to the influx of Gentiles and Gentile influence through the open door of the Christian sect.

Christianity became a new religion after Gentile Christians dwarfed the number of Jewish Christians and became vehemently anti-Jewish in order to create their own separate identity apart from the mostly non-messianic and persecuting Jews. Rabbinic and Christian Judaism, despite their parting of ways in beliefs and methods of worship, maintained many similarities, one of which was the avoidance of saying the Name of Yah, blessed be His Name:

> The practice of substituting YHWH for "LORD" was begun by the Jews hundreds of years before Christ. The Jews did not want to pronounce or mispronounce the name of YHWH out of reverence and also lest they violated the commandment that says, "You shall not take the name of the Lord your God in vain, for the Lord will not leave him unpunished who takes His name in vain" (Exodus 20:7). So, the Jews began substituting God's name [with Lord] . . . which is now Adonai. This practice is followed today in English translations of the Bible to show reverence for the Holy Name. Finally, since the early Hebrew text did not contain vowels but only consonants, it is not known exactly how to pronounce God's name. So, LORD is substituted for YHWH. (Slick)

I found this particular adoption of Jewish tradition strange for anti-Jewish Christians—and if you don't think Christians are anti-Jewish, study history.

The new generation of post-apostolic Christians, composed mostly of Gentiles by the end of Second Temple Judaism, turned their backs on many commandments of God. They turned their backs on the Day of Rest (Sabbath/Shabbat), Passover, and God's other appointed times, just to name a few. Nevertheless, their rejection of His commandments was not wholesale nor immediate. Even Ignatius of Antioch, considered to be a student of the apostle Y'hochanan (John) and third overseer (bishop) of Antioch, instructed the keeping of the Day of Rest in its appropriate spirit, although his words revealed his ignorance of Jewish practices and observances:

> Let us therefore no longer keep the Sabbath after the Jewish manner, and rejoice in days of idleness; for "he that does not work, let him not eat." For say the oracles, "In the sweat of thy face shalt thou eat thy bread." But let every one of you keep the Sabbath after a spiritual manner, rejoicing in meditation on the law, not in relaxation of the body, admiring the workmanship of God, and not eating things prepared the day before, nor using lukewarm drinks, and walking within a prescribed space, nor finding delight in dancing and plaudits which have no sense in them. And after the observance of the Sabbath, let every friend of Christ keep the Lord's Day as a festival, the resurrection-day, the queen and chief of all the days. Looking forward to this, the prophet declared, "To the end, for the eighth day." (Ignatius)

Ignatius evidently thought that the "Jewish manner" of keeping the Day of Rest was through rejoicing "in days of idleness." He did not know that Jewish observance of the Day of Rest spurned idleness and instead embraced meditation on the Word of God.

Although remnants of *talmidim* (disciples), from early Jewish Christians to the modern congregation of Seventh Day Adventists, continued to rest on His Day of Rest, the general and mainstream rejection of His Day of Rest by Christians finalized with Constantine the Great:

Even Constantine the Great . . . sanctioned the recognition of
Sunday as the sole day of rest, the "Sabbath," and thus consum-
mated the tendency that had been developing in the Christian
Church for nearly two centuries to substitute the day of Jesus'
resurrection for the Jewish Sabbath. (Singer, Vol. 10)

I clarify the first century practices as described by Ignatius of Antioch
concerning early Christians: they rested on the seventh day (Saturday)
with Jews, many even attending the synagogues, and then gathered
together in each other's homes to worship God and celebrate the resurrection of the Anointed One on the first day of the week (Sunday).

The Book of Acts indicates that the first church gathered daily
for worship in the Jerusalem temple and in the homes of believers, devoting themselves to instruction in the apostles' doctrine,
fellowship, prayer, and the Eucharist or Lord's Table (2:42-
47). Given their Jewish heritage and the example of Jesus, who
worshiped in the synagogues and temple (Luke 4:16; John 10:22-
23), it is only natural that the apostolic church retained temple
worship and Sabbath keeping along with the development of
Christian worship patterns for Sunday, the day of [the] Christ's
resurrection (Luke 24:1). (Elwell, Evangelical Dictionary)

Early Christians called the first day of the week "The Lord's Day"
(Sunday), but they still retained the seventh day (Saturday) as the Sabbath, as the Day of Rest. Even the Spanish language supports Saturday as
the Sabbath, Sabado, the seventh day of the week.

[The] words to designate . . . "Saturday" or *Sabado* and "Sunday"
or *Domingo*, in Spanish, were not adopted using the Roman
model of denomination. Saturday comes from the word of
Hebrew origin, that refers to the "Sabbat," the day of rest (in
the Jewish and Christian tradition, God rested the seventh day
of creation).

And finally, Sunday *Domingo* has its origin in a Latin word that means "the day of the God." (Etymological)

Many people will argue, but the historical fact is that the Day of Rest, the Sabbath, is the day most commonly known in English as Saturday.

I also clarify that no such thing as the Jewish Sabbath exists. The Jews did not create the Day of Rest. The Day of Rest solely belongs to Yah, blessed be His Name, and He created it for the benefit of humanity. The Day of Rest is not the Jewish Sabbath. The Day of Rest is the Lord's Sabbath,[12] and He shares it with all who draw close to Him.[13] Yah, blessed be His Name, owns the Day of Rest. Jews do not own the Day of Rest. Rather, Jews honor and respect God's Day of Rest.

While the majority of Christians blatantly spurned the commandment of the Lord by rejecting the fourth of the Ten D'varim (the Ten Words, the Ten Matters, inaccurately translated as the Ten Commandments), they somehow adopted a man-made tradition flimsily based on a stretched interpretation of the third of the Ten D'varim. In other words, Christian leaders and scholars are willing to adopt a Jewish man-made tradition, while at the same time, rejecting a clearly stated commandment. Allow me to further simplify it. Christian leaders are willing to avoid saying "YHVH, blessed be His Name," but have no qualms about ignoring the seventh day rest. I remind you of the Master's chastisement upon the religious leaders of His time, "You depart from God's command and hold onto human tradition" (Mark 7:8). I loathe the inconsistency of adopting the Jewish tradition of not saying His Name while rejecting the very commandment of God concerning His Day of Rest.

My point in these recent paragraphs concerning His Name and His Rest was to give you some historical perspective and a mild picture of grandiose theological debates to exhibit a point. Do not accept traditions given to you or instructed to you by some person or some society, even me. The majority is not always in the right. In fact, the majority is typically wrong (Matthew 7:13-14). No matter how well others support

12 Genesis 2:2-3; Matthew 12:1-13; Luke 6:1-10
13 Psalm 95:6-11; Mark 2:27-28; Hebrews 4:1-13

themselves with the Scriptures, be sure to study the Scriptures yourself (Acts 17:10-12), and grasp the fullness of the Scriptures within all of its contexts (2 Peter 3:15-18), both cultural and historical, but most importantly spiritual (1 John 2:27).

Heed the instruction of His Spirit while anchored in His written Word with its context intact. You can accurately understand His direction from His Spirit for you in your life without necessarily knowing the context of His written Word, but you will utterly fail to grasp the absolute truth without the full context. Truth is a belt that holds everything together.

Look around you. The doctrines of Christianity are falling apart because Christians built them outside the full context, outside the Truth. If you invent one loophole to circumvent the Instruction, from which the Prophets, the Good News, and the Apostolic Letters spring forth, it all withers. If you invent one loophole to circumvent the Instruction, you are attempting to circumvent HaShem (The Name), and you will soon see your doctrines fall apart one by one. If you invent one loophole to circumvent the teachings of the apostles, you are attempting to circumvent the Lord, and you will soon see your doctrines fall apart one by one. Your doctrines may remain intact for some time, even years, but I guarantee they will fall apart at the next intelligent challenge you face, unless you choose to hide your head in delusion. Thank God doctrine does not save us, but also keep in mind that faulty doctrine leaves us vulnerable to deception.[14]

I am not saying that past generations of Christians were all failures or that their doctrines were all failures. In the flesh, we will continue to err and sin. Martin Luther, for example, worked for the glory of the Kingdom when he pushed to have the Scriptures translated into the local language of his community. "But perhaps Luther's greatest achievement was the German Bible. No other work has had as strong an impact . . ." (Zecher). He also had his fair share of failures.

---

14 Deuteronomy 12:32; Deuteronomy 13:1-5 [Deuteronomy 13:1-6]; Ephesians 4:14-16; 1 Timothy 6:3-5; 2 Timothy 4:3-4; Titus 1:10-14

Luther worked against the Kingdom when he encouraged the persecution of the Jews and later provided fuel to Adolf Hitler with his writings:

> "Set fire to their synagogues or schools," Martin Luther recommended in *On the Jews and Their Lies*. Jewish houses should be "razed and destroyed," and Jewish "prayer books and Talmudic writings, in which such idolatry, lies, cursing, and blasphemy are taught, [should] be taken from them." In addition, "their rabbis [should] be forbidden to teach on pain of loss of life and limb." Still, this wasn't enough. Luther also urged that "safe-conduct on the highways be abolished completely for the Jews," and that "all cash and treasure of silver and gold be taken from them." (Gritsch)

What Luther and Hitler worked for evil, however, the Lord worked for good,[15] and now the global political scene has the current State of Israel, even if it is secular. The idea of Jews having their own country was a longshot of a dream before Hitler. Luther was not flawless. Although we falter in practice and doctrine, we continue to struggle and walk with Yah, blessed be His Name, trusting that He will *always* work to the greater good.

We continue our struggle with God, as we *talmidim* (disciples) of the Anointed One are engrafted into the commonwealth of Yisrael (Israel).[16] We continue our struggle with God because Yisrael means "he who struggles with God."[17] We are Yisrael, the commonwealth of Yisrael, the spiritual Yisrael.

We, as a community of *talmidim*, are metaphorically "the Church." A better descriptive, however, would be assembly. The word "church" etymologically comes from the Proto-Germanic *kirika*, which comes from the Greek word *kyriakon doma*, meaning the Lord's house (Harper, Church). In other words, church means "a physical place of worship," or temple.[18] No wonder many confuse the word "Church" to mean "a build-

---

15 Genesis 50:20; Romans 8:28

16 Genesis 22:18; Psalm 22:27; Isaiah 11:10-12; Isaiah 49:6; Ephesians 2:11-13;

17 Genesis 32:24-28 [B'reishit 32:25-29]; Philippians 2:12

18 Exodus 29:45; Leviticus 26:12; Isaiah 52:11; Isaiah 43:6; Hosea 1:10; 1 Corinthians

ing" rather than the group of *talmidim* (disciples). Translators used the word "church" to translate *ekklesia*, but we already have an English word for *ekklesia* from the Septuagint, the Greek translation of the Instruction and the Prophets. *Ekklesia* is best translated into English as congregation, assembly, or gathering. *Ekklesia* means the gathering of the people of God, and the people of God are Yisrael (Israel).

> The New Testament word for "church" is *ekklesia* . . . In classical Greek, the term was used almost exclusively for political gatherings. In particular, in Athens the word signified the assembling of the citizens for the purpose of conducting the affairs of the *polis* [city]. Moreover, *ekklesia* referred only to the actual meeting, not to the citizens themselves. When the people were not assembled, they were not considered to be the *ekklesia*. The New Testament records three instances of this secular usage of the term (Acts 19:32, 39, 41). The most important background of the term *ekklesia* is the Septuagint, which uses the word in a religious sense about one hundred times, almost always as a translation of the Hebrew word *qahal* . . . This is especially the case in Deuteronomy, where *qahal* is linked with the covenant. When we come to the New Testament, we discover that *ekklesia* is used of the community of God's people some 109 times (out of 114 occurrences of the term). (Elwell, Evangelical Dictionary)

Therefore, every time you see the word "church" in the Good News or the Apostolic Letters, read it as "congregation," "assembly," "gathering," "the people of God," "spiritual Yisrael," or "the commonwealth of Yisrael." The people of God existed since Hevel (Abel) (Hebrews 11) and were given a distinctive name under Ya'akov (Jacob).[19] In fact, the first appearance of *ekklesia/kahal* is in Genesis 28:3. Another notable appearance is in Exodus 12:6. Its final appearance in the Instruction is in Deuteronomy 31:30. We are spiritual Yisrael . . . waiting for the reunion with physical Yisrael.[20]

3:16-17; 2 Corinthians 6:14-18

19 Genesis 32:28; Genesis 35:10; Exodus 1:7; Exodus 17; Ephesians 2:11-22

20 Genesis 17:4-6; Genesis 22:18; Ezekiel 37; Romans 11:1-32

As the people of God, we should be more concerned with His commandments than human traditions.[21] As part of the commonwealth of Yisrael, we struggle with and obey the Instruction of HaShem (The Name) in following the complete example of the Anointed One because we love Him, not because we are attempting to enter His Kingdom by our own flawed efforts.[22] As the people of God, we call on Him by His Name, YHVH, blessed be His Name, because He revealed His Name to us and we belong to Him.[23]

My children, do not walk in the ways of human traditions, but rather walk in the Way of the Lord, in the commandments of Yah, blessed be His Name, as the Anointed One Himself lived them in the flesh. Christian denominations adopted the Jewish tradition of not pronouncing the Name of the Lord despite the animosity that Christians and Jews have for each other. I do not know why Christian elders adopted this tradition even while they discarded other commandments of HaShem, but I think it is foolish. Some scholars believe this tradition of not saying His Name started with the Jews sometime after Ezra and Nechemyah, soon after the rebuilding of the Temple.

> By the time that the Septuagint version of the Torah was translated in the third century BC, Jews avoided pronouncing the Tetragrammaton to avoid committing blasphemy; in reading the Scriptures, the name אֲדֹנָי (adonay, "Lord") was substituted, and the Septuagint translated this with the Greek word κύριος (kyrios, "Lord"). (Klippenstein)

The pronunciation of His Name was discouraged by the time the

---

21 Exodus 19:8; Isaiah 29:13-14; Matthew 15:7-9

22 Exodus 20:1-6; Deuteronomy 7:9; Deuteronomy 11; Joshua 22:5; Psalm 119:47-127; Daniel 9:4-19; Nehemiah 1:5-10; John 14:15-21; John 15:10; Romans 3:21-31; Ephesians 2:8-10; 1 John 5:2-3; 2 John 1:6

23 Exodus 3:13-15; Exodus 6:2-8; Exodus 9:16; Exodus 20:7, 24; Leviticus 19:12; Numbers 6:22-27; Deuteronomy 18:15-19; 2 Samuel 7:13; 1 Kings 8:1-29; 1 Kings 9:1-9; Psalm 89:19-29; Psalm 91:11-16; Joel 2:28-32 [Joel 3]; Isaiah 42:5-9; Isaiah 43:5-7; Isaiah 48:9-11; Isaiah 65:1; Amos 9:11-12; Nehemiah 1:5-10; Zechariah 13; Malachi 4:1-3; Acts 2:15-24; Acts 15:15-20; Revelation 19:12-16

Master walked the earth, and now it has been forgotten. The best guesses for the pronunciation are "Yahweh" and "Yehovah."

> Jehovah is the name for the Lord God occurring most frequently in the Old Testament (5,321 times). The actual Hebrew form of the word was *YHWH* (the Hebrew alphabet does not have vowels). We really do not know how the Hebrew pronounced the name (probably *Yahweh*, the Greek transliteration is *iaoue*). Because they were forbidden by the Commandments to take the name of the Lord in vain, they feared to pronounce the name of *Yahweh*, therefore they substituted in reading the word *Adonai*. After centuries transpired, they forgot how to pronounce *Jehovah* or *Yahweh*; and when scholars finally invented "vowel points" for written Hebrew, they gave to *Jehovah* the vowel points for *Adonai*, not knowing what the original vowel sounds had been.
>
> Scholars differ over the etymology of the name *JEHOVAH* (*YHWH*), but quite certainly it comes from a form of the verb "to be." This seems clear from the Lord's statement to Moshe (Moses) that "I AM" had sent him. "I AM THAT I AM" seems to amplify the name in a way that it could mean "the eternally existing One." Jesus seemed to identify with the name when he said to the Jews, "Before Abraham was, I AM" (John 8:58). Could it mean: "I AM the Way, the Truth and the Life" (John 14:16), "I AM the Light" (John 8:12), "I AM the Bread of Life" (John 6:35), and "I AM the Resurrection and the Life" (John 11:25)? With joy we sing, "He's everything to me." An abbreviated form of *Jehovah*, *JAH* is found forty-eight (48) times in the Old Testament (first in Exodus 15:2). It has the same meaning as *Jehovah*. It occurs mostly in the Psalms and it is always used in a context of PRAISE: ". . . extol him that rideth upon the heavens, by His name *JAH*. . ." (Psalm 68:4). (Duffield)

I simply say Yah (Strong's Concordance H3050), blessed be He for all eternity, since it is a shortened version of His Name and its pronunciation is a sure thing, with the first appearance in Exodus 15:26, although it is once again translated as LORD. I occasionally use Yahveh and Yehovah, blessed be His Name, but my uncertainty concerning their pronunciation makes my usage rare. The four Hebrew letters of His Name previously depicted reads as Yud-Hey-Vav-Hey, blessed be His Name, and I will sometimes say the letters in place of the guessed pronunciation.

You will encounter many twisted traditions concerning His Name, such as the tradition to abstain from even uttering His Name as I previously explained. The Sacred Name Movement that started in the 1930s is another twisting of the Truth from the opposite side of the spectrum.

> [My] main complaint against the SNO [Sacred Name Only] movement is not the use or non-use of the Name per se, but the fact that their linguistic superstition about "God" and "Lord" unnecessarily separates brethren from one another. Their linguistic superstition discredits SNO advocates and gives Christians and Jews an excuse to reject everything else that is being restored through the Messianic movement—the Sabbath, the Feasts, the dietary laws, etc. Paul warned Timothy about teachers who are continually "doting about questions and strifes of words, whereof cometh envy, strife, railings, evil surmisings [suspicions]" (I Timothy 6:4). I cannot think of a more accurate description of the SNO movement which has been driven by linguistic superstition since its inception . . .
>
> Hard-core SNO proponents are afraid to utter the words "God" or "Lord" when referring to the Creator. They insist that He must be addressed by His Hebrew Name. Most SNO literature gives a reader the impression that knowing the correct pronunciation of God's Hebrew name is more important than knowing God Himself . . .
>
> Indeed, many SNO proponents do not even consider the brethren their brethren. Christians who do not use the Hebrew names are often regarded as lost at best and as devil worshipers at worst. One large SNO organization printed these words in a newsletter last August: "Christianity calls 'God's' Son by the name 'Jesus.' Thus, those worshiping 'this son' are committing

spiritual adultery!!" This is from one of the more tolerant SNO organizations. Other SNO writers have flatly stated that Christians who use the words "God," "Lord," and "Jesus Christ" are actually worshiping Satan. (Botkin)

I think Botkin did an exemplary enough job of exhibiting the inanity of the Sacred Name Only movement that I do not need to further expound. I only mourn the misfortune of other groups mixing the SNO movement with the Hebrew Roots Movement (HRM). The names of the movements themselves should clearly delineate the obvious differences.

I know a former member of the Roman congregation, a former neo-Nazi, former Satanist, and former atheist all in one person who proclaimed to me his belief in the One True God simply because of His Name. He said that The Name was too profound to have been schemed by the minds of humanity. I am sure you can find many books on the profundity of His Name. While I do believe that knowing His Name is of grave importance, I believe having an understanding of the meaning of His Name is of greater importance.

So far, I perceive the intended meaning of His Name to be "HE WHO IS," or "I AM," pointing to the fact that He has always existed, that He is not created, and that He is the source of existence. I am admittedly only glossing over the heavenly expanse of His identity. Plumb the depths of His written Word to know Him for yourself. Knowing His character is more important than knowing His Name. Knowing His identity is more important than knowing His Name. More important than pronouncing His Name is to live such a life as accurately represents Him and His righteousness.[24]

Do not misunderstand me. I am not saying that knowing His Name is unimportant. Knowing His Name is important as well. He gave it to us so that we may know our God, but keep your priorities rightly aligned. Relationship and action are more important than knowledge, although knowledge is indeed a key part to relationship and action.

---

24 Isaiah 52:5; Ezekiel 36:21; James 2:14-24; Romans 2:21-29

CHAPTER TWO

TRINITY

MY CHILDREN, BEWARE the traditions of humanity; make the written Word of God your anchor, your plumb line, and your ultimate reference for Truth.

I challenge you to search the Scriptures and find the word—trinity. Go ahead. Take the time. I mean it. Go and find the word "trinity" in the Scriptures, whether in the Instruction or the Prophets or the Good News or the Apostolic Letters. I am referring only to the Scriptures and not some commentary of man. Don't cheat and look at the commentaries. Simply find the word in the Scriptures, and feel free to use Strong's Exhaustive Concordance or BlueLetterBible.org online. Put this book down and go find it.

No luck? Do you find it at least strange that a major word of Christian doctrine does not appear anywhere in the Scriptures? Let's try another word. How about Christmas? While you're searching, search for Easter.

If Christians were still in the position to burn people at the stake, the majority would denounce me as a heretic and proceed to burn me because of such questions and challenges. Such is the state of the sinful nature of humanity. If atheists want to blame Christianity itself rather than man's sinful nature for stake burning practices, then I wonder what excuse they have for communist Russia and China's treatment of malcontents.

As central as the word might be in mainstream Christianity, you will not find the word "trinity" anywhere in the Scriptures. The *Oxford Dictionary of the Christian Church* has this to say concerning the Trinity doctrine:

> Though the word "Trinity," first used . . . by Theophilus of Antioch (c. AD 180), is not found in Scripture, Christian theologians have seen [foreshadows] of the doctrine in the biblical narrative; in the OT, for example, the appearance of the three men to Abraham (Genesis 18) was held by the Fathers to foreshadow the revelation of the threefold nature of God. In the NT the most influential text was the reference to the three Persons in the baptismal formula at the end of Matthew (28:19), but there are other passages held to have Trinitarian overtones, such as the Pauline benediction of 2 Corinthians 13:14. From the biblical language concerning Father, Son (or Logos), and Spirit, Trinitarian doctrine developed, as the Church's expansion led to the need for reflection, confession, and dialogue. (Cross)

The first time a person used the word "trinity" to define Yah, blessed be His Name, was eighty years after the death of the last apostle, eighty years post-apostolic leadership, and eighty years of Gentile majority with their Greek philosophy originating from pagan philosophers. As central as the word and the doctrine was for Christians concerning the identity of HaShem (The Name), none of the apostles mentioned it. Not one author of the Scriptures mentioned it.

Do you find that lack of connection at the very least . . . disconcerting? Furthermore, again from the *Oxford Dictionary of the Christian Church* concerning the doctrine of the Trinity, "These . . . views echoed those of contemporary Platonists, who envisaged three eternal divine powers arranged in descending order of dignity." A Platonist is one who follows Platonism, and that is "the philosophy of Plato or his followers, especially that relating to Plato's theory of 'ideas' or 'form,' in which abstract entities ('universals') are contrasted with their objects ('particulars') in the material world" (Soanes).

Plato was born 428 BC into a pagan culture and taught by a pagan teacher, Socrates. Scholars ascribe "the identification of the One with the good" to Plato, as well as the Indefinite Dyad, meaning the unlimited two (Tarán). He also built an altar to the Greek Muses, Greek idols, at his academy (Tarán).

Such was the Christian distaste for Jews that they would rather turn to pagan philosophers 400 years before the Master rather than Jewish sages such as Hillel, the founder of the House of Hillel, and Shammai, founder of the House of Shammai, in order to understand Jewish writings. I call particular attention to Hillel and Shammai because they both lived prior to the announcement of the Anointed One by Y'hochanan the Immerser (John the Baptist) and thus did not have the anti-Christ influence and bias that forthcoming Jewish philosophers had.

So that you know, the most popular of these anti-Christ Jewish philosophers include Akiva ben Yosef (AD 40–137), Sh'lomo Yitzchaki, also known as Rashi (AD 1040–1105), Moshe ben Maimon, also known as Maimonides or Rambam (AD 1135–1204), and Yisrael ben Eli'ezer, also known as Baal Shem Tov (AD 1700–1760). When reading the works of any of these Jewish philosophers, be extremely cautious of their teachings due to the nature of their anti-Christ bias. I would, in fact, advise you to not bother reading them, considering the copious other choices you have of good books written by followers of the Anointed One.

Never in the history of Yisrael (Israel) did any prophet or philosopher understand YHVH, blessed be His Name, as dual, though Yisrael was well aware of the Spirit of God since Genesis 6:3, or Numbers 11:25-29, or Judges 3:10. Though the Instruction and the Prophets include the Father and the Spirit of God, never once do you find the word or mention of a "binity." Nevertheless, I still have yet to read *Two Powers in Heaven* by Alan Segal, suggested to me by an elder whom I respect. The book purportedly provides support for a Hebrew idea of dual powers prior to the Word becoming flesh.

Although the Good News and the Apostolic Letters were written in Greek, and not necessarily well-written Greek, they were still written by Jews who followed Jewish methods of thinking. Loukas/Luke was the exception to the rule because he was a Gentile. Sha'ul (Saul/Paulos/Paul) himself was one of the P'rushim (Pharisees) and accustomed to *halachic* debates. *Halachic* debates are discussions concerning the interpretations of the Scriptures. The word *halachah* comes from the Hebrew word *halach*, which means "to go," as in the way that you should go, the way you should choose and do and live. The Hebrews focused on action, how the Word of God affected your behavior. When all the apostles, who were Jews, left this world and Gentiles took the reign of leadership, however, Christianity took some crazy theological turns.

Where the Hebrews focused on action, the Greeks focused on abstract ideas. If you take pagan Plato's "the One" together with his "Indefinite Dyad," you get three. You stretch Plato's philosophy over five hundred years to the Anointed One and His Good News, shut away the culture of the authors, add some prestidigitation, and you reach the doctrine of the Trinity. How did they jump from One God to the doctrine of the Trinity with the single new revelation of the Anointed One?

If the Father and the Spirit was always considered One, then when adding the Word, wouldn't that then be: $1 + 1 = 2$? One plus one does not equal three. One plus Y'hoshua (Jesus) does not equal trinity. The Jews, and the apostles by inclusion, understood God to be One God in the Instruction and the Prophets. The Good News and the Apostolic Letters exhibited the Anointed One, and He never separated the Father from the Spirit, maintaining Oneness. The Anointed One Himself said that He was One with the Father. Something isn't correctly adding together. All I keep reading in the Scriptures is—One.

The doctrine of the Trinity is the result of Western pagan methods of attempting to pigeonhole Semitic writing concerning HaShem (The Name) into Western culture. It is no wonder that Jews today cannot fathom the idea. Even others outside Christianity analyze the doctrine of the Trinity and find it to be a stretch of reasoning. Of course, Christians will ignorantly quote 1 Corinthians 1:20-29 as their scapegoat answer for every disagreement they encounter. The verse clearly states that the cruci-fied Anointed One, not the doctrine of the Trinity, is the stumbling block that baffles the wise and the strong. The Scriptures do not even claim the word "trinity."

Most Christians either do not know history, the history of the Scriptures, even the Scriptures themselves, or, at the very least, the culture and psychology of the authors of the Scriptures. Many American Christians, for example, are quicker to quote the words or ideas of theologians before they can quote the written Word of God. If they can quote the written Word of God, they can typically quote a few key verses taken out of context in order to support their favorite theologian's ideas.

Even worse, many American Christians can more easily quote a movie than they can the Scriptures, and even I am guilty of this same disappointment as well. This ignorance hurts us all and diminishes our understanding of our God. Take note that I am not calling movies evil. I am simply pointing at our failure of priorities. The Lord, and by extension His written Word, should always be our first love,[25] our primary focus.

The entry from the *Oxford Dictionary of the Christian Church* concerning the Trinity mentioned three key verses for the doctrine; they are Genesis 18, Matthew 28:19, and 2 Corinthians 13:14. Let us examine them and carefully consider the supposed Scriptural defense for the doctrine of the Trinity. Weigh for yourself its soundness, or lack thereof.

First is Genesis 18, where three men approach Avraham. Genesis 18:22 states that two of the three men left to go to S'dom (Sodom) and Amora (Gomorrah) and that Avraham was alone with YHVH, blessed be His Name. Genesis 19:1 then identifies two spirit messengers/angels arriving to S'dom in the evening. A more likely explanation than the doctrine of the Trinity is that a physical manifestation of YHVH, blessed be His Name, appeared to Avraham along with two physical manifestations of spiritual representatives, more commonly called angels. These two spiritual representatives then left for S'dom and Amora, stayed with Lot, and helped Lot and his family evacuate the city.

Interestingly enough, Genesis 19:24 says, "Then YHVH caused sulfur and fire to rain down on S'dom and Amora from YHVH out of the sky." Did you catch that? Allow me to use a microscope and zoom in a little.

---

25 Deuteronomy 4:35-40; Deuteronomy 10:12-20; 1 John 4:19; Revelation 2:2-5

"Then YHVH . . . caused sulfur and fire to rain down . . . from YHVH out of the sky." Does that sound like two? Some One caused sulfur and fire . . . from Some One else out of the sky. Yah, blessed be His Name, said that "You cannot see My face, for no man can see Me and live" (Exodus 33:20)! Yet we have Avraham face to face with YHVH, blessed be His Name, having a conversation. Then we strangely have the two seemingly separate appearances of His Name in one sentence, in one event. There is more here than meets the eye, but it is not the doctrine of the Trinity. Hold this thought to the very end.

Let's examine the defense of the second referenced verse for the doctrine of the Trinity. Matthew 28:19-20: "Having gone, then, make people from all nations into *talmidim* [disciples], immersing them into The Name of the Father and the Son and the Holy Spirit, teaching them to obey everything that I have commanded you, and remember, I am with you always, even until the end of the age." Most people can count, and thus they count the Father, the Son, the Holy Spirit, and reach the number three, the basis of the doctrine of the Trinity. Nevertheless, I see the verse acknowledging only one Name, although it does not provide that Name.

To this case I add more support, and that is Revelation 1:4-6, Revelation 3:1, Revelation 4:5, and Revelation 5:6. Some can count. I can read. We see a phrase "the seven Spirits of God" in the Revelation verses. These verses shed light (no pun intended) upon the *menorah* (lampstand) of the Temple. Yeshayah (Isaiah) also explained these seven Spirits of God long before Y'hochanan (John) wrote the book of Revelation. Yeshayah described the seven Spirits of God as (1) the Spirit of YHVH, blessed be His Name, (2) the Spirit of Wisdom, (3) the Spirit of Understanding, (4) the Spirit of Counsel, 5) the Spirit of Power, (6) the Spirit of Knowledge, and (7) the Spirit of the Fear of HaShem (Isaiah 11:2). What happens now? Is YHVH, blessed be His Name, Seven in One and One in Seven? Instead of Trinity, should we now use Heptinity? If we take seven plus two (the Father and the Son), should we rather use Nonity? Do you find these proposals ludicrous? I do.

Follow the background information. Biblical, and therefore Jewish, poetry commonly maintains a pattern of couplets or triplets in order to make parallel statements that increase insight, understanding, and clarification. Stephen A. Geller tells us through a review of Douglas Stuart that "there are underlying connections between lines of a couplet or triplet in Hebrew poetry that obviously go far beyond the presence simply of synonyms, antonyms, or 'other.'"

Take Isaiah 1:3, for example, which reads, "An ox knows its owner, and a donkey its master's stall; Yisrael does not know, my people do not consider." The relationship of familiarity between "ox and owner" was given in parallel to the relationship of "donkey and master's stall." Also, "Yisrael" is given in parallel to "My people," and "to know" is given in parallel with "to consider." Yah, blessed be His Name, did not mean something different from Yisrael when He spoke of "My people." "My people" was simply a different way of expressing Yisrael. You could say that the second word, "My people," grew deeper than the first word, "Yisrael." You could argue that He used the second word to make His statement more personal. He moved from saying "Yisrael" to saying "My people." The Lord also used two words to clarify His people's relationship with Him during the time of Yeshayah, and that was a lack of knowledge and familiarity as well as a lack of discernment and perception. You could argue that the second word of accusation, "a lack of understanding or recognition," went deeper than the first phrase, "a lack of knowledge and familiarity." He was saying at first that His people were not well familiarized with Him, and secondly, much worse, they couldn't even distinguish Him from the idols surrounding them.

You will find in many books of the Scriptures the presence of Hebrew poetry with similar importance in its composition, recognizable only to the Hebrew trained eye. Such poetry commonly appears in the format of couplets, meaning two lines that share a parallel meaning, and sometimes as triplets, meaning three lines. In fact, I would boldly guess that the majority of the Prophets follow the patterns of Hebrew poetry.

The last verse used to support the doctrine of the Trinity, according to the *Oxford Dictionary of the Christian Church*, was 2 Corinthians 13:14, which reads, "The grace of the Lord Yeshua the Messiah, the love of God, and the fellowship of the Holy Spirit, be with you all."

To take these three parts as separate is to imply that God does not have grace, or we do not have fellowship with our Lord Y'hoshua (Jesus), or that love is not a fruit of His Spirit. This is, however, not the case, as Scripture clearly tells us. In addition, to take these three parts as separate is to imply that the Lord Y'hoshua and the Holy Spirit is not God. If these three parts were three distinct "Persons," then that would mean that only the Father was God and the other two were not, according to this particular verse, since the title God was very clearly only given to the One unmentioned (He being the Father). If we, however, study this verse with the understanding that Sha'ul (Saul/Paulos/Paul) was Jewish and naturally operated as a Jew in Jewish culture, and that he was familiar with Jewish Biblical poetry, then perhaps we can gain further insight.

Let us now take the understanding of Hebrew poetry and apply it to 2 Corinthians 13:14. If we took the verse and divided it into three lines, we would get:

a. The grace of the Lord Yeshua (Jesus)

b. The love of God

c. The fellowship of the Holy Spirit

We can find verses in which grace is described as coming from the Father, the Son, and the Holy Spirit.[26] We find love in the Father, the Son, and the Holy Spirit.[27] We also find verses in which we have fellowship with the Father, the Son, and the Holy Spirit.[28] If grace, love, and fellowship each do not come from separated "Persons," but rather all from One God, then the conclusion should be obvious concerning the identity of YHVH, blessed be His Name.

The Father is YHVH, blessed be His Name. The Lord Y'hoshua

---

26 Genesis 24:27; Genesis 32:10; Genesis 39:21; Exodus 15:13; Exodus 20:5-6; Exodus 34:6-7; Numbers 14:18-19; Deuteronomy 5:8-10; Psalm 5:7; Psalm 119:41-42; Ezra 3:11; Nehemiah 1:5; John 1: 17; Acts 15:11; Acts 20:24; Romans 1:7; Romans 5:15; Hebrews 10:29

27 Deuteronomy 7:7-10; Deuteronomy 10:15; Zephaniah 3:17; 1 John 3:1; Ephesians 6:23; Titus 3:3-7; 2 John 1:3; Romans 15:30-32; Galatians 5:22-23

28 Psalm 25:14; Psalm 89:6-7; Proverbs 3:32; Amos 3:5-7; 1 Corinthians 1:9; 1 John 1:1-3; 2 Corinthians 13:14; Philippians 2:1-2

the Anointed One (Jesus the Christ) is YHVH, blessed be His Name. The Holy Spirit is YHVH, blessed be His Name. He is One. To say "the Father, the Son, and the Holy Spirit" is *not* to "name" three different "Persons," but rather is to say "God, God, and God" in the same method that the Master often emphasized His points with "Truly, Truly."[29] The Father, the Son, and the Holy Spirit in 2 Corinthians 13:14 is not "naming" three different "Persons," but rather is to say "God gives grace," "God loves you," and "God will always be with you." God is One.

Many questions, ideas, and arguments arose in the beginning of Christianity that moved the early Christians to build the doctrine of the Trinity as a hedge of protection around the Anointed One. One such question was how could God the Son die but not God the Father? Considering that the Father and the Son are One, the Father did not die on the cross, did He? I have no idea how the metaphysical technicalities work. I'll be sure to ask HaShem (The Name) when I cross over into the next life since I don't think He'll answer that question this side of life. For now, all I know is what the Scriptures say. Where they remain silent, so will I. I will not put the Lord into a triangular box simply to satisfy my yearning to understand, much like the ancient Greeks invented stories and constellations to grasp the stars. I am content with mysteries, filing them in my mind until the opportunity presents itself to obtain complete answers (1 Corinthians 13:12). All I know is that there is only One True God.

The Oneness of the Father with His Word born flesh is a mystery (John 6:59-69). I have heard many attempts to explain the mystery of the Father, the Son, and the Seven Spirits of God, but they all fall short of satisfying. Even I have my own explanation: the Father touches this world as depicted by His self-designed dwelling (Exodus 26:34-35) through His right arm, which is His Expression, His Word, even His Word born flesh, the Bread of Life . . . and His left arm, which is His Spirit, even the Seven Spirits of God. If the Word/Bread is the right hand and the Spirit/Meno-

---

29 John 1:51; John 3:3-11; John 5:19-25; John 6:26-53; John 8:34-58; John 10:1-7; John 12:24; John 13:16-38; John 14:12; John 16:20-23; John 21:18; Psalm 41:13; Psalm 72:19; Psalm 89:52

rah is the left hand in the Temple, then that means the person entering the Temple is facing the back of HaShem (Exodus 33:17-23). He expresses His Word born flesh as His Son to best convey extension, identity, and yet Oneness. Just as you cannot separate a person's words from the person, you cannot separate the Word born flesh from the Father.

Nevertheless, these explanations, even my own, all strike me as weak attempts, stretches of logic, seemingly reaching but still failing to hit the mark. I have come to the point of contentment concerning the mystery of the identity of God. I know some brothers and sisters in the Way who are honest with themselves and with the Truth who still struggle to understand this mystery. I understand that He touches the world through His Spirit and His Word, even His Word born flesh. I understand that we use the pronoun "He" to denote God because of His positional authority as God and not as a representation of actual gender.

Meanwhile, I recognize the innately feminine Hebrew noun "Ruach HaKodesh" for the Holy Spirit, and thus we, both man and woman, originate equally from Him.[30] Yet the relationship of His Word to Himself remains a mystery to me. I have decided to rest peacefully in His Name and wait patiently until I cross over from this life into Paradise or His Kingdom to see clearly.[31] I refuse to be so arrogant as to demand understanding *right now*, like a petulant child, demanding the understanding of the infinite Spirit (John 4:24) with a finite fleshly mind. He is not the Christian Trinity. He is not the Jewish S'firot (ten forces that God uses to interact with humanity). He told us who He is. He is YHVH, and blessed be His Name.

My children, my greatest hope and yearning for you is that you will trust the One True God, the Father (symbolized by the *kaporet*/covering/mercy seat in the Holiest Place of the Temple),[32] Son (symbolized by the *lechem haPanim*/the bread of Faces in the Holy Place of the Temple),[33]

---

30 Genesis 1:27; 1 Peter 3:7

31 Exodus 34:29-35; 1 Corinthians 13:12

32 Exodus 25:17; Exodus 25:22; Exodus 26:34; Leviticus 16:2; 1 Chronicles 28:11-18; Luke 18:13-14; Romans 3:21-26; Hebrews 2:17; Hebrews 9:3-5; 1 John 2:1-2; 1 John 4:10

33 Exodus 25:30; Exodus 40:23; Numbers 4:7; 1 Samuel 21:6; Matthew 12:1-8; Luke 6:1-5; Ezekiel 44:1-3; Exodus 16:4-7, 14-21; Isaiah 54:13; Jeremiah 31:34; John 6:31-

and Seven Spirits (symbolized by the *menorah*/lampstand in the Holy Place of the Temple),[34] whose name is YHVH, blessed be His Name, and whose Anointed One is Y'hoshua (Jesus), who is worthy to be praised. Trust Him for all things and especially for salvation from eternal death. I believe in One God who reveals Himself in numerous expressions of His Spirit and Word. I believe the physical manifestation of YHVH, blessed be His Name, is Y'hoshua the Anointed One. The One who met with Avraham was Y'hoshua the Anointed One before He was born flesh. I believe Y'hoshua the Anointed One rained down sulfur and fire from the Father in the sky. I believe YHVH, blessed be His Name, is the Father, the Son, and the Holy Spirit . . . and the Spirit of Wisdom, the Spirit of Understanding, the Spirit of Counsel, the Spirit of Power, the Spirit of Knowledge, and the Spirit of the Fear of YHVH, blessed be His Name. I believe that HaShem (The Name) is infinite. I do not limit Him to a number. For all I know, He could be infinite in One and One in infinite.

Hebrew poetry also helps me to understand from 2 Corinthians 13:14 that I can perceive Yah, blessed be His Name, from different angles, from different revealed perspectives. If I can understand that the Lord is both judge and savior, then I can understand Him as Father, Word, and Spirit. I understand Him as infinite, perceivable according to His written and living Word, but still One God and only One God. I refuse to accept the so-called wisdom of pagan philosophy. I refuse to hem my God into a triangle.

HaShem (The Name) is beyond our complete understanding on this side of life[35]; I am content to know Him as He reveals Himself without

---

65; Exodus 15:6; Deuteronomy 33:2; Psalm 17:7; Psalm 18:35; Psalm 20:6; Psalm 44:3; Psalm 48:10; Psalm 60:5; Psalm 63:8; Psalm 80:14-19; Psalm 89:13; Psalm 98:1; Psalm 108:6; Psalm 110; Matthew 22:41-45; Mark 12:35-37; Luke 20:41-44; Daniel 7:13; Matthew 26:63-64; Mark 14:60-62; Luke 22:67-69; Psalm 16:8-11; 2 Samuel 7:12-17; Psalm 89:3-4; Psalm 132:11; Acts 2:22-36; Psalm 118:15-16; Psalm 137:5; Psalm 138:7; Isaiah 41:10; Isaiah 48:13; Isaiah 62:8; Mark 16:19; Acts 5:31; Acts 7:55-56; Romans 8:33-34; Ephesians 1:18-21; Hebrews 1:3; 1 Peter 3:21-22; Revelation 1:12-19

34 Exodus 25:31-35; Exodus 26:35; Leviticus 24:4; Numbers 8:1-4; 2 Chronicles 13:11; Isaiah 11:2; Zechariah 4:1-6; Hebrews 9:2; Revelation 1:4; Revelation 2:5; Revelation 4:5

35 Proverbs 3:5-12; Isaiah 55:8-9; 1 Corinthians 13:9-13

needing to restrict Him into the triangle symbol (Trinity) of Christians and their theology or even the tree symbol (S'firot) of Jews and their Kabbalah. All I know is what He tells me, and His written Word says nothing about Trinity, but rather His written Word gives me His Name, into whom I immerse myself, into the Father, Son, and Spirit (Matthew 28:19). He is—simply—YHVH, and blessed be His Name.

CHAPTER THREE

HISTORY

MY CHILDREN, JUST as knowing the context of the surrounding events and times is important to understanding a particular statement in the Scriptures, so is knowing history, specifically the history of the Gentile Christian congregation, important to understanding the present condition of the *talmidim* (disciples) of the Anointed One.

I provide for your reference a list of well-known and influential Gentile Christian elders and leaders throughout the history of Christianity:

- Clement of Rome (AD 1st century)

- Ignatius of Antioch (AD 35 – 107)

- Polycarp of Smyrna (AD 69 – 155)

- Justin Martyr (AD 100 – 165)

- Quintus Septimius Florens Tertullianus of Carthage (AD 155 – 240)

- Origen Adamantius of Alexandria (AD 184 – 254)

- Athanasius of Alexandria (AD 295 – 373)

- Basil of Caesarea (AD 329 – 379)

- Gregory of Nazianzus (AD 329 – 390)

- Aurelius Ambrosius of Milan (AD 340 – 397)

- John Chrysostom of Constantinople (AD 349 – 407)

- Eusebius Sophronius Hieronymus or Jerome (AD 347 – 420)

- Augustine of Hippo (AD 354 – 430)

- Gregory the Great of Rome (AD 540 – 604)

- Giovanni di Pietro di Bernardone (AD 1181 – 1226)

- Tommaso d'Aquino (AD 1225 – 1274)

- John Wycliffe of England (AD 1331 – 1384)

- Jan Hus of the Kingdom of Bohemia/Czech Republic (AD 1369 – 1415)

- Martin Luther of Germany (AD 1483 – 1546)

- Huldrych Zwingli of the Swiss Confederation (AD 1484 – 1531)

- William Tyndale of England (AD 1494 – 1536)

- Jean Calvin of France (AD 1509 – 1564)

- John Knox of Scotland (AD 1513 – 1572)

- John Smyth (AD 1570 – 1612)

- Robert Browne (AD 1550 – 1633)

- George Fox (AD 1624 – 1690)

- John Wesley (AD 1703 – 1791)

- Thomas Campbell (AD 1763 – 1854)

- Barton Stone (AD 1772 – 1844)

- John Darby (AD 1800 – 1882)

- Søren Kierkegaard (AD 1813 – 1855)

- James White (AD 1821 – 1881)

- Daniel Warner (AD 1842 – 1895)

- Phineas Bresee (AD 1838 – 1915)

- Albert Simpson (AD 1843 – 1919)

- Charles Parham (AD 1873 – 1929)

- Karl Barth (AD 1886 – 1968)

- Clive Staples Lewis (AD 1898 AD – 1963)

I direct your attention to Barton Stone, who said, "The divinity in him we acknowledge was eternal, because all the fullness of Godhead was in him. But we cannot acknowledge two eternal, distinct beings, possessed of infinite power, wisdom . . . nor can they without contradicting the first article of their faith." In other words, he did not accept the Anointed One as pre-existing as HaShem (The Name) pre-existed, meaning uncreated and outside the boundaries of time. He was not the first elder to be confused by the doctrine of the Trinity. In fact, we can find earlier examples in Arius (AD 250–336), elder in Alexandria, Egypt/Kemet, and Michael Servetus (AD 1511–1553). Arius and Servetus, however, were burned at the stake and labeled heretics by the majority of elders and authorities of their time. Somehow, Barton Stone escaped the same fate. Stake burning must have lost its popularity by the 18th century. The leaders in the above list, however, mostly adhered to mainstream Trinitarian doctrines and shaped Christianity to become what it is today.

I designed a ridiculously extreme oversimplification of the Christian family tree, a history of the congregations, so to speak.

ILLUSTRATION FOR THE HISTORY OF CHRISTIAN DENOMINATIONS

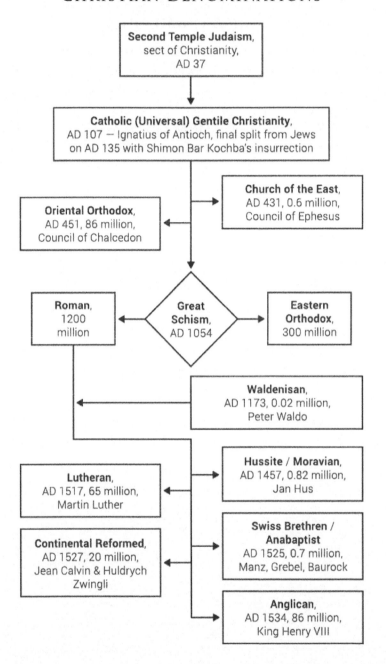

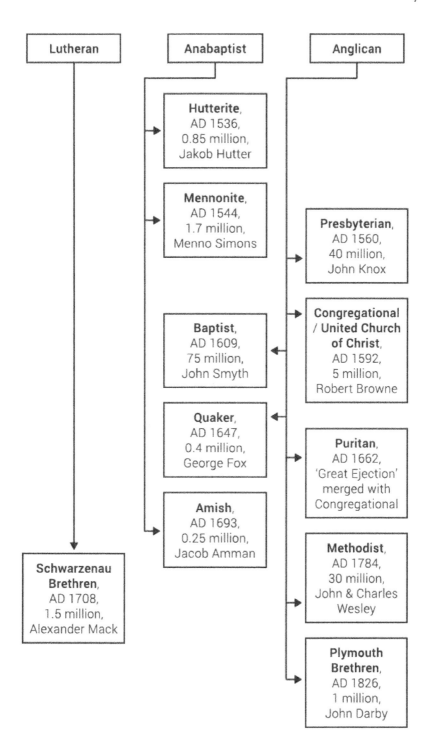

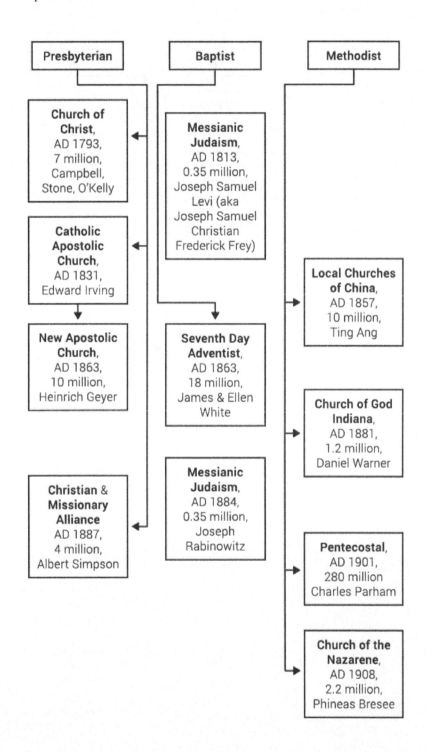

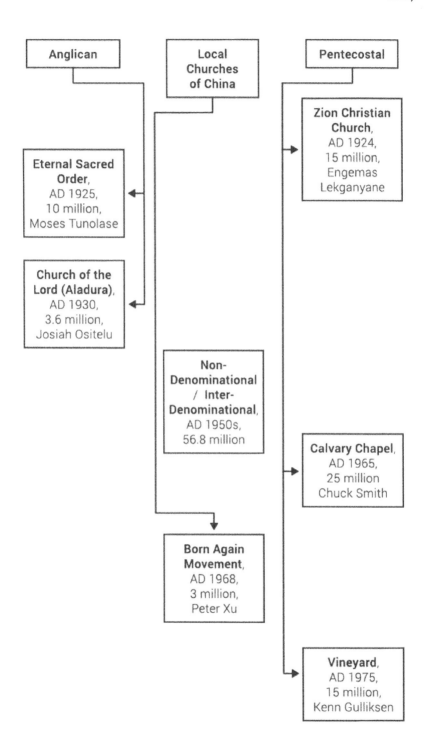

I see the congregations in the illustration as organized into four large groups: (1) congregations that are observant to the entirety of the commandments of God, (2) congregations that represent the earliest tradition of unified Gentile Christians, (3) liturgical Protestant congregations, and (4) non-liturgical Protestant congregations. I will clarify the term "liturgical" later, but for now, study the patterns in the illustration.

This small piece of history covered in the illustration begins with a commandment observant people (Second Temple Judaism), extending to the Gentile nations of the world,[36] progressing to widespread protest of corruption and abuse,[37] further evolving to the shedding of trivialized rituals and traditions,[38] and finally reaching the reemergence of a commandment observant people (Messianic Judaism, Seventh Day Adventist), even to embrace the people whom God never forsook. He said He would never leave nor forsake Yisrael (Israel).[39] He said He desired to gather them and that He would return for them.[40] He doesn't break His Word.[41]

You will notice that Messianic Judaism seems to disappear at the end of the illustration because it is unmentioned. Messianic Judaism made its debut in 1813, 1863, and again in 1884, but it did not reach more common recognition until the 1950s. In fact, extensive coverage of Messianic Judaism remained absent until the turn of the millennium. The population of Messianic Jews in Israel was only five to seven thousand in the 1990s. Their numbers jumped to ten thousand in 2008 and then twenty thousand in 2013. Global estimation of members of Messianic Judaism in 2013 was 300,000 (Statistics). We are seeing a rise of *talmidim*

---

36 Roman, Eastern Orthodox, Oriental Orthodox, Church of the East

37 Waldensian, Hussite, Lutheran, Reformed, Anglican, Presbyterian, Congregational, Methodist, New Apostolic Church, Church of the Nazarene, Zion Christian Church, Eternal Sacred Order, Church of the Lord Aladura, Vineyard

38 Anabaptist, Hutterite, Mennonite, Baptist, Quaker, Puritan, Amish, Schwarzenau Brethren, Church of Christ, Plymouth Brethren, Local Churches of China, Church of God Indiana, Christian and Missionary Alliance, Pentecostal, Non-denominational, Calvary Chapel, Born Again Movement

39 Exodus 32:12; Numbers 14:13; Joshua 7:9; 1 Samuel 12:22; Psalm 106:8; Jeremiah 14:21; Romans 11:1-12

40 Exodus 6:6-7; Matthew 23:37-39; Luke 13:34-35; Romans 11:25-32

41 Numbers 23:19; Isaiah 40:8; Matthew 5:18

(disciples) who desire to obey the commandments of Yah, blessed be His Name, because they love Him and place His Word above their surrounding culture, even above Western cultural Christianity.

Of all the congregations, my favorite is the Messianic Judaism congregations. They have the strongest claim to restorationism, meaning restoring the *talmidim* of the Anointed One back to first century Christianity. Messianic Judaism claims authority based on an ancient understanding (Jeremiah 6:16) of the Scriptures according to historical and cultural context. My only problem with them as a group is their chaotic disorganization and chasmal doctrinal variations. Nevertheless, these congregations offer what I feel to be the closest reflection of first century Christianity.

My second favorites are the Non-denominational/Inter-denominational congregations, especially those that use the Hebrew Roots Movement (HRM) in their understanding and application of the Scriptures. Non-denominational and Inter-denominational congregations, who come from the non-liturgical group, offer the freedom to seek God and the freedom to build relationship with God as He reveals Himself to the individual. My problem with them is that too many of them follow in the footsteps of mainstream Westernized/Gentile Christian theology. These Non-denominational and Inter-denominational congregations, however, still offer a space for those who desire to seek God without being hammered into robots of regurgitated theology.

My third favorite, coming from the earliest tradition of unified Gentile Christians, is the Eastern Orthodox congregation. They have the longest, and therefore oldest and strongest, claim to an unbroken chain of Gentile Christian orthodoxy, stretching as far back as second century Christianity. Their label of "Orthodox" suits them well. My only problem with them is their belief in transubstantiation[42] and that Miryam (Mary), the mother of Y'hoshua the Anointed One (Jesus the Christ), is sinless.[43] While I may disagree with them on some matters, they still offer the best

---

42 Genesis 9:4; Acts 15:19-20

43 Psalm 14:1-3; Psalm 53:1-3; Galatians 3:22; Romans 3:9, 23; Romans 5:11-13; Romans 11:32

claim to Gentile Christian orthodoxy over any other congregation who would like to commandeer the word and label of "orthodoxy." I still would never formally join them, and they would never accept me into fellowship with them because I do not believe in the doctrine of transubstantiation.

I have no favorites among liturgical Protestants because I do not have much experience with them. I may have attended the occasional service from a variety of their congregations, but I suppose I never saw the point of liturgy unless I joined the oldest forms of Gentile liturgy, being Roman or Eastern Orthodox. I do, however, admire the teachings of John Wesley who founded the Methodist congregation.

I admire Seventh Day Adventists for their desire to love God through His commandments.[44] They seriously consider the exhortation of the Master, "Why do you call Me, 'Lord, Lord,' and do not do what I say" (Luke 6:46). They understand Him when He says, "Yes indeed! I tell you that until heaven and earth pass away, not one *yud* or stroke will pass from the Torah until everything that must happen has happened" (Matthew 5:18). I, however, find them overly strict, even so far as teaching against imbibing alcohol when the Scriptures are clearly balanced on the matter.[45] They also do not believe in an eternal hell.[46] They believe that spirits who do not wish to have life, to have relationship with the Creator, will reap complete and utter destruction and thereafter cease to exist. Religious circles label this belief annihilationism. Seventh Day Adventists do not believe that we have immortal spirits in the image of Yah, blessed be His Name.

Interestingly, this belief in annihilationism does not originate with them. According to Jews:

---

44 John 14:15, 21; John 15:10; 1 John 5:2-3; 2 John 1:6

45 Genesis 27:28-29; Genesis 49:8-12; Leviticus 10:8-11; Numbers 6:1-21; Deuteronomy 14:22-26; Judges 13:3-5; Psalm 104:14-15; Proverbs 20:1; Proverbs 23:31-33; Proverbs 31:4-7; Amos 9:11-15; Matthew 26:26-29; John 2:1-11; Ephesians 5:18-20; 1 Timothy 3:1-13

46 Matthew 18:8; Matthew 25:46; 2 Thessalonians 1:9; Jude 1:7, 12-13; Revelation 14:11; Revelation 19:3; Revelation 20:10

Only truly righteous souls ascend directly to Gan Eden [Garden of Paradise], say the sages. The average person descends to a place of punishment and/or purification, generally referred to as Gehinnom.

The name is taken from a valley (*Gei Hinnom*) just south of Jerusalem, once used for child sacrifice by the pagan nations of Canaan (II Kings 23:10). Some view Gehinnom as a place of torture and punishment, fire and brimstone. Others imagine it less harshly, as a place where one reviews the actions of his/her life and repents for past misdeeds.

The soul's sentence in Gehinnom is usually limited to a twelve-month period of purgation before it takes its place in Olam Ha-Ba [world to come] (Mishnah Eduyot 2:9, Shabbat 33a). This twelve-month limit is reflected in the yearlong mourning cycle and the recitation of the Kaddish (the memorial prayer for the dead).

Only the utterly wicked do not ascend to Gan Eden at the end of this year. Sources differ on what happens to these souls at the end of their initial time of purgation. Some say that the wicked are utterly destroyed and cease to exist, while others believe in eternal damnation (Maimonides, Mishneh Torah, Law of Repentance, 3:5-6). (Rose)

Rabbinical Jews generally do not believe in an eternal hell because the first mention of an eternal hell is in the Apostolic Scriptures. Nevertheless, they consider it a possibility. Until Seventh Day Adventists can address Matthew 18:8, Matthew 25:46, 2 Thessalonians 1:9, Jude 1:7, 12-13, Revelation 14:11, Revelation 19:3, and Revelation 20:10, I stand wholly upon the belief of an eternal hell. Either way, the belief in hell or no hell does not change my life in the slightest fashion. I follow and obey God because I love Him, not because of a fear of eternal "fire."

This informational overview of the different congregations is by no means inerrantly accurate. It is not fully comprehensive or exhaustive. I had to group some congregations together for the sake of brevity, but I tried to include as many as space and sense allowed. I also included their estimated populations in the world (2015) and the person or movement that influenced their genesis just for your reference. I did not provide the illustrations and information as a citable resource, but for you to have a vague idea of the various congregations and estimated dates and numbers. Hopefully, you will find patterns that I have missed. At the very least, you will have a hint of an idea of the movement of God Almighty over the years through the morphology of Christian denominations.

CHAPTER FOUR

ORTHODOXY

MY CHILDREN, KNOW the Truth so that you may discern between the things of HaShem (The Name) and the perverted things of humanity, between the commandments of God and the traditions of humanity.

You will most likely encounter the word 'orthodoxy' somewhere in your journey to seek and know Yah, blessed be His Name. Orthodoxy is an interesting word. It means "a belief or way of thinking that is accepted as true or correct." Its etymology is Greek, mixing *orthos* (right, true) with *doxa* (opinion), thus meaning "right opinion." The word also implies original, age, ancient, and the support of many generations.

The word orthodoxy implies authority, but who has the authority to label something as orthodoxy? Who has the authority to claim something as authoritative? Elders or leaders of any community have the authority to label something as orthodoxy. Elders and leaders are also human and able to err. Thus, you have disagreements of orthodoxy between the latter group of theologians (John Wycliffe–John Knox) with the earlier group (Clement–Gregory). You can find disagreements of orthodoxy between the Catholic and Protestant congregations. You can find disagreements of orthodoxy between almost every congregational group that currently exists.

Using orthodoxy as the foundation for your beliefs is like building your house on shifting sand. The Master lectured on building houses on sand (Matthew 7:26-27). The problem with orthodoxy is that you will find various types of orthodoxies, even an orthodoxy for each congregational group, and they do not all agree with each other. I prefer to rely upon the Lord alone, upon the instruction of His Spirit, always anchored and tested by His written Word, and completely exemplified by the role model and standard of His Word born flesh, His Anointed One.

Some will use the argument of the "orthodoxy of the faith" as a defense for the doctrine of the Trinity. They will cite such historical figures as mentioned in the previous chapter for any case in which they use "orthodoxy" as authority. To fully grasp the idea of orthodoxy, however, you must first become familiar with the word "liturgy":

> Liturgy (*leitourgia*) is a Greek composite word meaning originally a public duty, a service to the state undertaken by a citizen. Its elements are *leitos* (from *leos=laos*, people) meaning *public,* and *ergo* (obsolete in the present stem, used in future *erxo*, etc.), *to do. . .*
>
> At Athens the *leitourgia* was the public service performed by the wealthier citizens at their own expense, such as the office of *gymnasiarch,* who superintended the gymnasium, that of *choregus,* who paid the singers of a chorus in the theatre, that of the *hestiator,* who gave a banquet to his tribe, of the *trierarchus,* who provided a warship for the state. The meaning of the word liturgy is then extended to cover any general service of a public kind. In the Septuagint, it (and the verb *leitourgeo*) is used for the public service of the temple (e.g., Exodus 38:27; Exodus 39:12, etc.). Thence it comes to have a religious sense as the function of the priests, the ritual service of the temple (e.g., Joel 1:9; Joel 2:17, etc.). In the New Testament, this religious meaning has become definitely established. In Luke 1:23, Zachary goes home when "the days of his *liturgy*" (*ai hemerai tes leitourgias autou*) are over . . .
>
> So in Christian use, liturgy meant the public official service

of the Church that corresponded to the official service of the Temple . . ." (Fortescue)

To clarify some terminology, "Mass" is the Roman service of worship, taken from the Latin word for "dismissal" because of the closing blessing at the end of every service. As a side note, the Eastern Orthodox calls their service of worship the "Liturgy."

> [An] Apostolic Liturgy in the sense of an arrangement of prayers and ceremonies, like our present ritual of the Mass, did not exist. For some time the Eucharistic Service was in many details fluid and variable. It was not all written down and read from fixed forms, but in part composed by the officiating bishop . . . All [ceremony] evolves gradually out of certain obvious actions done at first with no idea of ritual, but simply because they had to be done for convenience. The bread and wine were brought to the altar when they were wanted, the lessons were read from a place where they could best be heard, hands were washed because they were soiled. Out of these obvious actions, ceremony developed . . . It follows then, of course, that when there was no fixed Liturgy at all, there could be no question of absolute uniformity among the different Churches. (Fortescue)

To clarify, the "Holy Eucharist" in the previous quote refers to the breaking of bread (Acts 20:7). "Bishop" comes from the Greek word *episkopos*, which means overseer.[47] This is different from the word presbyter or elder, which comes from the Greek *presbyteros*.[48]

And yet the whole series of actions and prayers did not depend solely on the improvisation of the celebrating bishop. Whereas

---

47 Acts 20:28; Philippians 1:1; 1 Timothy 3:1-7; Titus 1:5-9; 1 Peter 2:25

48 Matthew 15:2; Matthew 16:21; Matthew 21:23; Matthew 26:3, 47, 57; Matthew 27:1, 3, 12, 20, 41; Matthew 28:12; Mark 7:3, 5; Mark 8:31; Mark 11:27; Mark 14:43; Mark 15:1; Luke 7:3; Luke 9:22; Luke 15:25; Luke 20:1; Luke 22:52; John 8:9; Acts 2:17; Acts 4:5, 8, 23; Acts 6:12; Acts 11:30; James 5:14; Acts 14:23; Acts 15:2, 4, 6, 22-23; Acts 16:4; Acts 20:17; Acts 21:18; Acts 23:14; Acts 24:1; Acts 25:15; 1 Timothy 5:1-2, 17-20; Titus 1:5-6; Hebrews 11: 2

at one time scholars were inclined to conceive the services of the first Christians as vague and undefined, recent research shows us a very striking uniformity in certain salient elements of the service at a very early date. The tendency among students now is to admit something very like a regulated Liturgy, apparently to a great extent uniform in the chief cities, back even to the first or early second century. In the first place the fundamental outline of the rite of the Holy Eucharist was given by the account of the Last Supper. What our Lord had done then, that same thing He told His followers to do in memory of Him. It would not have been a Eucharist at all if the celebrant had not at least done as our Lord did the night before He died. So we have everywhere from the very beginning at least this uniform nucleus of a Liturgy: bread and wine are brought to the celebrant in vessels (a plate and a cup); he puts them on a table—the altar; standing before it in the natural attitude of prayer, he takes them in his hands, gives thanks, as our Lord had done, says again the words of institution, breaks the Bread and gives the consecrated Bread and Wine to the people in communion. (Fortescue)

The Roman and Eastern Orthodox congregations call the bread the "Holy Eucharist," meaning the "set-apart body of the Anointed One," because they believe that the bread transforms into the actual flesh of the Anointed One. Thus, they capitalize "B" in bread and "W" in wine to denote the transubstantiation of the bread and wine into the body and blood of the Anointed One.

To clarify some of the mentioned rituals, washing hands before handling the bread and wine most likely did not result from having soiled hands, but rather from the tradition of Jews to ritually wash their hands before eating.[49] Also, the blessing that the Roman priest says before handling the bread and wine is the same as the blessing that the Jews say before eating bread and drinking wine. It is the same blessing that the Jews

---

49 Matthew 15:1-2; Mark 7:1-5

say during Passover, and most likely the same blessing that the Master said during His last supper with His *talmidim* (disciples) and for all His meals.

While Gentile Christians forgot this connection and now say "grace" over their meals to bless the food, Jews and the Master and the early *talmidim* never blessed food. They instead blessed HaShem (The Name) for His gift of food. Notice that the phrase "the food" did not exist in the original manuscripts of Matthew 14:19 and Mark 6:41. Gentile translators who were ignorant of Jewish culture and practices inserted the phrase "the food" into the verses. Our Master never blessed food. He blessed God. Nevertheless, the Apostolic Letters mention at least one time that blessing the food is appropriate—when there is a possibility that the food was part of a sacrifice to idols.[50]

I find humor in the attempt of using orthodoxy as a valid defense by non-liturgical Protestants. They will rely upon the writings of Clement of Rome, Ignatius of Antioch, and Polycarp of Smyrna, despite the fact that these men built the foundation for the institution of the Catholic (meaning "universal") congregation. They will accept these three and yet deny the doctrines of the Catholic congregation that these same three theologians built. Aurelius Ambrose of Milan, Eusebius Sophronius Hieronymus (Jerome), Augustine of Hippo, and Gregory the Great influenced the Western side of the Catholic congregation, which later became the Roman congregation. Basil of Caesarea, Athanasius, Gregory of Nazianzus, and John Chrysostom influenced the Eastern side of the Catholic congregation, which later became the Eastern Orthodox congregation.

I may not agree with the early Gentile theologies, but at least I can understand how someone from the Roman or Eastern Orthodox congregation can cite and stand upon the words of Chrysostom, Augustine, Polycarp, Ignatius, and Clement. I can even stretch my acceptance to include the liturgical Protestant congregations such as the Lutheran (AD 1521), Anglican/ Episcopalian (AD 1534), Presbyterian (AD 1560), Congregational/United Church of Christ (AD 1592), and Methodist (AD 1784) congregations. I cannot, however, fathom how non-liturgical con-

---

50 Daniel 1; Acts 15:19-21; 1 Corinthians 8; 1 Corinthians 10; Revelation 2:20; 1 Timothy 4:1-5

gregations such as Baptists and Pentecostals can call upon these ancient sources for their doctrinal and traditional support.

> Protestants think of themselves as people of the Book, not hampered by human tradition. They think of Catholics as, at best, followers of traditions for whom the Bible is secondary. That is a huge misconception: Protestants are *also* people of tradition. No one reads the Bible objectively. People who claim to "just read the Bible" really read it through the eyes of a tradition they've already accepted, whether that be Fundamentalist, Calvinist, Pentecostal, Baptist or one of many others. *Everyone* depends upon tradition, but not everyone recognizes it. (Ray)

These non-liturgical groups feel entitled to malign the Roman congregation for their man-made traditions, yet they themselves adopt what traditions they do have, such as Easter, Christmas, and the Day of Rest on the first day of the week, from the very same doctrinal roots they disdain.

Some non-liturgical Protestants go so far as to label the Roman congregation (their "parent" congregation) as a cult in hopes of authenticating their own theological authority. This accusatory attitude simply mirrors the general Gentile Christian attitude to their Hebrew roots. If we can invalidate our parents, we can usurp the throne of their authority.

I do not understand how non-liturgical Protestants can call the Roman congregation a cult and yet stand upon the doctrines of Clement, Ignatius, and Polycarp. Clement, Ignatius, and Polycarp built the Catholic doctrines of the Roman and Eastern Orthodox congregations. I also do not understand how non-liturgical Protestants refer to the doctrines of Wycliffe, Luther, Calvin, and Knox as the "orthodoxy of the faith." Do they not realize that these men supported, preached, and practiced a liturgy? Non-liturgical Protestants, of which Anabaptists and Baptists are the oldest, cannot claim these men as their orthodoxy since these men supported liturgy, as can be found in the Lutheran, Anglican/Episcopalian, Presbyterian, Congregational/United Church of Christ, and Methodist congregations. Either the Baptist and Pentecostal congregations must relinquish any claim to "the orthodoxy of the faith," or they must only rely upon the orthodoxy of the doctrines proposed by John Smyth, Henry Jacob, and Richard Blunt. Non-liturgical congregations can use neither the doctrines of Clement, Ignatius, and Polycarp, nor Wycliffe, Luther, and Calvin as orthodoxy for a defense of their doctrines. If non-liturgical congregations continue to maintain their defense of orthodoxy on such early figures as Ignatius of Antioch, Athanasius of Alexandria, and Augustine of Hippo, then they must concede that the Roman congregation has a stronger stance upon orthodoxy.

I laugh at the irony that many non-liturgical Protestants will label the Roman congregation as a cult, yet they celebrate Christmas, ignore the Lord's Day of Rest or misname the first day of the week as the Lord's Day of Rest, and hold to the doctrine of the Trinity. The Roman and Eastern congregations started such things. I smell the hint of hypocrisy in maintaining some parts of a tradition while denouncing other parts of the same tradition. Hypocrisy, to me, is adopting some of the same methodologies of the "parent" while scorning the "parent" for their practices. They practice the same arrogant rebellion to their "parent" as their "parent" did to the "grand-parent," as the Roman congregation did to their Hebrew roots. It is a vicious cycle. At least the Eastern Orthodox congregation still maintains relatively closer ties to their Hebrew roots. I can understand disagreement and separation due to differences in beliefs . . . but the gall to call the parent congregation a cult baffles me.

Protestants touted Sola Scriptura (by Scripture alone), Sola Fide (by faith alone), and Sola Gratia (by grace alone) as their motto when they rebelled against the authority of the Roman congregational elders. I personally strive to adhere to the idea of "by Scripture alone," but as revealed and instructed by the Spirit of God and educated in the context of culture, language, and history. I challenge Christmas-celebrating Protestants who tout Sola Scriptura to find the word "Christmas" or the occasion of the celebration of Christmas, the annual celebration of the Word born into flesh, in the Scriptures. "Under Calvinist Puritan and separatist influences in Britain and Europe, many Protestant groups who eventually emigrated to America rejected the Christian year and its feasts as 'abominations' . . . Christmas itself was not observed until the nineteenth century" (Webber,

Vol. 5, p. 42). If you study American History, you will find that only Catholic, Lutheran, and Anglican congregations celebrated Christmas. Non-liturgical Protestants strayed from Sola Scriptura when they adopted the traditions of "Christmas" from the very "parent" they called heathen.

Another word for "the Christian year and its feasts" is the liturgy, and non-liturgical Protestants, in my experience, generally disdain liturgy.

> Thus, most early Baptists followed the Calvinists in discarding calendars of "feasts and fasts," and in deemphasizing liturgical ceremony. This approach became so deeply entrenched that, even in to the early twentieth century, some Baptists of North America declined to observe Christmas and other Christian festivals and continued to uphold the related principle that every Lord's Day (Sunday) was just like any other." (Webber, Vol. 5, pp. 5-6)

I myself held the same belief for a number of years. I did not discover the Hebrew roots of the Christian liturgy, even in my Roman doctrinal upbringing, until I started digging into the Hebrew roots of the written Word of Yah, blessed be His Name. The more I studied and learned and understood, the more parallels I saw in the Catholic liturgy with Hebrew culture and liturgy.

> Although the liturgies of the Orthodox, Roman Catholic, Anglican, and certain Protestant communions may seem forbiddingly complex to members of nonliturgical Protestant traditions, the heart of the Communion service in all the liturgical groups is the great prayer and thanksgiving and blessing over the bread and wine. The prayer's roots extend all the way to the Jewish liturgy Jesus himself used. (Webber, Vol. 6, p. 251)

Yes, the liturgies of the various liturgical Christian congregations have Hebrew roots, though Christian congregations themselves might be ignorant of that fundamental relationship.

Christmas is now widely celebrated in America, even by Baptists, and even by atheists and followers of other religions. Its modern popularity is easy to explain. The non-liturgical Protestants who adopted Christmas after a history of rejecting it, adopted it for its worldly seductions and for its pleasures of gifts and entertaining symbols. Let me be clear. Their adoption of the holiday had nothing to do with the worship of HaShem (The Name).

You will find the focus of the liturgical keepers of the holiday (Roman, Episcopalian, Lutheran) to generally be the celebration of the Word becoming flesh, while non-liturgical congregations' focus will be on gifts. You will never find a cancelled service or Mass in a liturgical congregation when Christmas coincidentally falls on Sunday. You will find some non-liturgical congregations, however, who put more weight on Christmas morning presents than morning worship of Yah, blessed be His Name. It is not uncommon to find a cancelled service in a non-liturgical congregation when Christmas Day coincidentally occurs on Sunday. Thus, you easily find atheists, agnostics, and members of other religions participating in Christmas.

Who doesn't like a day to celebrate presents? It feeds the fleshly selfish desires, even if they justify themselves with the occasional charitable donation to a poor family. Observe families, Christian and otherwise, who celebrate Christmas and ask yourself if fellowship, prayer, and instruction consume most of their holiday, or if presents and worldly conversations do. You will soon discover why non-Christians can so easily adopt such man-made holidays.

Christians in America are fighting to "keep Christ in Christmas." It is time to leave the liturgical calendar and holidays to those who understand the liturgy and worship HaShem (The Name) through the liturgy. Christmas is inherently a part of Gentile Christian liturgy. If a congregation rejects liturgy, they must also reject "the Christian year and its feasts," such as Christmas, to avoid hypocrisy.

As for those outside spiritual and physical Yisrael (Israel), let them have their Winter Solstice and Saturnalia back, which still includes most of the "fun" trappings and appearances of the "Christmas season," such as the date of its celebration, the evergreen tree, holly and ivy decorations, yule log, wreaths, mistletoes, orb decorations, candles and lights, human-shaped biscuits, singing from house to house, and gift-giving, all wrapped in fancily disguised self-gratification as they mob rush retailers to satisfy their consumer idols.

As for me and my house, we will keep the appointed times of God and dust off the Gentile additions, many of which drip with pagan connotations. When you become an adult and have your own "house," your own family, I hope you continue with the same set-apartness and remember to refrain from disdaining others' different methods of worship. Protect your mind from disdain to protect your heart from evil. Humility is the Way of God.

I reject the idea of "by faith alone'" because it attempts to deny the entire writings of Ya'akov (James), the kinsman of Y'hoshua the Anointed One (Jesus the Christ) and overseer of the congregation at Yerushalayim (Jerusalem). Sola Fide denies the written Word of God (James 2:24). "The book received its harshest treatment from Martin Luther. Luther emphasized Paul's doctrine of justification by faith so strongly that he had difficulty accepting James (cf. Rom. 3:27-30; James 2:20-26). Luther regarded James as an 'epistle of straw,' but he did quote it approvingly on several occasions" (Lea). No motto of a *talmid* should ever contradict even a simple interpretation of the Word.

I will not delve into semantics at this time, but I do wholeheartedly support "by grace alone," which, mind you, is understood differently between Calvinists and Arminians.

Orthodoxy can also be categorized, not by congregation, but by topic. In other words, one could separate the orthodoxy of the doctrine of the Trinity apart from other doctrinal statements or practices. Separating and isolating doctrinal statements allows groups to claim the orthodoxy of a particular belief while rejecting the orthodoxy of other connected beliefs. Thus, a Baptist can claim the orthodoxy of the doctrine of the Trinity while rejecting the orthodoxy of the doctrine of the liturgy.

Nevertheless, why should I give value to a statement of orthodoxy concerning the doctrine of the Trinity from someone who denies a statement of orthodoxy concerning the liturgy? The doctrine of the liturgy, for example, which can be traced back to Jewish liturgy, is even older than the doctrine of the Trinity. Should I simply accept a person's opinion that a single doctrinal orthodoxy is better than the other? Either orthodoxy stands together or falls together. I do not accept a cut and paste ideology. Such practices coincide too much with building one's own idol or fashioning a religious smorgasbord of convenience to satisfy one's own desires.

The strongest orthodoxy for Gentile Christianity is found in the practices and doctrines of the Roman and Eastern Orthodox congregations. They have stood the tests of time, defended their doctrines throughout the ages, and can live at peace with each other. Conversations concerning reunification between the two groups ebb and flow in seriousness throughout the years. While I do not agree with much of Roman doctrine and practices, I can at least commend them for their fight against the confusion of the early years; I commend them for their solidarity, their commitment, their perseverance, and submission to authority. The more I learn, the more I also appreciate the Eastern Orthodox congregation, which I believe holds the oldest of orthodox beliefs in a Gentile Christian age.

My response to the orthodoxy of the Roman and Eastern Orthodox congregations is Sola Scriptura. I have no intent of disdain or offense. I have only passion for the Truth, and I will be held accountable according to my understanding, talents (Matthew 25:14-30), and mina (Luke 19:11-27) before the judgment seat of Yah, blessed be His Name. I will not depend upon others, even in places of authority, for my responsibilities on the Day of Judgment. They will not be able to take the blame for the wrong doctrines I inherit from them, and my resulting actions dependent on such doctrines. Pagan influence is proven in Gentile Christianity. HaShem (The Name) is set-apart. I hold to the orthodoxy of the Scriptures and the Jewish apostles, not to pagan-influenced Gentile philosophy and traditions.

Repeating my previous statement, I am not saying that past generations of Christians were all failures or that their doctrines were all inaccurate. I am not saying that the full gamut of Christian congregations is or was all failure. I believe each congregation stands to serve their purpose. The parting of ways between the Christian sect and P'rushim (Pharisees) sect of Second Temple Judaism was to create an environment for Gentiles to flourish in their relationship with Yah, blessed be His Name, without the hindrances of messianic Jews who insist that Gentile Christians must become like Jews.[51]

The Catholic (universal) congregation bourgeoned for a thousand years until the Great Schism, which I believe to be the beginning of what I deem restorationism. I am not specifically referring to the Restoration Movement in America started by Barton Stone (AD 1801) and Thomas Campbell (AD 1809), but rather to the overall principle of restorationism. I am definitely not referring to the New Apostolic Movement with its claims of a return to the appointments of apostles, which I do not trust, considering none of the current appointments are Jews nor eyewitnesses of the Anointed One. I also do not believe they were directly sent by HaShem (The Name) Himself. Restorationism, however, concerns the return of the Gentile congregations to first century Christianity.

> The first volume of Gilbert Burnet's History of the Reformation of the Church of England (1679) sought to establish beyond all doubt that, "the design of the Reformation was to restore Christianity to what it was at first." In 1687 the clergyman, Simon Patrick (1626–1707), later bishop of Ely, asserted that "the Religion of the Church of England, by Law established, is the true Primitive Christianity." The "Deliverance" of the Revolution of 1688–1689 provided the perfect context to affirm that the "Protestant Religion" in England was "Primitive Christianity Restored." Thereafter, this assertion became the mainstay of Anglican apologetics and an assumption of the faithful. Taking it as a given that appeals to primitive Christianity were various and inherently contestable both within and without the Church of England, which was obviously neither a static, nor monolithic institution, the basic claim of this essay is that such appeals were not only subtly distinct from the process of citing specific Church Fathers but were indicative of an emerging ideology that was actually formative in establishing the very intellectual and

---

51 Galatians 2:14; Galatians 6

cultural context by which such citations were perceived to have authority in the Reformations. Put another way, the authority of the Fathers would have been vastly diminished had an ideology of Christian primitivism not existed. (Manning)

In other words, the leaders of the Protestant Reformation would have had much weaker authority in their movement without the idea of "Christian primitivism," or restorationism, of restoring the Gentile congregations to first century Christianity.

Persecution seems to be the anvil upon which we see the rise of the people of Yah, blessed be His Name. We see the proof in the generation of Yisrael (Israel) that left the wilderness and entered the Promised Land under the leadership of Y'hoshua (Joshua), previously Hoshea, son of Nun (Numbers 13:16). We see the proof in the early Jewish believers who strived side-by-side with the apostles. We see the proof in the early Catholic (Universal) congregation, who grew in spiritual strength due to the persecution by the Roman Empire before the policy changes of Roman emperors Constantine (AD 306–337) and Theodosius (AD 379–392). We see the proof in the early generations of Protestants during the Reformation. We see the proof in the Blacks who survived slavery and endured the Jim Crow laws. We see the proof right now in the Local Churches of China. Comfort, however, breeds weakness, corruption, and disintegration.

While the Catholic congregation blossomed for the first thousand years after the resurrection and ascension of the Master, so too did restorationism thrive for the next thousand years. Christianity progressed, according to my personal estimation and research, through the following path:

- Great Schism, AD 1054
- Protestant Reformation of the 16th century
- Great Ejection of the 17th century
- Holiness Movement of the 18th century
- Sabbatarianism and Millennialism of the 19th century

- Charismatic Movement of the 20th century

- Hebrew Roots Movement (HRM) of the 21st century

The first thousand years built the ideal environment for Gentiles' growth in Yah, blessed be His Name, much like the growth of Yisrael in Egypt. The second thousand years brought and is bringing Gentiles back to first century Christianity.

The Great Schism saw a humbling of *talmidim* (disciples) to the Instruction of the Lord. It saw the rejection of idolatry in obedience to the second of the Ten D'varim (Ten Words, Ten Matters, Ten Subjects) of God and the core of the decision of the Council of Yerushalayim (Jerusalem) (Acts 15:19-20).

The Protestant Reformation brought intimacy with the Lord for the common person. It brought the Scriptures, and thus the Truth, into a language that the local communities, and therefore the common person, could read for themselves, know God, and have a personal relationship with Him. The Great Ejection provided freedom from man-made restrictions in order to seek Him as He revealed Himself through His written Word. It helped implement newly discovered Truth into one's life. It gave them freedom from routine tradition, a freedom to seek God Almighty according to His written Word and apart from Gentile orthodoxy.

The Holiness Movement imbued *talmidim* with amplified passion for God Most High and His righteousness. It encouraged them to protect their hearts with His righteousness and to lead lives of service, lives set-apart for Yah, blessed be His Name, and His purpose. While Christianity spread from Europe and the Middle East to the Americas, Asia, and again to Africa, Sabbatarianism and Millennialism, both of which drew closer to Jewish and early Christian practices and beliefs, came into the field.

Then we saw the Charismatic Movement of the 20th century, which brought our attentions to Pentecost (Fiftieth Day), the day that the Jews flooded Yerushalayim to celebrate Shavu'ot (Weeks), the day that the Spirit of God empowered His people, the day that the Christian sect of Judaism started, and the day that Jews celebrated the official giving of His commandments to Moshe (Moses). Now we have the HRM, which brings clarity to all the Scriptures according to the context of the authors, the Hebrew language and culture, the historical practices, and the lives and leadership of the apostles, even the teachings and earthly life of the Anointed One.

Some criticize the Hebrew Roots Movement (HRM) because it obviously does not follow the ideology of mainstream Gentile Christianity. I add that many criticisms attacked other earlier pioneering movements. The Romans criticized the Eastern Orthodox and vice versa. The Romans with a membership of 1.2 billion and the Protestants with a membership of 800 million still criticize each other. Evangelicals and Seventh Day Adventists lobby criticisms at each other. Criticisms are constructive in that a person can use them to study and weigh the accusations, enabling them to discern cultic from Scripturally reliable beliefs . . . even if and when they are disagreeable. Criticisms can also be destructive in the sense that they are generally in a spirit of hate, disdain and arrogance, or ignorance.

Critics say that the Hebrew Roots Movement (HRM) misinterprets the Instruction and the Good News. The opposite stands. The HRM, with an understanding of the context of culture and history and time and language, desires to correct the misinterpretation of the Instruction and the Good News. They say that the HRM insists on keeping the fourth of the Ten D'varim (Ten Words), what mainstream Christians call the fourth of the Ten Commandments. Indeed, the HRM supports the entirety of the Ten D'varim.

They criticize the HRM for its use of the Instruction and the Prophets as their guide for religious practices and beliefs. Indeed, all the apostles, especially Sha'ul (Saul/Paulos/Paul), the apostle to the Gentiles, used the Instruction and the Prophets as their guide for religious practices and beliefs. The early Christians for many years only had the Instruction and the Prophets until the Good News and Apostolic Letters were written, copied, and circulated.

Critics censure the HRM by demanding that the Greek version of the Scriptures supersedes the Hebrew version. They must have lost their minds. Firstly, I cannot rationalize taking a translation above the original language. Secondly, all the translations, whether in Hebrew, Greek,

Aramaic, English, or any other language, are authoritative in some way (Nehemiah 8:8).

They also criticize eating kosher. The HRM doesn't promote a kosher diet, which is dictated by Rabbinical Judaism, but a dietary restriction on meat according to what Yah, blessed be His Name, said was clean to eat, even as early as Noach (Genesis 7:2). Eating animal meat that is unclean to eat is described by HaShem (The Name) to be *to'evah* (Deuteronomy 14:3-20), appearing in various Scriptural translations as a detestable thing, abominable thing, or disgusting . . . punishable by death or excommunication.[52] The Lord says the same thing of any form of sexual immorality as He defines it (Leviticus 18), worshiping statues or making statues for worship,[53] murder of children,[54] persuading someone away from HaShem (Deuteronomy 13:12-15), offering "damaged goods" as a sacrifice to God (Deuteronomy 17:1), idolatry,[55] witchcraft of all varieties (Deuteronomy 18:9-14), cross-dressing (Deuteronomy 22:5), monetary Temple offerings from prostitution and those outside covenant with God Almighty (Deuteronomy 23:18), remarrying one's previously remarried ex-wife (Deuteronomy 24:1-4), and cheating for monetary gain (Deuteronomy 25:13-16).

There are, however, some dietary leniencies for those not physically Yisrael (Israel) but grafted into Yisrael (Deuteronomy 14:21). These criticizers against the HRM cannot maintain logic or consistency when they disdain everything on the previous list of *to'evah* but make an exception for God Most High's diet plan. These criticizers also disdain the celebration of God's appointed times, yet they have no qualms about celebrating Christmas with all its accoutrements in pagan roots.

These criticizers, however, have a valid point in that there are many

---

52 Genesis 43:32; Genesis 46:34; Exodus 8:26; Leviticus 18:22, 26-27, 29, 30; Leviticus 20:13; Deuteronomy 7:25-26; Deuteronomy 12:31; Deuteronomy 13:14; Deuteronomy 14:3; Deuteronomy 17:1, 4; Deuteronomy 18:9, 12; Deuteronomy 20:18; Deuteronomy 22:5; Deuteronomy 23:18; Deuteronomy 24:4; Deuteronomy 25:16; Deuteronomy 27:15; Deuteronomy 32:16

53 Deuteronomy 7:25-26; Deuteronomy 27:15

54 Deuteronomy 12:31; Deuteronomy 18:9-10

55 Deuteronomy 17:2-5; Deuteronomy 20:18

flaws, inaccuracies, and unscriptural beliefs within the HRM. The HRM is fairly new, and nothing controls or standardizes the movement. Just as with all movements, from the Protestant Reformation to the Charismatic Movement, many sub-groups propagate within each dynamism. From the Protestant Reformation to the Charismatic Movement, from the Lutherans to the Assemblies of God, only a small number of congregations survive the birthing pains of movements. Only time will tell which groups will survive the HRM. So far, my votes are for the First Fruits of Zion led by Boaz Michael and the Seed of Abraham led by Avram Yehoshua, although I still do not fully agree with either group.

The HRM is so varied as to include the full gamut, from Jews raised under the Sinai Covenant who are now ordained Baptist leaders, to Gentiles striving to be more Jewish than Jews themselves. I am saddened to see Jews turn their back on the Sinai Covenant in order to enter into the New Covenant (e.g., Jews for Jesus organization), knowing that no covenant should ever be invalidated, but rather they build on top of each other (Galatians 3:15).

I am also saddened to see Gentiles striving to be more culturally Jewish, striving to obey the commandments of HaShem (The Name) the way the Jews obey them, rather than striving to obey the commandments the Way the Anointed One exemplified obedience for us.[56] He did not, for example, encourage the title of master (rabbi).[57] He criticized the P'rushim (Pharisees), the religious ancestors of Rabbinical Judaism, for many of their practices and interpretation of the Instruction (Matthew 23). The Master did, however, share more in common with the P'rushim than He did any of the other sects.

I also agree with the HRM criticizers that no additional writings (i.e., Mishnah, Talmud, Zohar, etc.) should ever be seen as equal to the Instruction, the Prophets, the Good News, and the Apostolic Letters. By all means, read the Mishnah and Talmud as commentary if you wish, but always with the understanding that they were written by authors of an

---

56 Matthew 15:1-20; Matthew 23:23; Mark 7:1-23; Luke 11:42
57 Matthew 23:1-10; Matthew 26:25, 49; Mark 9:5; Mark 11:21; Mark 14:45; John 1:38; John 4:31; John 9:2; John 11:8

anti-Christ persuasion. Also, the time you spend on the Scriptures should always dwarf the amount of time that you spend on commentary. Sharpen your mind with the Word of God, not commentary.

In addition, the Zohar should be avoided at all costs. It is the main inspiration for Kabbalah, which is simply a Jewish form of witchcraft that mainstream religious Jews somehow accepted into their midst. I have seen its dangers firsthand in the lives of people dear to me. It can even confuse the minds of those who have the anointing of HaShem with its philosophical babble and evasively longwinded nonsense.

The HRM, despite its flaws, stands as a bridge back to 1st century Christianity, to the ancient paths.[58] The Charismatic Movement stands as a reminder that the Spirit of God still works supernaturally in our earthly world.[59] The Sabbatarians stand as examples of hearts that desire the blessing of the commandments of Yah, blessed be His Name.[60] The Holiness Movement stands as an example of hearts that desire the righteousness of HaShem (The Name).[61] The Great Ejection stands as a pillar of love for the Truth.[62] The Protestant Reformation stands as a pillar of passion to know the Lord and His Way directly from His own written Word apart from the traditions of man.[63] The Roman congregation stands as a pillar of unity and order.[64] The Eastern Orthodox congregation represents the oldest Gentile Christian orthodoxy; they are the "history keepers."

---

58 Deuteronomy 18:15-18; Jeremiah 6:16; Zechariah 8:20-23; John 4:22; Acts 2:46; Romans 11

59 Numbers 11:29; Matthew 7:21-23; 1 Corinthians 12; Romans 12:6-8

60 Exodus 20:8-11; Psalm 119; Isaiah 56:2-7; Matthew 12:1-13; Matthew 24:20; Mark 2:23-28; Luke 6:1-10; Luke 13:10-17; Luke 14:1-6; John 7:21-24

61 Deuteronomy 16:20; Isaiah 1:16-17; Isaiah 56:1; Micah 6:8; Matthew 5:10; Matthew 23:23; James 4:17; 1 Thessalonians 5:15; Galatians 6:8-10; Romans 2:7-29; Romans 12:20-21; 2 Corinthians 13:5-7; Colossians 3:17

62 Joshua 24:14; Ezekiel 33:1-20; John 4:23-24; 2 Thessalonians 2:8-12; 1 Corinthians 5:8; 1 Corinthians 13:1-6; 2 Corinthians 13:8; Ephesians 5:6-10

63 Deuteronomy 12:32; Deuteronomy 13:1-5 [Deuteronomy 13:1-6]; Isaiah 29:13-24; Nehemiah 8:8; Matthew 15:1-9; Acts 17:10-12; Romans 15:4; 1 Timothy 1:8-11; 1 Timothy 4; 1 Timothy 6:1-12; Titus 1:10-16; Titus 2:1; 2 Timothy 3:16-17

64 Exodus 19:8; Exodus 35:1; Leviticus 8:1-5; Psalm 133; 2 Chronicles 30:11-12; Acts 1:14; Acts 2:46; 1 Corinthians 1:10; Philippians 1:27-28; Hebrews 10:23-25

No trend exists among the members of the Roman or Eastern Ortho-dox congregations of leaving a congregation simply because they do not hear what they want to hear, jumping from congregation to congrega-tion until they find a teacher who caters to them or tickles their ear. If a member disagrees with some doctrine or practice, that person simply maintains and stands for their beliefs with the enduring hope of changing the congregation from within.

The Eastern Orthodox stands as a pillar of the wisdom that can be found in tradition.[65] For example, the Eastern Orthodox congregation worships God with prayers that are mostly, if not all, sung, just as in Jewish worship, to symbolize dancing smoke rising from the altar of incense (Revelation 8: 3). They celebrate the resurrection of the Anointed One on Pascha (Greek for Passover) instead of Easter (named after the North Umbrian Germanic tribe's idol of fertility) on the first day of the week following the Jewish Passover (Leviticus 23:11). Both the Roman and Eastern Orthodox congregations stand as examples of endurance in the face of persecution. We all have our purpose as individuals, as congre-gations, and within movements.

Take the good of each movement, but always remain skeptical, weigh-ing them by the only standard of Truth, which is the Word of God. I have seen the good, but also the glaring misinterpretations of the Scriptures. Be on guard and cling to the orthodoxy of the apostles.

---

65 Job 12: 12; Proverbs 10: 8; Proverbs 13: 1; Jeremiah 6: 16; Jeremiah 18: 15-17; 2 Thessalonians 2: 15; 2 Thessalonians 3: 6; 1 Corinthians 11: 2; Hebrews 13: 7

CHAPTER FIVE

WORD

MY CHILDREN, IF we are to know Yah, blessed be His Name, we must know His revelation of Himself to humanity. HaShem (The Name) reveals Himself to us through both His Spirit and His Word. His Word is more than just His written Word. His Word is completely revealed through the physical embodiment of the emanation of His Word, the incarnation of His Word . . . His Word born flesh, being Y'hoshua the Anointed One (Jesus the Christ).[66]

The Jews view Torah as the Law of God, meaning the first five books of the Scriptures, the books of the Instruction, the books of the Law: (1) B'reishit (Beginning), (2) Sh'mot (Names–Names of God), (3) Vayikra (Calling–calling for the people of God), (4) B'midbar (Desert/Wilderness–the struggles of the people of God in the wilderness), and (5) D'varim (Words–last words of Moshe) (Block). I prefer the Hebrew titles for the books of the Torah, which they take from the first word in each book. The titles neither add nor subtract from the written Word of HaShem. Later Jewish translators, however, attached their own Greek titles to the Pentateuch (Greek meaning Five Scrolls): Genesis (generations–these are the generations of), Exodus (going out–mass departure

---

66 John 1: 1-5, 9-11, 14

from Mitzrayim/Kemet/Egypt), Leviticus (Levites–relating to the Levites), Numbers (relating to the numbering of the tribes), Deuteronomy (Second Law–the second declaration of the Law) (Block). Both sets of titles provide their own insight.

The actual translation for the Hebrew "Torah" into English is "Instruction."

> The expression derives from two Greek words *penta*, "five," and *teuchos*, "vessel, container," and refers to the first five books of OT. . .but Jewish canons label these books collectively as the Torah, which means "Teaching, Instruction." In English Bibles these first five books are commonly called "Law." This designation is misleading because it misrepresents the content of the Pentateuch. (Block)

Torah Resources International further supports Block:

> The Hebrew word, torah . . . is derived from a root that was used in the realm of archery, yareh . . . Yareh means to shoot an arrow in order hit a mark. The mark or target, of course, was the object at which the archer was aiming. Consequently, torah, one of the nouns derived from this root, is, therefore, the arrow aimed at the mark. The target is the truth about God and how one relates to Him. The torah is, therefore, in the strict sense instruction designed to teach us the truth about God. Torah means direction, teaching, instruction, or doctrine. We should note that the usual translation of this word as law is not quite accurate. One of the most common ways that torah . . . is rendered in the Septuagint (LXX) is by using the word nomos . . . The Greek word nomos, however, has a variety of uses, among which, to be sure, is law, but it is certainly not limited to law. Following the precedent set by the LXX, the Newer Covenant Scriptures consistently render the Hebrew torah by the term nomos. This is where things begin to become confusing. Sometimes, in the New Covenant Scriptures, it is appropriate to translate nomos as law. However, other times

it is more appropriate to render it as God's teaching/instruction, or simply to transliterate the term as Torah. The context of the word is always the final determiner of its meaning. There are at least two other related Hebrew words derived from the same root as torah. The first is the word for teacher, moreh . . . A moreh is one who imparts instruction to his/her students. The second important word is parent, horeh . . . This indicates to us that one of the primary roles for a parent is to teach and instruct the child. (Torah)

Even the Jews agree: "The Septuagint rendered the Hebrew *torah* by the Greek *nomos* ('law') . . . The designation of the Torah as *nomos* . . . has historically given rise to the misunderstanding that Torah means legalism" (Bard). Thus, Torah is more accurately the Instruction of Yah, blessed be His Name, more so than the Law of God.

Over the years, "Law" became synonymous with "Torah" as early as the translation of the Instruction to the Septuagint around the 3rd century BC. So, while the past two-thousand-year interpretation of Torah is "Law," the accurate translation is "Instruction." Although they are both valid within their contextual circles, I prefer "Instruction" in place of "Law" for accuracy's sake, and in place of "Torah" for the sake of an English-speaking audience, except within the context of quotes.

Continuing on the clarification of semantics concerning the Anointed One, the Jews linked Wisdom together with Torah. "In 10:1 (335) the reference to Proverbs 3:8 substitutes Torah for Wisdom and declares in keeping with Philo's structural Logos that the pillars of Torah are the pillars of the world . . . Surely this implies the role in creation played by the preexistent Torah" (Ellens). Ellens makes the point that the Instruction of God and the Spirit of Wisdom are preexistent, meaning they are divine and not created, making both Instruction and Wisdom facets of Yah, blessed be His Name. Furthermore, Keener made the connection of Wisdom and Torah with the Word of God:

Philo also connects creation with the law of Moses, and by arguing that the universe was created in harmony with Moses' law and that those who obey the law obey Nature, he explicitly identifies Moses' law with the universal natural law that philosophers conceived as pervading the cosmos . . . As early as the second century B.C.E., Jewish writers indicated God's prior design for creation rooted in knowledge or wisdom . . . Texts connect creation by God's word with creation by his wisdom or Torah . . . Not only was the world created by Word, Wisdom, and Torah, it was sustained by Word, Wisdom, and Torah. (Keener, John, p. 380)

We also historically see that Jews personified Wisdom and Torah, and Keener takes the next step to explain Y'hochanan (John) the apostle's use of the Greek "Logos" in John 1:1:

The image of divine Wisdom was almost certainly more widespread than the personification of Torah in John's day; the former was available to all readers of the LXX [Septuagint] and their pupils, whereas the latter seems to have flourished particularly in Pharisaic circles. A neutral term like Logos could draw on associations with personified Wisdom already offered in Hellenistic Judaism, without compromising its bridge to the Torah, which was also recognized as God's Word. (Keener, John, p. 361-362)

Logos is Greek for "word," and is the Greek word that Y'hochanan the apostle used in John 1:1 to describe Y'hoshua the Anointed One. According to Keener, Wisdom was more popular with the Hellenistic Jews or Hellenists while Torah was more popular with the Hebraic Jews or Hasidim, making "Word" the bridge or middle ground between Wisdom and Torah.

The Word may also be personified in second-century B.C.E. 1 Enoch, a work of Palestinian provenance. The Wisdom of Solomon is clearer: God's all-powerful Logos came down from heaven to slay the first-born immediately before the exodus. Rabbinic texts sometimes personified the Word. The rabbinic mystic work 3 Enoch objectifies the Word of God as Dibburiel, one of Metatron's seventy names. The "progressive hypostatization of the

Word in Judaism" may well include the Memra concept of the Targumim as one illustration. (Keener, John, p. 351)

While non-messianic Jews ascribe the Word of God to Dibburiel, the Scriptures ascribe the Word of God to Y'hoshua the Anointed One.

First Enoch, 2 Enoch, and 3 Enoch are, despite their similar titles, three books written by different authors across different time periods. They all share the same title due to the person who appears in all three works, being Chanok (Enoch).[67] Neither non-messianic Jews nor Christians currently consider these books as inspired by HaShem (The Name) except for the Ethiopian Orthodox congregation, who consider only 1 Enoch as inspired (Barry, Enoch). First Enoch was also "popular in Judaism and Christianity during the centuries immediately preceding and following Jesus' birth" and was supposedly quoted by Y'hudah in Jude 1:14-15 (Hiehle). First Enoch is divided into five parts: Chapters 1-36 as the "Book of the Watchers," Chapters 37-71 as the "Parables," Chapters 72-82 as the "Astronomical Enoch," Chapters 83-90 as the "Book of Dream," and Chapters 91-108 as "Enoch's Testament" (Hiehle).

The Astronomical Book may be the earliest of the Enochic writings, followed by the Book of the Watchers; both of these texts can be dated to the late third or second century BC, prior to the Maccabean revolt. Since it is not included among the Dead Sea Scrolls, the [Parables] of Enoch could then be understood as the most recent of the books of 1 Enoch. VanderKam dates it between the first century BC and first century AD. (Hiehle)

Second Enoch and 3 Enoch, however, are neither considered to be early works relative to the rest of the Scriptures, nor considered inspired by mainstream Judaism or Christianity. "The author of 2 Enoch is unknown, but is often proposed that it was composed by a Jew in Palestine or Egypt, and was later added to by Jewish and Christian writers . . . Suggestions for the date of 2 Enoch range from the first century AD to the 10th century AD" (Thornhill). As far as I am concerned, 3 Enoch is not any more reli-

---

67 Genesis 5:18-24, Hebrews 11: 5

able than 2 Enoch in reference to divine inspiration. The original title for 3 Enoch was Sefer Hekhalot, meaning "Book of Palaces," and its authorship attributed to Ishmael, a historical Jewish elder (Odor).

> The Jewish mystical movement that birthed 3 Enoch draws from traditions found in Old Testament prophetic texts, such as Ezekiel's visions of heaven (Ezekiel 40-48) and of the chariot of God (Ezekiel 1; 3 Enoch 24), as well as Isaiah's vision of God's throne (Isaiah 6) . . . The text seems to be a compilation of Enochic stories gathered over several centuries, and its final form dates to the fifth or sixth century AD. (Odor)

Only one Christian congregation considers 1 Enoch as inspired by Yah, blessed be His Name. In addition, it is purportedly quoted in the Apostolic Letters. The authenticity of 2 Enoch and 3 Enoch, however, are dubious at best. Nevertheless, Judaism, which allows Kabbalistic witchcraft to pollute all of its areas, uses all three books as sources for their philosophy.

The Jewish mystical movement referenced by Odor is the *ma'aseh merkavah*, which means "the workings of the chariot," coming from Yechezkel's vision in Ezekiel 1. "*Ma'aseh merkavah* . . .was among the earliest movements in Jewish mysticism . . . The early mystics—the predecessors of kabbalists—meditated on the image of the fiery chariot to develop a fuller understanding of God" (SparkNotes Editors). *Ma'aseh merkavah* and Kabbalah are supposedly based on the Instruction, but the commandments of HaShem (the Name) clearly speak against witchcraft.[68] In addition, we have the warnings of God through Yechezkel: "Woe to the seamstresses of magic charms on wrists, who make amulets for the heads of every stature in order to hunt human lives" (Ezekiel 13:18b)! A short online search for "Kabbalah," "amulets," and "charms" should prove to you the obvious relationship between Kabbalah and witchcraft.

---

68 Exodus 22:18; Leviticus 19:26, 31; Leviticus 20:6, 27; Deuteronomy 18:9-14; 1 Samuel 15:23; 1 Samuel 28;2 Kings 21:6; 1 Chronicles 10:13-14; 2 Chronicles 33:6; Isaiah 8:19-20; Isaiah 44:25; Isaiah 47:8-14; Acts 8:9, 18-22; Acts 13:6-12; Galatians 5:19-21; Revelation 9:20-21; Revelation 21:8; Revelation 22:15

Some kabbalists will claim that amulets and charms are the result of Hermetic Qabalah, a European distortion of Jewish Kabbalah. They will claim that Jewish Kabbalah is more akin to philosophy than witchcraft, but you will find just as many talismans and amulets offered for sale from Jewish websites as you will from Gentile websites. Observe www.kabbala. co.il and Itzhak Mizrahi, for example. Witchcraft also does not restrain itself to tangible objects and casting of spells, but also extends to ways of thought and mystical patterns. I also respond with a warning from apostle Sha'ul. "Beware so that no one will take you captive through philosophy and vain deception according to the kabbalah of men, according to the elemental spirits of the world, and not according to the Messiah" (Colossians 2:8) (Orthodox Jewish Bible). The more common translation for Colossians 2:8 uses "tradition" instead of "kabbalah," but the use of the word "kabbalah" by the Orthodox Jewish Bible is nevertheless interesting and telling.

You will find within Judaism the belief in a supernatural figure named Metatron. He appears not only in the Talmud, but also in all three works of 1 Enoch, 2 Enoch, and 3 Enoch. Of these works, the earliest is 1 Enoch, specifically in the section recognized as the "Parables," which is the isolated section that could have been written as late as AD 100. The rest of 1 Enoch was written earlier, which to my knowledge does not mention Metatron. The Babylonian Talmud mentions him in Chagigah 15a, Sanhedrin 38b, Sanhedrin 94a, Avodah Zarah 3b, Zevachim 16b, and Chullin 60a. Targum Yerushalmi also refers to him in Genesis 5:24, Exodus 24:1, and Deuteronomy 34:6. He also appears in the Midrash on Lamentations and in Chapter 6 of Midrash Tanchuma Va'etchanan, concerning Deuteronomy 3:23 through Deuteronomy 7:11 (Singer, Volume 8).

The Scriptures say that Chanok (Enoch) did not die, but instead simply disappeared from the earth (Genesis 5:24). The common belief is that Yah, blessed be His Name, took Chanok, still alive in the flesh, to be with Him. Ancient Jewish texts claim that Chanok transformed into an angel named Metatron, which means "guide" from the Latin *metator*, fitting Volume 2 of Adolf Jellinek's Beit ha-Midrash: "[Metatron] is the most excellent of all the heavenly host, and the guide to all the treasuries of my [God]" (Singer, Volume 8). Other titles attested to Metatron are "prince of the presence," "prince of the ministering angels," "mighty scribe," "the lord of all the heavenly hosts, of all treasures, and of secrets," who "bears the lesser divine name" (Singer, Volume 8).

> The Zohar defines his nature exactly by declaring that he is little lower than God . . . The ancients had already noticed that the numerical value of the letters in the word "Metatron" correspond with those of the word "Shaddai," and "Metatron" is also said to mean "palace" ("metatrion"), and to be connected with the divine name [place], etc. (Singer, Volume 8)

My first impression of the ancient written understanding of Metatron is that the ancients suffered from identity crises concerning the supernatural figure. In some cases, He is compared to HaShem (The Name) Himself. In some cases, he is thought to be Chanok transformed.

Nothing in the Scriptures ever hints that a man could ever become an angel. The difference between an angel and a human is the fact that a human was at some point trapped in flesh. In addition, the angel comes from the position of complete knowledge of the Lord, while a spirit in flesh, the human, comes from a position of ignorance.

When an angel rejects HaShem, there is no repentance or reconciliation. They rejected the Lord fully knowing who He is. In other words, they fully rejected Him with complete understanding of their decisions and who God is. When humans die and leave their bodies, they are still considered humans, not angels, and humans usually reject God in ignorance. The Scriptures do not mention a salvation for angels as it does for humans.

I propose that Metatron is a completely mythical figure, mentioned only after the time of Y'hoshua the Anointed One (Jesus the Christ) and the result of Jewish occultism, even tainted with anti-Christ biases. The ancient non-messianic Jews may have simply created Metatron and Dibburiel to dismiss the personification of the Word of God in the Scriptures as Y'hoshua the Anointed One. The Word of God is not Dibburiel or Metatron or Chanok. The Word of God, the Logos of God, is Yah, blessed be His Name. We know the Word of God in flesh, the Logos of God in flesh, by His earthly Name—Y'hoshua the Anointed One.

A side-note concerning the previous quote from Singer: the Jewish method of giving numerical values to letters is called Gematria and its earliest mention is by Eliezer ben Yose the Galilean in the second century (Singer, Volume 5). As with Gentile Christian philosophy after the leave-taking of the apostles, I put no stock in non-messianic Jewish philosophy after the death and resurrection of the Master, Y'hoshua the Anointed One (Jesus the Christ). My reaction to non-Scriptural Hebrew literature, as with all literature that is not considered genuine Scripture, is caution. I personally do not put any stock in such things as Gematria, but I also recognize that there is a possibility of usefulness and accuracy and Truth in it, especially considering such things as the mark and name and number of the Beast (Revelation 13:16-18). At the same time, there is just as much a possibility that Gematria is a man-made invention absent of any divine inspiration, revelation, or wisdom. I advise you to stay away from Gematria. You have more efficient avenues to gain revelation, understanding, and wisdom (i.e. the Spirit of God).

In addition to the Greek "Logos," we have the additional support of the Aramaic "Memra." The online *Jewish Encyclopedia* defines Memra as, "'The Word,' in the sense of the creative or directive word or speech of God manifesting His power in the world of matter or mind; a term used especially in the Targum as a substitute for 'the Lord' when an [expression described as having human form or human attributes] is to be avoided" (Kohler). Both the Aramaic "Memra" and the Greek "Logos" equates to the English "Word."

Targum Onkelos is the Babylonian Targum, consisting only of Aramaic translations of the Instruction. Targum Yonatan is the Babylonian Targum, consisting only of Aramaic translations of the Prophets. Targum Yerushalmi I and II is the Jerusalem Targum, also called the Palestinian Targum or Targum Psuedo-Jonathan, and exists today only in fragments. Yah, blessed be His Name, approved this practice of translating His written Word into other languages as early as the time of Nechemyah (Nehemiah 8:8). The estimated date of writing for the Targums is not known, but the scholarly guess is after the birth, death, and resurrection of the Anointed One. For example, Onkelos was reputed to be the nephew of Roman emperor Hadrian and the author of Targum Onkelos (Singer, Volume 9), presumably the first of the Targums.

Onkelos lived approximately AD 30-120. Targum Onkelos, Targum Yonatan, and Targum Yerushalmi I and II replaced the Name of Yah, blessed be His Name, with the phrase "the Memra of God," which means "the Word of God," in their translations. This replacement was not consistent but rather an intermittent occurrence in the Targums, showing us that YHVH, blessed be His Name, is interchangeable with the phrase "the Word of God." As much as Jews would like to separate the Targum Memra from the Good News Logos, and as much as Gentiles would like to make the Good News Logos a new unique theology separate from Jewish thought and belief, the link between Logos, Memra, the Anointed One, and HaShem (The Name) is obvious to the unbiased seeker of Truth.

As if the previous points were not enough, we see further connections and support within the translations. Throughout Psalm 119, the Hebrew for "Word" (Devar) and the Hebrew for "Instruction" or "Law" (Torah) are interchangeable. In similar fashion, the Greek for "Word" (Logos) and the Greek for "Law" (Nomos) are interchangeable in the Septuagint translation of the same chapter (Kittel):

> In order to place the Gospel of John squarely in Jewish context, this theory proposes that *logos* is best understood as the incarnated Torah. The theory is based on some parallels between "word" and "law" in the LXX (Psalm 119:115); thus, one could translate John 1:1 as Jacobus Schoneveld did: "In the beginning was the Torah, and the Torah was toward God, and Godlike was the Torah." (Estes)

While I do not agree with the specific word choices of Schoneveld's interpretation of John 1:1, specifically "Godlike," he nevertheless displays the clear relationship between "Torah" and "Word." While I see kabbalists as sorcerers, and Jewish elders were often historically at odds with them, the "kabbalists taught that the Torah is a living organism . . . Ultimately, it was said that the Torah is God" (Bard). In other words, these various sources display Wisdom, Torah (Instruction), and Word (Logos, Memra) as interchangeable. Thus, you could read John 1:1 as:

- In the beginning was the Word, and the Word was with God, and the Word was God.

- In the beginning was the Logos, and the Logos was with God, and the Logos was God.

- In the beginning was the Memra, and the Memra was with God, and the Memra was God.

Or:

- In the beginning was the Torah, and the Torah was with God, and the Torah was God

- In the beginning was the Instruction, and the Instruction was with God, and the Instruction was God.

- In the beginning was Wisdom, and Wisdom was with God, and Wisdom was God.

The Scriptures speak for themselves.

Y'hoshua the Anointed One (Jesus the Christ) is the Word of YHVH, blessed be His Name, the Logos of God, the Memra of God. A prophet is a person who speaks under divine inspiration. Thus, they are mouthpieces. When the prophets spoke the Word of God as HaShem (The Name) inspired them, they spoke Y'hoshua the Anointed One. Y'hoshua is more than a mouthpiece; He is the very Word of God, the Word who later was born in flesh.

CHAPTER SIX

CHRIST

MY CHILDREN, THE prophecies of the Anointed One as prophet and priest are fulfilled, so wait patiently for His sure return to complete the prophecies of the Anointed One as king.

The Anointed One, Christos in Greek and Mashiach in Hebrew, has very specific connotations. Yah, blessed be His Name, gave instructions on the specific anointing oil that He designated for anointing (Exodus 30:22-33). The anointing is a special method of choosing. The anointing oil consists of myrrh, spice from the inner bark of *cinnamomum verum* (commonly called true cinnamon), spice from the leaves of *acorus calamus* (commonly called sweet flag), and spice from the inner bark of *cinnamomum iners* (commonly called cassia), mixed together in olive oil, all with specific measurements.

The punishment for misusing this oil or creating it for personal use was excommunication (Exodus 30:32-33), removal from fellowship with the people of God. The purpose of the anointing oil was to formally ordain a person as prophet, priest, or king.[69] Nevertheless, no one used the special anointing oil to anoint Moshe (Moses) as prophet or Malki-

---

69 Exodus 30:30; 1 Samuel 10:1; 1 Kings 1:34, 45; 1 Kings 19:15-16; 1 Chronicles 16:22; Psalm 105:15

Tzedek (Melchizedek) as priest or king, or Y'hoshua the Anointed One (Jesus the Christ) as the prophetic Word of God born flesh, the High Priest of the Order of Malki-Tzedek, or the King of Kings.

Y'hoshua the Anointed One was born from a young woman of marriageable age, even a virgin. This was unlike Adam, who He created completely from earth.[70] Thus the Anointed One is the unique and only begotten Son of God,[71] and at the same time the Last Adam as explained by Sha'ul (Saul/Paulos/Paul).[72] The phrase the "sons of God" has many meanings. It can mean spirits without flesh,[73] spirits in flesh who trust and obey God,[74] or those who have been resurrected into their glorified bodies.[75]

The spirit messenger, the angel, of God addressed Y'hoshua the Anointed One as the Son of God (Luke 1:35). Y'hochanan the Immerser (John the Baptist), considered a prophet by many in ancient Yisrael (Israel), addressed the Anointed One as the Son of God (John 1:34). The Enemy wanted to see if the Anointed One was the Son of God[76] and came to the conclusion that He was, in fact, the Son of God.[77]

The elders of Yisrael condemned the Anointed One on that very same single accusation that Y'hoshua Himself claimed to be the divine Son of God.[78] One of the Roman soldiers present at His death recognized the accuracy of the claim and misjudgment of the accusation of blasphemy.[79] Most importantly, and despite the dissenting claims of others that He never did, the Anointed One Himself confirmed His own title as the Son of God (John 10:30-36).

---

70 Genesis 2:7; Genesis 3:15; Isaiah 7:14; Matthew 1:20-23; Luke 1:26-31; Galatians 4:4

71 Psalm 2; John 1:14-18; John 3:18

72 Genesis 2:7; 1 Corinthians 15:45-53

73 Genesis 6:2-4; Job 1:6; Job 2:1; Job 38:4-7

74 Romans 8:14; Galatians 3:26

75 Luke 20:34-36; Romans 8:18-23

76 Matthew 4:3-6; Luke 4:3-9

77 Matthew 8:29; Mark 3:11; Luke 4:41

78 Matthew 26:63-66; Luke 22:66-71

79 Matthew 27:54; Mark 15:39

There was definitely an obvious meaning of the divine in the specific title of "Son of God," especially linked to the HaOlam Haba, the World to Come.[80] Some say that the Jews initially had no issue with linking the Anointed One to the Son of God, with linking Y'hoshua (Joshua/Yeshua/Jesus) to God Himself, but they did (Acts 9:18-25). Nevertheless, we see the written testimony of the Jewish Sha'ul, known as Paulos among Greek speakers, a member of the sect of the P'rushim (Pharisees) (Acts 23:6), even a former disciple of the renowned Gamliel I (grandson of Hillel who founded the House of Hillel). Sha'ul testified that Y'hoshua was, in fact, the only unique begotten Son of God. Yes, some members from the sect of the P'rushim also belonged to the sect of the Christians at the same time (Acts 15:5). We also know that at least one person from the sect of the Zealots was in the sect of the Christians, even an apostle (Acts 1:12-14), but I digress. Sha'ul's testimony was that Y'hoshua the Anointed One was the unique Son of God.[81]

You will find, with some examination, a commonality between the sons of God. You can observe them through two perspectives. The first perspective is that they are all spirits, in flesh or without flesh, who serve Yah, blessed be His Name. The second perspective is that they are all beings without earthly fathers. There is an overlap in the two views.

The first perspective of the sons of God are all those who serve the Lord, including the spiritual representatives of HaShem (The Name), commonly known as angels, as well as the earthly representatives of HaShem, commonly called Yisrael (Israel) or talmidim of the Anointed One. The second perspective of the sons of God includes all beings who have no earthly father. We find spirits, commonly called angels and demons (Genesis 6:2), Adam (Luke 3:38), also known as the First Adam, and Y'hoshua the Anointed One, also known as the Last Adam (1 Corinthians 15:45), in this second perspective.

There is, however, only one specific mention of a unique begotten Son scattered in a few verses.[82] The second perspective, rather than the first

---

80 John 1:47-49; John 11:27; John 19:7

81 Galatians 2:20; Romans 1:1-7; Ephesians 4:9-13

82 1 Samuel 7:12-16; Psalm 2:7; John 1:14-18; John 3:16-18; Acts 13:32-33; Hebrews

perspective, more closely addresses the topic of the Anointed One as the unique Son of God. I exhibit this train of thought to show you that there can be multiple interpretations to the title "Son of God."

C. S. Lewis, in *Mere Christianity*, is correct in his deduction: Y'hoshua the Anointed One (Jesus the Christ) was either who He claimed to be, or a demonic false prophet, or a madman. The Instruction of Yah, blessed be His Name, and the ancient Jewish legal system did not condemn you for being a "son of God" in the sense of being a human devotee of God. It did not condemn you for being a Torah-keeping anointed one. The ancient Jewish legal system, however, condemned you for blasphemy, such as claiming to be the Son of God in reference to being God, or of God, meaning divine. The Sanhedrin, the Jewish court, condemned Y'hoshua the Anointed One for only one reason: He claimed to be the Son of God in the sense of being God. History attests to His existence. History attests to the only accusation that led to His execution and death on the cross.

Atheists may claim whatever they wish, but history clearly states the reason for His death: He claimed to be divine. Atheists may claim that He was a good teacher but not God, yet that reasoning does not fit logical deduction, which they so often claim to be the motto for their lives. A good teacher does not strive to deceive the masses. If Y'hoshua was not deceiving the masses, then He was the Anointed One as He claimed to be, the only begotten Son of God . . . and thus also a good teacher.

Muslims say He was a prophet but not God, yet that reasoning also does not fit logical deduction. A true prophet does not strive to deceive people. At least the Jews maintain logic and consistency and, sadly, uphold their accusation that Y'hoshua the Anointed One was a liar, a false prophet. Y'hoshua the Anointed One (Jesus the Christ) announced Himself to be the unique and divine Son of God, was accused by a formal Jewish court that such a claim was false, was accused by a formal Roman court of treason by claiming to be a king not authorized by Caesar, and thereby executed because of their judgment of blasphemy and treason, respectively. Again, Y'hoshua was either who He said He was, a liar, or a madman.

1; Psalm 110:1-4; Hebrews 5:5-6; 1 John 4:9

Any modern court would take a single eyewitness as proof, especially without any definitive opposition. We have more than a single eyewitness of His resurrection and the manner of His resurrection. We have 500 witnesses (1 Corinthians 15:3-6), my guess being 120 men (Acts 1:10-15) and 380 women and children (Acts 1:14; Matthew 14:21). We have more than a single eyewitness of His ascension. We have the Instruction and the Prophets as witnesses, which I will continue to expound later. We have YHVH, blessed be His Name, Himself, as a witness by His Word,[83] and a witness by His works.[84] We have today the testimony from tens of thousands of brothers and sisters in the Way, the testimony of Him working in their lives and in their hearts, of miracles and healings, of various levels of spiritual warfare, and of supernatural guidance and direction that defies mundane explanations.

Y'hoshua the Anointed One (Jesus the Christ) is the High Priest of the Order of Malki-Tzedek (Melchizedek), and the priests' primary purpose is service to God. Where the prophet was the mouthpiece, the priests were the hands and feet of YHVH, blessed be His Name. Their primary service was intercession for the people—blessing them,[85] facilitating their thanksgiving to God,[86] and facilitating communion between humanity and the Lord.[87]

Merriam-Webster defines the word "communion" as "an act or instance of sharing." The term "communion" comes from the Latin word

---

83 Psalm 2:7; Isaiah 11:10; Isaiah 42:1-4; Matthew 3:16-17; Matthew 12:15-21; Matthew 17:5-6; Mark 9:6-8; Luke 9:34-36

84 Exodus 4:1-9; Exodus 7:3-5, 17; Exodus 8:18-19; Exodus 9:13-16; Exodus 14:18-31; Exodus 16:12-15; Deuteronomy 4:32-40; Joshua 3:7-17; Joshua 4:20-24; 1 Kings 18:36-39; Daniel 3; Mark 2:3-12; Mark 16:20; John 3:1-2; John 5:36; John 10:37-38; John 14:10-11; John 20:30-31; Acts 2:22-24; Acts 14:3; 2 Corinthians 12:12; Hebrews 2:2-4

85 Genesis 14:19; Numbers 6:23-27; 1 Samuel 2:20

86 Genesis 14:20; Leviticus 27:30; Numbers 18:21-26; Deuteronomy 14:22-29; 2 Chronicles 31:5; Nehemiah 13:12; Malachi 3:10

87 Genesis 14:18; Leviticus 1:7-17; Leviticus 2:2-16; Leviticus 3:11-16; Leviticus 4:3-35; Leviticus 5:6-18; Leviticus 6:6-26; Leviticus 7:5-34; 1 Samuel 2:22-36; 1 Samuel 7:5; 1 Samuel 8:6; 1 Samuel 12:19-23; Matthew 8:4; Luke 5:14; Numbers 6:1-21; Acts 21:20-26

communio, which means "fellowship, mutual participation, a sharing" (Harper, Communion). In ancient Middle Eastern culture, a meal was the most intimate form of sharing between two parties, outside the institution of marriage, of course (Exodus 24:9-11). In terms of humanity's relationship with God Almighty, a meal with Him took many forms. Malki-Tzedek, the first priest mentioned in the Scriptures, initiated the first divine meal with bread and wine, not much different from Y'hoshua the Anointed One.[88] The many Temple sacrifices were also forms of communion, forms of mutual sharing via a "meal," with portions given to God Most High and other portions eaten either by the priests or those bringing the sacrifice[89] or both.

The sacrifices are as follows:

- *Olah*[90] – burnt offering of dedication

- *Minchah*[91] – offering of thanksgiving, typically grain

- *Zebach sh'lamim*[92] – peace offering of communion/fellowship

- *Milu*[93] – priesthood ordination offering of fulfillment

---

88 Matthew 26:26-28; Mark 14:22-24; Luke 22:17-20

89 Leviticus 2:3, 10; Leviticus 3:16; Leviticus 6:16-18, 26-29; Leviticus 7:5-18, 28-34

90 Genesis 8:20; Genesis 22:1-13; Exodus 10:25; Exodus 18:12; Exodus 20:24; Exodus 29:18-46; Leviticus 1:3-17; Leviticus 5:7-10; Leviticus 6:9-12; Leviticus 7:8; Leviticus 17:8-9; Leviticus 22:18-20; Leviticus 23:12, 18; Numbers 28-29; Deuteronomy 12:5-27; Job 1:5; 1 Samuel 15:22; 2 Samuel 24:22-25; Psalm 20:3; Psalm 40:4-8; Psalm 51:16-17 [Psalm 51:18-19]; Isaiah 1:10-17; Isaiah 43:22-24; Isaiah 56:6-8; Micah 6:6-8; Hosea 6:6; Jeremiah 7:21-23; Jeremiah 33:17-18

91 Genesis 4:3-5; Exodus 29:41; Leviticus 2:1-15; Leviticus 6:14-15, 20-23; Leviticus 7:9-10; Leviticus 10:12; Leviticus 14:10-31; Leviticus 23:13, 16, 18, 37-38; Numbers 5:12-28; Judges 6:18; Judges 13:19-23; 1 Samuel 3:14; 1 Kings 18:28-36; Psalm 20:3; Psalm 40:4-8; Psalm 45:12; Psalm 96:8; Psalm 141:2; Isaiah 1:13; Isaiah 19:21; Isaiah 43:23; Isaiah 66:3, 20; Jeremiah 14:12; Jeremiah 33:17-18; Daniel 9:20-21, 27; Zephaniah 3:10; Malachi 1:10-14; Malachi 2:11-14; Malachi 3:3-4

92 Exodus 20:24; Exodus 24:5; Exodus 29:28; Exodus 32:6; Leviticus 3:1-9; Leviticus 7:11-37; Leviticus 9:3-4, 18-22; Leviticus 17:5; Leviticus 19:5; Leviticus 22:21; Leviticus 23:19; Numbers 6:14-18; Numbers 10:10; Numbers 15:8-9; Numbers 29:39; Deuteronomy 27:6-7; Judges 20:26; 1 Samuel 11:15; 2 Samuel 6:17-18; 2 Samuel 24:21-25; 1 Kings 8:63-64; 1 Kings 9:25; Amos 5:21-24; Ezekiel 46:12

93 Exodus 29:22-34; Leviticus 7:37-38; Leviticus 8:22-33

- *Para adumah* (Numbers 19) – red heifer offering of purification
- *Chatat*[94] – sin offering for covering
- *Asham*[95] – guilt offering for covering

The *olah, minchah, zebach sh'lamim, milu, para adumah, chatat*, and *asham* were the different forms of *korbanot* (plural of *korban*). While the *minchah* was typically a grain offering, Hevel (Abel) offered the firstling of his flock, and Eliyah's (Elijah's) ox sacrifice was an offering of thanksgiving, and David even called the evening *olah* as a thanksgiving offering. The Scriptures also label some of these sacrifices an *ish'shah* (sacrifice or offering by fire),[96] such as the *olah*,[97] *minchah*,[98] *zebach sh'lamim*,[99] *chatat*,[100] *asham* (Leviticus 7:5), *milu* (Leviticus 8:28), and even the *nesekh* (drink offering of sacrifice and suffering) (Numbers 15:8-10).

The common word used in English translations for *korbanot* is "offerings." Offering, however, loses the meaning of the word. *Korban* means "something brought near to the altar," but its root word is *karav*, which means "to draw near." The altar was a gateway to the Lord,[101] so bringing a *korban* was akin to 'drawing close' to Yah, blessed be His Name. Even the author of the letter to the Hebrews was obviously aware of this relationship (Hebrews 10:1).

The Jews already understood that the *chatat* (sin offering) and *asham* (guilt offering) were never meant to take away sins (Hebrews 10:4), in

---

94 Exodus 29:14, 36; Exodus 30:10; Leviticus 4; Leviticus 5:5-13; Leviticus 6:25-30; Leviticus 7:7; Leviticus 10:16-20; Leviticus 12:6-8; Leviticus 14:19-31; Leviticus 16; Leviticus 23:15-21; Numbers 15:22-31; Numbers 18:9; Ezekiel 45:17

95 Leviticus 5; Leviticus 6:6; Leviticus 7:1-7; Leviticus 14:1-32; Leviticus 19:20-22; Numbers 6:11-12; 1 Samuel 6:1-17; Isaiah 53:10

96 Leviticus 21:6, 21-22, 27; Numbers 15:13-14; Numbers 18:17; Numbers 28:1-25; Deuteronomy 18:1

97 Exodus 29:18; Exodus 29:41; Exodus 30:19-20; Leviticus 1:9, 13, 17; Leviticus 8:21

98 Leviticus 2:2-3, 9-11, 16; Leviticus 6:17; Leviticus 10:12-13; Leviticus 24:5-9; Numbers 29:13, 36

99 Leviticus 3:3, 5, 9, 11, 14, 16; Leviticus 7:29-35

100 Leviticus 4:35; Leviticus 5:12

101 Genesis 28:16-18; Genesis 35:1-3; Revelation 6:9-11

disagreement with mainstream Christian misunderstanding of Jewish doctrine. In fact, the *chatat* and *asham* were for unintentional sins, sins done in ignorance.[102] They were not for intentional sins. Repentance, turning away from sin and returning to God, was ever the only solution for intentional sin and outright rebellion.[103] Jews understood this fact. Y'hochanan the Immerser, Y'hoshua the Anointed One, and the apostles said the same thing.[104] The author of the letter to the Hebrews was not stating anything new in Hebrews 10:1-4.

The various forms of *korban* (offering) were the methods of drawing close to the Lord, the methods of communion, the methods of mutual sharing, the methods of drawing close with the necessary covering over unintentional sins . . . not methods of forgiveness for intentional sins. A person who sinned intentionally, who outright rebelled against HaShem (The Name) and His commandments, had no *korban* available to him because, for all intents and purposes, he was not trying to draw near to God. Forgiveness for intentional sins of the repentant person relied solely upon the loving-kindness/grace of Yah, blessed be His Name.

The offeror could not approach the altar with his/her *korbanot*. Only the priest could approach the altar and facilitate the offeror's drawing close to the Lord through their *korban*. A mediator was necessary for all who desired to draw close with the exception of the high priest, Moshe (Moses), and the patriarchs, Avraham, Yitzchak (Isaac), and Ya'akov (Jacob). One can argue, however, that Y'hoshua the Anointed One (Jesus the Christ) is the mediator for all—past, present, and future. He is even the mediator for the patriarchs, Moshe, and the high priests. One can also argue that the fathers were the mediators, Noach for his children (Genesis 8:20), Iyov for his children (Job 1:5), Avraham for Yitzchak and Yitzchak for Esav and Ya'akov (Genesis 22:1-18), and Ya'akov for his

---

102 Leviticus 4:2, 22, 27; Leviticus 5:15, 18

103 Genesis 3:19; Genesis 4:6-7; Numbers 5:5-7; Job 42:1-6; 1 Kings 8:47; 2 Chronicles 6:37; Psalm 7:11-12; Psalm 32:5; Psalm 85; Isaiah 27:9; Jeremiah 5:1-13; Jeremiah 8:4-22; Ezekiel 14:5-11; Ezekiel 18; Luke 16:25-31; Luke 17:4; Acts 8:20-22; Revelation 2-3; Revelation 9:20-21; Revelation 16:8-11

104 Matthew 3:1-2; Matthew 4:11-17; Matthew 11:20; Mark 1:14-15; Mark 6:7-12; Luke 13:1-5; Acts 2:37-38; Acts 3:16-21; Acts 17:30-31; Acts 26:19-20

children (Genesis 31:54). Nevertheless, who interceded for Iyov, Avraham, and Moshe? We can see Malki-Tzedek (Melchizedek) interceding for Avraham, but Iyov (Job) and Moshe remain without mediators if not for Y'hoshua the Anointed One.[105]

Y'hoshua the Anointed One (Jesus the Christ) is not relegated to the high priest who brings an animal for a *korban*, covering and cleansing the physical flesh, but rather He is the High Priest who brings Himself as the *korban* (offering), covering and cleansing the spirit (Hebrews 9:6-14). He is more than just the *asham* (guilt offering) to cover and cleanse us from ignorant sin by His shed blood, from cheating and stealing from others, which also is a sin against HaShem (The Name), and from sin against the things set-apart for the Lord.[106] He is also more than the *chatat* (sin offering) to cover and cleanse us from all unintentional sins, also by the shedding of His blood, His life, which is in the blood.[107] More than these two *korbanot*, He is the ultimate *olah* (burnt offering), the only life that completely dedicated Himself to the service and purpose of Yah, blessed be His Name.[108]

He is the *minchah* (grain offering), the life of praise and thanksgiving and glorification of HaShem (John 6:31-58). He is the *nesekh* (drink offering), the life of humility and obedience exhibited by His sacrifice and suffering.[109] He is the *zebach sh'lamim* (peace offering) through whom we have fellowship with God.[110] He is the *milu* (ordination offering) through whom we receive the ordination as priests, inaugurated servants

---

105 Exodus 20:19; Galatians 3:19-20; 1 Timothy 2:5-6; Jeremiah 31:31-34; Hebrews 8:6; Hebrews 9:15; Hebrews 12:18-24

106 Isaiah 53:10; Leviticus 5:6-7, 15-19; Leviticus 6:6, 17; Leviticus 7:1-7, 37

107 Isaiah 53:4-6; John 1:29; 1 Corinthians 15:1-5; Romans 3:21-26; Romans 4:23-25; Romans 5:6-9; 2 Corinthians 5:21; Hebrews 9:26; Hebrews 10:3-18; Hebrews 13:10-12

108 John 3:13; James 1:17; Ephesians 4:8-10; Hebrews 2:10; Hebrews 5:9-10; Hebrews 7:28

109 Acts 1:3; 1 Peter 2:21-25; 1 Peter 4:1-2; Hebrews 2:9, 18; Hebrews 5:8; Hebrews 13:13

110 Genesis 14:18; Exodus 24:9-11; Psalm 42:1-2; Luke 14:12-14; Luke 15:11-32; John 1:14-18; John 14:1-3; John 17:20-21; Romans 5:1-11; Ephesians 2:1-18; Revelation 19:7-9

in the Order of Malki-Tzedek (Melchizedek).[111] He is the *para adumah* (red heifer), whose shed blood cleanses us from the corruption of death and from sin and its effects.[112] More than the *korbanot*, He is the Way for forgiveness of intentional sins, the vessel of God's loving-kindness and salvation, and the empowerment unto obedience through a clean conscience.[113]

Furthermore, Y'hoshua the Anointed One (Jesus the Christ) came from the tribe of Y'hudah (Judah), from the line of King David, not only from Yosef his adopted father, but also through Miryam (Mary) his earthly mother.[114] A messenger, Y'hochanan the Immerser (John the Baptist), prepared the people for the work and instruction of the Anointed One.[115] Although Y'hochanan the Immerser was not Eliyah (Elijah), an angel of God and the Anointed One Himself revealed that Y'hochanan was a type of Eliyah.[116] The Lord addressed the Anointed One's return rather than His initial coming when Malachi prophesied concerning Eliyah's actual physical reappearance.[117] Y'hoshua the Anointed One was a prophet and mediator like Moshe (Moses), neither one anointed by the priests of the Order of Aharon; they both descended or will descend twice, the first time for intercession and the second time in glory.[118] The Jewish elders would value Him at thirty pieces of silver[119] and pierce Him,[120]

---

111 1 Peter 2:4-10; Revelation 1:4-6; Revelation 5:10; Revelation 20:6

112 Numbers 19; Hebrews 13:10-13

113 Matthew 9:1-8; Matthew 26:27-28; Mark 2:1-12; Luke 5:17-26; Luke 7:40-50; Luke 24:45-47; Acts 2:38; Acts 5:31; Acts 10:43; Acts 26:15-18; Psalm 32:1-2; Romans 4:5-8; Ephesians 1:7-12; Ephesians 4:32; Colossians 1:13-14; Colossians 2:13-14; 1 John 2:12

114 Genesis 49:10; 2 Samuel 7:12-13; Isaiah 9:7; Matthew 1:6-18; Luke 1:32-33; Luke 3:23-33; Romans 1:3; Hebrews 7:14

115 Isaiah 40:3-5; Matthew 3:1-3; Mark 1:2-4; Luke 3:1-6; John 1:19-23

116 Malachi 4:5-6; Matthew 11:14; Luke 1:13-17

117 Malachi 4:5-6; Revelation 11:3-6

118 Deuteronomy 18:15-16; Acts 3:19-23; Acts 7:30-40; Exodus 32:11-19; Luke 2:7-38; Exodus 34:29; Isaiah 19:1; Daniel 7:13; Luke 21:27; Matthew 17:1-5; Mark 9:2-8; Luke 9:28-36; 2 Peter 1:16-18

119 Zechariah 11:12-13; Matthew 26:14-16

120 Zechariah 12:9-10; Matthew 27:35; Mark 15:24; Luke 23:33; Luke 24:38-40; John

but His bones would remain unbroken.[121] He resurrected as prophesied by King David and confirmed by eye-witnesses.[122] Stephanos (Stephen), the Jewish martyr with a Greek name, witnessed the current status of the unique Son of God. Now Y'hoshua the Anointed One is the right hand of God, returned to glory.[123]

I have shown to you the prophecies that Y'hoshua the Anointed One (Jesus the Christ) fulfilled. He fulfilled two of the three available positions of anointed one, specifically prophet and priest. We now await His return as King[124] at the trumpet sound.[125] Here is where the appointed times of HaShem (The Name) play a critical role. Now we await His return on the appointment Day of the Loud Blast, otherwise known as the Feast of Trumpets or Yom T'ruah.

19:34-37; John 20:25-27

121 Exodus 12:46; Psalm 34:20; John 19:33-36

122 Psalm 16:8-10; Matthew 28; Mark 16; Luke 24; John 20-21; Acts 2:25-28, 34-35

123 Exodus 15:6-12; Deuteronomy 33:2-3; Psalm 17:7; Psalm 18:35; Psalm 20:6; Psalm 21:8; Psalm 44:3; Psalm 48:10; Psalm 60:5; Psalm 63:8; Psalm 80:15-19 [Psalm 80:16-20]; Psalm 98:1; Psalm 108:6; Psalm 118:15-16; Psalm 138:7; Isaiah 41:10; Isaiah 48:13; Isaiah 62:8; Psalm 110:1-5; Matthew 22:44; Mark 12:36; Luke 20:42; Matthew 26:64; Mark 16:19; Luke 22:69; Acts 2:25-34; Acts 7:55-56

124 Isaiah 11:1-9; Jeremiah 23:5-6; Jeremiah 33:14-16; Ezekiel 34:11-31; Ezekiel 37:21-28

125 Isaiah 27:13; Zechariah 9:11-17; Matthew 24:30-31; 1 Thessalonians 4:16; 1 Corinthians 15:52; Revelation 11:5

CHAPTER SEVEN

PSALMS

MY CHILDREN, BE attuned to even the smallest details of the Scriptures, discerning between translator inserts (Mark 7:18-19) and the inspired words. Even such seemingly trivial things as a pronoun (Matthew 23:1-3), division of chapters,[126] numbering of verses, names (Acts 13:9-10), and organization and titles of books and chapters,[127] can drastically change, obfuscate, or mislead the meaning of His Word.

Some writings in the Prophets, from Judges to Malachi, or Judges to Chronicles depending on the canon, may not appear to be prophetic in nature, or at least they do not appear prophetic until the completed events reveal them to be prophetic. Following that train of thought, I find the canonical division of the Instruction and the Prophets by non-messianic Jews to be interesting. Every time the Anointed One referenced the Scriptures, He merely called them "the Instruction and the Prophets."[128] The Jewish apostle with the Greek name of Philippos (Philip) from Beit Tsaida (Bethsaida) also called them "the Instruction and the Prophets" (John 1:45). Sha'ul (Saul/Paulos/Paul) the apostle called them "the Instruction and the

---

126 Deuteronomy 12:32; Deuteronomy 13
127 Genesis, Exodus, Leviticus, Numbers, Deuteronomy
128 Matthew 5:17; Matthew 7:12; Matthew 11:13; Matthew 22:40; Luke 16:16

Prophets" (Acts 24:14-15). The Gentile believer Loukas (Luke) called them "the Instruction and the Prophets" (Acts 28:23). In fact, you will find only one reference, being Luke 24:44, in which you can find a tripartite division of the Scriptures—the Instruction, the Prophets, and the Psalms.

Noting the abundance of references for only a bipartite division, I take the single tripartite reference in Luke 24:44 with the grain of salt. In other words, I do not see the single tripartite reference as formally declaring an official division of the books into three parts. Perhaps the Anointed One still used the bipartite division and singled out Psalms from the Prophets because He mostly quoted from it, but not treating it as a third separate section.

> Furthermore, external evidence used to argue for an early tripartite canon is reassessed. Theodore Swanson (1970) and John Barton (1985) have argued for a bipartite canon of the Torah and the Nevi'im in which the latter remained open (BCE) and was later formed into divisions (CE). They have found support for this position in reinterpreting the Prologue to Sirach in which the three-fold reference to a supposed section of the cannon refers probably to other non-sacred writings (Swanson 1970: 125-31; Barton 1986: 47-48). Thus Swanson (1970: 326) concludes his learned study: "there is no unambiguous evidence of the tripartite Scripture prior to the *baraita* of *Baba Bathra* 14b" [Babylonian Talmud]. Ulrich's (1993) preliminary assessment of the evidence from Qumran indicates a pluriform Scripture as far as the textual base is concerned as well as the pluriform Judaism. The canon was bipartite, consisting of the Torah and the Nevi'im with Daniel among the latter, but this second division was growing too large ("stretched too far") and a third section was being created which eventually resulted in the Writings. (Dempster)

So why would it matter that the Jews saw the Scriptures as two parts prior to and during the time of the Anointed One and as three parts after the destruction of the Temple? You need to understand the meaning of names and labels and titles. The "Instruction" is obviously the Instruction that God gave to Moshe (Moses) and the "Prophets" are obviously the words of the prophets thereafter.

Now pay close attention.

The "Writings," the Ketuvim, are all the words that the Jews consider to be neither the Instruction of God nor the message of God through the prophets. In other words, the Jews chose not to see the Ketuvim as prophetic. I repeat myself. The Jewish canon of the Instruction and the Prophets views the Ketuvim as not prophetic. "Unlike the Torah and the books of the Prophets (Nevi'im), the works found in Ketuvim do not present themselves as the fruits of direct divine inspiration" (Ketuvim). The Jewish canon places the following books into the Ketuvim (what they do *not* consider to be prophetic books): Psalms, Proverbs, Job, the Song of Songs, Ruth, Lamentations, Ecclesiastes, Esther, Daniel, Ezra, Nehemiah, and 1 & 2 Chronicles.

I find too much convenience and coincidence in the fact that the Jews created a third category of Ketuvim (Writings) after they failed to vanquish the Christian sect and suppress the teachings of the apostles. I am suspicious of the fact that the ancient non-messianic Jewish elders conveniently moved Psalms into a non-prophetic category after Christian teachings spread, teachings that linked the prophecies in Psalms to Y'hoshua the Anointed One (Jesus the Christ). Now every new Jewish generation accepts the Psalms as non-prophetic and propagates the continued denial of the revelation of the Anointed One.

Now that I have addressed the prophetic nature of Psalms despite Jewish prestidigitation, let us look to Psalm 22. In this case, I specifically use the Jewish Publication Society's (JPS) version in order to assuage the Jewish claims that Christian translators twisted the words of the Scriptures to suit their theology. I, of course, used the Name of God where appropriate instead of the substituted title "LORD" in the JPS translation. I included the JPS notation of uncertainty in translation or meaning by the use of italics and the following symbols: < >. I used asterisks * and parentheses () for my personal notes on further clarification. I used the Christian numbering system on verses, however, for ease of reference since most of our translations at home follow the Christian system.

Psalm 22

(0) For the leader; on a *<ayyeleth ha-shahar>*. A psalm of David.

(1) My God, my God,

why have You abandoned me;

why so far from delivering me

and from my anguished roaring?

(2) My God,

I cry by day—You answer not;

by night, and have no respite.

(3) But You are the Holy One, (or "But You are holy")

enthroned,

the Praise of Israel. (or "enthroned upon the praises of Israel")

(4) In You our fathers trusted;

they trusted, and You rescued them.

(5) To You they cried out

and they escaped;

in You they trusted

and were not disappointed.

(6) But I am a worm, less than human;

scorned by men, despised by people.

(7) All who see me mock me;

they curl their lips, (literally "they open wide with a lip")

they shake their heads,

(8) "Let him commit himself to [YHVH];

let Him rescue him,

let Him save him,

for He is pleased with him."

(9) You <*drew me*> from the womb,

made me secure at my mother's breast.

(10) I became Your charge at birth;

from my mother's womb You have been my God.

(11) Do not be far from me,

for trouble is near,

and there is none to help.

(12) Many bulls surround me;

mighty ones of Bashan encircle me.

(13) They open their mouths at me

like tearing, roaring lions.

(14) My life ebbs away: (literally "I am poured out like water")

all my bones are disjointed;

my heart is like wax,

melting within me;

(15) my vigor dries up like a shard;

my tongue cleaves to my palate;

You commit me to the dust of death.

(16) Dogs surround me;

a pack of evil ones closes in on me,

like lions <*they maul*> my hands and feet.

(17) I take the count of all my bones

while they look on and gloat.

(18) They divide my clothes among themselves,

casting lots for my garments.

(19) But You, O [YHVH], be not far off;

my strength, hasten to my aid.

(20) Save my life from the sword,

my precious *life* from the clutches of a dog. (literally "only one")

(21) Deliver me from a lion's mouth;

from the horns of wild oxen *rescue* me. (literally "answer")

(22) Then will I proclaim Your fame to my brethren,

praise You in the congregation.

(23) You who fear [YHVH], praise Him!

All you offspring of Jacob, honor Him!

Be in dread of Him, all you offspring of Israel!

(24) For He did not scorn, He did not spurn

the *plea* of the lowly; (or "plight")

He did not hide His face from him;

when he cried out to Him, He listened.

(25) *Because of You I offer praise* in the great congregation; (literally "From You is my praise)

I pay my vows in the presence of His worshipers.

(26) Let the lowly eat and be satisfied;

let all who seek [YHVH] praise Him.

Always be of good cheer!

(27) Let all the ends of the earth pay heed and turn to [YHVH],

and the peoples of all nations prostrate themselves before You;

(28) for kingship is [YHVH's]

and He rules the nations.

(29) <All those in full vigor shall eat and prostrate themselves;

all those at death's door, whose spirits flag,

shall bend the knee before Him.>

(30) Offspring shall serve Him;

[YHVH's] fame shall be proclaimed to the generation to come;

(31) they shall tell of His beneficence

to people yet to be born,

for He has acted. (Jewish Publication Society)

A Jewish teacher, born and raised under the Sinai Covenant, once told me that a not uncommon Jewish practice was to pray by mentioning an entire Psalm through simply quoting only the first and last lines of that Psalm. "By having the first and last line, they make us think of the whole 'Kriat Sh'ma' and get to include it without actually including it" (Kimmel). Some Christians are not unaware of this pattern and practice. Karla Oakley Anderson, director of Children's Ministries, speaker for Christian Women's Conferences, and associate minister for two congregations, wrote an entire book on this topic.

> If you will remember . . . rabbis would frequently quote from the first line of a scriptural text, then the congregation of Jews would follow by quoting the rest of that section, and lastly, the rabbi would say the last verse to close . . . He quoted the first and last line of Psalm 22. As the rabbi, the teacher, Jesus was teaching and fulfilling Scripture as He was dying so that we might believe! He was not asking why he had been abandoned. He was not the misunderstood martyr. God had not turned His back on His Son. Jesus said these words with a loud voice to fulfill the Scripture that told all of these things would happen—and that His Father had not abandoned Him as [His] accusers had said. (Anderson)

Understand that if John 19:30 is indeed the Master quoting the end of Psalm 22, then that would change quite a few current Christian doctrines based on the Master's last words on the cross, "It is finished."

Perhaps instead of "It is finished," He simply said, "Finished" or "Done."

On the cross, Jesus again evokes images from the Psalms, when He cries out "Eloi, Eloi, lema sabachthani?" which means, "My God, my God, why have you forsaken me?" (Mark 15:34), a line directly from Psalm 22:1. In his last breath, he then utters, "It is finished" (John 19:30), which may be an allusion to the final line of Psalm 22:31, "He has done it." In quoting the first and last line, He signals that the entire psalm is about Him. The lamenter in the psalm unjustly suffered, as did Jesus. In just a few words, Jesus proclaims that He is the ultimate lamenter. (Barry, Psalms)

Psalm 22 was the cry of our Master, Y'hoshua the Anointed One (Jesus the Christ), as He hung dying on the cross. He wasn't asking if God the Father was forsaking Himself, God the Son, but rather He was exhorting and teaching Psalm 22 to His audience. Even while dying in excruciating pain, He was teaching and exhorting.

Note the uncertainty of Jewish translators in Psalm 22:16, specifically the phrase "they maul." Christian translators use the phrase "they pierce." Go figure. The biases playing on the hearts and minds of the translators become obvious. Non-messianic Jews will choose a word as far removed from the circumstances of Y'hoshua the Anointed One (Jesus the Christ) as possible while Christians will choose a word to more closely identify the text to the Master. Let us examine other translations:

Psalm 21:16 – For many dogs have compassed me: the assembly of the wicked doers has beset me around: they pierced my hands and my feet. (Brenton LXX En)

Psalm 22:17 – For the wicked, who may be compared to many dogs, have surrounded me; an assembly of evildoers have encircled me; they bite my hands and feet like a lion. (The Aramaic Bible, Volume 16: The Targum of Psalms)

I would say lions biting my hands and feet would resemble something like piercing my hands and feet.

Meanwhile, let us look at the various translations for a passage that might shed light on Psalm 22:16, which is Zechariah 12:10.

But I will fill the house of David and the inhabitants of Jerusalem, the spirit of pity and compassion; and they shall lament to Me about those who are slain, wailing over them as over a favorite son and showing bitter grief as over a first-born. (Tanakh)

And I will pour upon the house of David, and upon the inhabitants of Jerusalem, the spirit of grace and of supplication; and they shall look unto Me because they have thrust him through; and they shall mourn for him, as one mourneth for his only son, and shall be in bitterness for him, as one that is bitterness for his first-born. (JPS 1917)

And I will pour upon the house of David and upon the inhabitants of Jerusalem the spirit of mercy and compassion, and they shall entreat me because they were exiled; and they shall mourn for an only son and shall lament for him as they lament for a firstborn. (The Aramaic Bible, Volume 14: The Targum of the Minor Prophets)

And I will pour upon the house of David, and upon the inhabitants of Jerusalem, the spirit of grace and compassion: and they shall look upon me, because they have mocked me, and they shall make lamentation for him, as for a beloved friend, and they shall grieve intensely, as for a first-born son. (Brenton LXX En)

I will pour out on the house of David and on the inhabitants of Jerusalem, the Spirit of grace and of supplication, so that they will look on Me whom they have pierced; and they will mourn for Him, as one mourns for an only son, and they will weep bitterly over Him like the bitter weeping over a firstborn. (NASB95)

The apostles and authors of the Good News and the Apostolic Letters already understood the status of Y'hoshua the Anointed One (Jesus the Christ) as the firstborn.[129] Along with firstborn, we see the Zecharyah (Zechariah) titles of "favorite son," "only son" three times, and "beloved

---

129 Psalm 89:27-29; Luke 2:7; John 1:14-18; John 3:16-18; Romans 8:29-30; Colossians 1:15-18; Hebrews 1:6; 1 John 4:9; Revelation 1:4-6

friend." Except for the post-ascension Targum, we note that the One mentioned as "an only son," as a "firstborn son," is prophesied to be slain,[130] thrust through (as with a spear) (John 19:34-37), mocked,[131] and pierced.[132] Those verses are suspiciously close to describing the manner of death of Y'hoshua the Anointed One. In fact, if we study the rest of Psalm 22, we will find more glaring "coincidences."

As much as Jews would like to hide it, they have a historically accepted, if not popular, perspective that these Zechariah verses could concern an anointed one, and not necessarily pertain to Yisrael (Israel) the nation.

> First, the Talmud witnesses to belief in a Messiah descended from Joseph. Second, this Messiah ben Joseph is slain, although his slayer is unnamed. Third, Zechariah 12:10 is taken as applying to him. Fourth, Zech. 12-13 is taken as implying a causal link between his slaying and the slaying of the evil *yetzer*. (Mitchell, p. 79)

I think the masses of Jews unfortunately put their trust in flawed humanity, even in their respected leaders, elders, and sages, and their "elite" interpretation of the Scriptures. Do they simply disregard and deny correlations just because their elders say there are no correlations? They are no different than mainstream Christianity who unquestioningly feed from the hand of their priests, pastors, and elders.

Our Master started His prayer of Psalm 22 with the first verse as attested in Matthew 27:46 and Mark 15:34. Psalm 22:6-8, 11-13, and verse 17 speaks of the loneliness and mockery that He would endure and fulfilled according to Matthew 26:31-35, 40, 67-75; Matthew 27:38-44; Mark 15:29-32; and Luke 23:35-39. Psalm 22:9-10 was implied as fulfilled according to Matthew 1:18-25, Luke 1:26-45, and John 1:14.

Studying the effects of crucifixion, which is how the Anointed One

---

130 Matthew 27:50; Mark 15:37; Luke 23:46; John 19:30
131 Matthew 27:29-31, 39-44; Mark 15:16-20, 29-32; Luke 23:11, 35-38; John 19:2-3
132 Matthew 27:35; Mark 15:25; Luke 23:33; John 19:17-18

died,[133] confirms Psalm 22:14-15. Psalm 22:18 was also fulfilled according to Matthew 27:35-36, Mark 15:24, Luke 23:34, and John 19:23-25. Psalm 22:19-21 and verses 24 and 29 were fulfilled according to Matthew 28:1-10, Mark 16:1-11, Luke 24:1-12, and John 20:1-18. Psalm 22:22 and verses 25-26 were fulfilled according to Matthew 28:16-20, Mark 16:14-18, Luke 24:36-51, John 20:26-31, Acts 1:3-15, Acts 26:22-23, and 1 Corinthians 15:3-6. The Apostolic Letters and history itself give testimony to the fulfillment of Psalm 22:30-31. Only Psalm 22:27 is left to fulfill . . . and He does not break His Word. He will return to complete it.

The testimonies of those who witnessed the cry of Psalm 22 from the Master's mouth as He was dying on the cross are not just wild claims of modern Christians two thousand years removed. These are the testimonies of eyewitnesses of the Anointed One recorded in historical documents that overwhelm the standards of accuracy compared to all other historical documents treated as authoritative.

As far as historical documents that meet scientific standards of accuracy, only the Instruction and the Prophets exceed the dependability of the Good News and the Apostolic Letters. The Zoroastrian documents were written almost 1,300 years after Gathas of Zoroaster, the writings of Siddhartha Gautama 600 years after, and the Quran 100 years after Islam's founder. Instead, we have the Good News and Apostolic Letters written within the first forty years after the ascension of the Anointed One, before the destruction of the Temple in AD 70. We also have a fragment of an original document of the Good News according to Markon (Mark) from as early as the first century (Wallace).

> There have been plenty of claims that things contradict the biblical account, but the Bible has a habit of being proved right after all. I well remember one of the world's leading archaeologists at Gezer rebuking a younger archaeologist who was "rubbishing" the Bible. He just quietly said, "Well, if I were you, I wouldn't rubbish the Bible." When the younger archaeologist asked "Why?" he replied, "Well, it just has a habit of proving to be right after

---

133 Matthew 27:35; Mark 15:24; Luke 23:33; John 19:18

all." And that's where I stand. Professor Nelson Glueck, who I suppose would be recognized as one of the top five of the 'greats' in biblical archaeology, gave a marvelous lecture to 120 American students who were interacting with the Arabs. He said, "I have excavated for 30 years with a Bible in one hand and a trowel in the other, and in matters of historical perspective, I have never yet found the Bible to be in error." Professor G. Ernest Wright, Professor of Old Testament and Semitic Studies at Harvard University, gave a lecture at that same dig. He made the point that (because of the researches associated with the Hittites and the findings of Professor George Mendenhall concerning what are called the Suzerainty Covenant Treaties between the Hittite kings and their vassals) it had become clear that the records of Moses, when dealing with covenants, must be dated back to the middle of the second millennium BC. That's about 1500 BC. Also, that those writings should be recognized as a unity. In other words, they go back to one man. That one man could only be Moses. I went to Professor Wright later and said, "Sir, this is very different from what you've been putting out in your own writings." He looked at me and said, "Clifford, for 30 years I've been teaching students coming to Harvard to train for the Christian ministry; I've been telling them they could forget Moses in the Pentateuch, but at least in these significant areas of the covenant documents that are there in the Pentateuch, I've had to admit that I was wrong." They were two scholastic giants. One says, "I've excavated for 30 years and I've never found the Bible to be in error"—basically that's what he was saying. The other says, "For 30 years I've been wrong." (Wilson)

All human courts today regard eyewitnesses as authoritative. Yet for some rebellious reason the world twists their standards in order to deny the eyewitness of the apostles so that they can comfortably deny the revelation of Yah, blessed be His Name.

The more things change, the more things stay the same. We have gone from sticks and stones to nuclear bombs; we have gone from run-ning to flying in airplanes—yet humanity still rebels against HaShem (The Name), just as Adam did. Ignore as some might, but the correlation between Psalm 22 and the life of the Anointed One is obvious, His prayer of Psalm 22 at the end of His earthly life—poignant.

For those who exercise the ears of their spirit, let them hear. Y'hoshua the Anointed One is the unique and divine Son of God, the Word of God born flesh.

CHAPTER EIGHT

YESHAYAH

MY CHILDREN, OUR Master quoted Psalms and the prophet Yeshayah (Isaiah) the most from the books of the Prophets in order to reveal His identity to the people.

Y'hoshua the Anointed One (Jesus the Christ) was not anointed with the anointing oil, just as neither Moshe nor Malki-Tzedek (Melchizedek) were anointed with the anointing oil. He was instead anointed with the Spirit of God.[134] The author of the letter to the Hebrews best explains how and why Y'hoshua the Anointed One is the high priest, using Genesis 14:18-20 and Psalm 110:4 to build his case from both the Instruction and the Prophets. The priest's main purpose is service through blessing the people, facilitating the thanksgiving of the people, and facilitating communion/fellowship between HaShem (The Name) and the people of God. Y'hoshua the Anointed One blesses us,[135] facilitates our thanksgiving,[136]

---

134 Numbers 11:24-29; Matthew 3:16-17; Mark 1:10-11; Luke 3:21-22; Isaiah 61:1-3; Luke 4:16-21; John 1:29-34; Acts 10:38

135 Luke 24:50-51; Hebrews 7:1-3, 20-22; Romans 8:31-34

136 Deuteronomy 14:22-29; Deuteronomy 26:12; Matthew 25:34-46; Acts 2:43-47; 1 Thessalonians 5:18; Deuteronomy 25:4; 1 Corinthians 9:3-14; 1 Timothy 5:17-19; 1 Corinthians 16:1-4; Galatians 2:10; Romans 15:25-29; 2 Corinthians 9; Ephesians 5:20-21; Colossians 3:15-17; 1 Peter 2:4-5; Hebrews 7:23-25; Hebrews 12:28-29; Hebrews 13:15-16

and facilitates our communion/fellowship with the Lord.[137] You will also find an ancient document among the Dead Sea Scrolls called 11Q13 or 11QMelchizedek that show the connection between Malki-Tzedek and the anointed one mentioned in Isaiah 61:1-3.

> The eschatological interpretation of these passages concerns "captives" who are the "inheritance of Melchizedek." Melchizedek makes these captives return, proclaims liberty to them, and frees them from the debt of their iniquities. Clearly, then, Melchizedek is seen as personally enacting a jubilee on behalf of the "captives" who are somehow associated with him (his "inheritance"), in much the same way that Isaiah 61:1-2 portrays a messianic figure personally enacting jubilee on behalf of the "poor of Zion" . . . The "to proclaim liberty to the captives" is the quintessential activity of the "anointed of the spirit" of Isaiah 61:1-2; Melchizedek is taking on the role of the "anointed of the spirit" . . . The eschatological Day of Atonement is identified as "the year of grace of Melchizedeck," which is quite a remarkable phrase. It is an unmistakable reference to Isaiah 61:2a, "to proclaim a year of favor to the Lord," which in turn is a clear evocation of the image of the jubilee year. However, Melchizedek has taken the place of the LORD . . . Be that as it may, in this line of 11QMelch, the Day of Atonement is now being described as a jubilee year through the use of Isaianic images . . . At first, the stress on Melchizedek as executor of God's vengeance may seem at odds with the imagery of the Day of Atonement and jubilee, neither of which say much about vengeance. The immediate impetus for the wedding of the concepts of proclamation of liberty and execution of vengeance is to be found in Isaiah 61:2, in which, as seen above, the two movements are juxtaposed . . . There are also some implicit elements of vengeance associated with the Day of Atonement and jubilee in the pentateuchal texts. In the Day of

---

137 Matthew 26:26-28; Mark 14:22-24; Luke 22:19-20; Romans 4:24-25; Romans 8:3-5; Ephesians 5:1-2; 1 Peter 2:21-25; Hebrews 7:26-28; Hebrews 9:11-14, 27-28; Hebrews 10:10-18; Hebrews 13:10-14

Atonement, there is in a sense an implicit act of judgment against the people of Israel, yet the divine vengeance/wrath is diverted through the sacramental ritual to the scapegoat and the sacrificial goat, each of whom bear the people's sins and the attendant divine vengeance, though in two different modes. As for the jubilee, it was noted above that the institution of the jubilee seems closely related to the institution of the redeemer . . . and that the two biblically-mandated duties of the [redeemer] are redemption of the kinsman (Leviticus 25:25-55), and vengeance on the kinsman's enemy (Numbers 35:16-34). (Bergsma)

In similar fashion, we see the letter to the Hebrews displaying the connection between Y'hoshua the Anointed One and Malki-Tzedek (Melchizedek). Then consider the teaching of the Master, "Today, as you heard it read, this passage of the Scriptures was fulfilled," (Luke 4:21b) concerning Isaiah 61:1-3. To summarize:

1.   The letter to the Hebrews explains the connection between Y'hoshua the Anointed One and Malki-Tzedek the High Priest.

2.   The Dead Sea Scrolls document, 11Q13, explains the connection between Malki-Tzedek the High Priest and the Anointed One prophesied in Isaiah 61:1-3.

3.   Y'hoshua the Anointed One announces that He is the Anointed One in Isaiah 61:1-3 (Luke 4:16-21).

Wrapping the three points together, Malki-Tzedek (Melchizedek) the Anointed One prophesied in Isaiah 61:1-3 and Y'hoshua the Anointed One (Jesus the Christ) could very well be the same One. At the very least, you see their relationship and connection. Y'hoshua the Anointed One is the High Priest of the Order of Malki-Tzedek (Hebrews 5:1-10).

Y'hoshua the Anointed One is the King of Kings for whom we wait, although even now He rules the spiritual realm[138] and the hearts of His

---

138 Genesis 1:2; Numbers 16:22; Numbers 27:16-19; Job 1:6-12; Job 38; Psalm 110; Matthew 22:41-46; Acts 2:33-36; Acts 5:31; Acts 7:55-56; Romans 8:33-34; Ephesians 1:18-21; Colossians 3:1; Hebrews 1:3-13; Hebrews 8:1-2; Hebrews 10:11-25; Hebrews 12:1-2; 1 Peter 3:21-22

talmidim (disciples) in the earthly realm.[139] The Jews deny Y'hoshua as the Anointed One because He did not fulfill the kingly prophecies concerning the Anointed One in the Instruction and the Prophets,[140] ignoring the fulfillment of the priestly prophecies. They are correct in that He did not fulfill the kingly prophecies, but He will accomplish them upon His return.[141]

Just as the Jews are awaiting the kingly revelation of the Anointed One, so are we loyally and diligently awaiting the return of our King. The untimely spiritually born apostle, Sha'ul (Saul/Paulos/Paul), and the beloved apostle, Y'hochanan (John), both shared the revelation that Y'hoshua the Anointed One is the King of Kings and Lord of Lords.[142]

If you have no relationship with Him, then truly you have nothing to trust. We do not trust blindly, but rather we trust His return because we trust His fulfilled Word, the fulfillment of the priestly prophecies of the Anointed One. We trust because of a real experience of intimate relationship with the Creator of the world, and He has proven and proves Himself time and again in our own lives, in even the smallest and mundane details.

The clearest revelation that Yah, blessed be His Name, gave of Himself to humanity is His Word born flesh, His Anointed One, Y'hoshua in Hebrew, Yeshua in Aramaic, Iesous in Greek (pronounced I-yeh-soo), Iesus in Latin (pronounced I-yeh-soos), Jesus in German (pronounced Yeh-sus), and finally Jesus in English. As Sha'ul the apostle said, "For in Him, bodily, dwells the fullness of all that God is" (Colossians 2: 9). He gave His Name, and that is YHVH, blessed be His Name. He revealed Himself in flesh through a virgin, by His Word, just as He created Adam from dust by His Word. He spoke from the beginning concerning His gift

---

139 Exodus 19: 5; Exodus 23: 22; Numbers 14: 24; Joshua 24: 20-24; Matthew 7: 21-27; Luke 6: 46-49; John 14:15-21; John 15:10; 1 John 5:2-3; 2 John 1:6

140 Zechariah 12:2-3; Zechariah 14:2-4; Zechariah 12:8-10; Deuteronomy 30:3; Amos 9:15; Isaiah 60:8-9; Jeremiah 16:14-16; Zechariah 14:2-4; Joel 1:1-2

141 Matthew 24:29-31; Mark 13:26-27; Luke 21:27; 1 Thessalonians 4:13-18; 1 Corinthians 15:51-53; Revelation 1:7; Revelation 14:14-16; Revelation 17:14; Revelation 19:11-21

142 John 1:18; John 14:8-11; 1 Timothy 6:13-16; John 1:29-36; Revelation 17:14; John 1:1; Revelation 19:11-16

of salvation. He revealed His gift of salvation, His outstretched arm,[143] the saving strength of His right hand,[144] the Light of His presence,[145] the Son of Man[146], the Wonderful Counselor,[147] the Eternal Father,[148] the Prince of Peace,[149] the Son of God,[150] even Mighty God[151] . . . as Y'hoshua the Anointed One, the only path, door, gate, Way of His salvation (John 14:6-31).

Non-messianic Jews also believe that the Anointed One will bring universal knowledge to all people that Yah, blessed be His Name, is the only God.[152] Jews must not realize how many people believed in the God of Avraham before Y'hoshua the Anointed One (Jesus the Christ) compared to how many people now believe in the God of Avraham after the Anointed One's resurrection and ascension. Nevertheless, I understand their point. The whole world does not yet believe that HaShem (The Name) is the only One True God. Again, this is something that Y'hoshua the Anointed One will fulfill upon His return.[153]

Non-messianic Jews believe that Christians pervert Isaiah 7:14, specifically the Hebrew word *almah*, to mean virgin. If we look at the Septuagint, we find the Greek word *parthenos*. Dictionary.com defines *parthenos* as "an epithet of Athena, meaning 'virgin.'" Remember that ancient Jewish scholars, not Gentiles, wrote the Septuagint as a translation of the Hebrew Scriptures into Greek.

---

143 Exodus 6:6; Deuteronomy 11:1-7; Psalm 136:10-22; Ezekiel 20:33-35

144 Psalm 20:6; Acts 7:55-56

145 Genesis 1:3; Psalm 44:3; John 1:4-5, 9; John 8:12

146 Psalm 80:17-19; Daniel 7:13; Matthew 9:6; Matthew 12:8, 39-40; Matthew 13:41-43; Matthew 17:9-12; Matthew 24:27-44; John 3:13-14; John 5:26-27; John 6:27; John 6:53; John 8:28; Acts 7:55-56

147 Isaiah 9:6; Mark 10:17-27; Luke 18:18-27

148 Isaiah 9:6; John 10:30

149 Isaiah 9:6; John 14:27

150 John 20:30-31; Acts 9:17-20; Hebrews 4:14; Hebrews 7:3; Hebrews 10:29; 1 John 3:5-8; 1 John 4:15; 1 John 5:5-20; Revelation 2:18

151 Isaiah 9:6; John 20:27-28

152 Isaiah 2:2-3; Micah 4:1-2; Zephaniah 3:9; Zechariah 8:23; Zechariah 14:9

153 Isaiah 45:22-25; John 1:1, 14; Romans 14:11; Philippians 2:9-11; Revelation 19

[Ptolemy] Philadephus, the king of Egypt, commissioned a translation of the Torah into Greek. To do the work he contacted Eleazar, the chief priest in Jerusalem at the time. Eleazar arranged for six translators from each of the twelve tribes of Israel. These seventy-two men became the namesake of the translation—"Septuagint" means 70 (apparently they rounded down) and is often referred to now as the "LXX," the Latin form of 70. By 200 to 150 BC, the Neviim and Ketuvim were also translated into Greek, completing the work. (Powell)

Now that we've established a lack of Christian bias upon the translation that led to the Septuagint, we see that the ancient Jews themselves understood Isaiah 7:14 to be saying "virgin." I have read some mental gymnastics in reasoning that still attempt to deny the obvious use of the word "virgin" in Isaiah 7:14, but they are all far stretches of the imagination and not solid logical deduction. I previously stated that the Hebrew Scriptures use the word *almah*, which, in all actuality, means "young woman of marriageable age."

Ever since the publication of the Revised Standard Version there has been a storm of debate over the translation of *'almah* in Isaiah 7: 14 as "young woman" instead of the King James "virgin." The commonly held view that "virgin" is Christian, whereas "young woman" is Jewish is not quite true. The fact is that the Septuagint, which is the Jewish translation made in pre-Christian Alexandria, takes *'almah* to mean "virgin" here. Accordingly, the New Testament follows Jewish interpretation in Isaiah 7:14.

Little purpose would be served in repeating the learned expositions that Hebraists have already contributed in their attempt to clarify the point at issue. It all boils down to this: the distinctive Hebrew word for "virgin" is *betulah*, whereas *'almah* means a "young woman" who may be a virgin, but is not necessarily so.

The aim of this note is rather to call attention to a source that has not yet been brought into the discussion. From Ugarit of around 1400 B.C. comes a text celebrating the marriage of the male and female lunar deities. It is there predicted that the goddess will bear a son. (For the translation, see my *Ugaritic Literature*, Rome, 1949, pp. 63-64) The terminology is remarkably close to that in Isaiah 7:14. However, the Ugaritic statement that the bride will bear a son is fortunately given in parallelistic form; in 77: 7 she is called by the exact etymological counterpart of Hebrew *'almah* "young woman"; in 77: 5 she is called by the exact etymological counterpart of Hebrew *betulah* "virgin." Therefore, the New Testament rendering of *'almah* as "virgin" for Isaiah 7:14 rests on the older Jewish interpretation, which in turn is now borne out for precisely this annunciation formula by a text that is not only pre-Isaianic but is pre-Mosaic in the form that we now have it on a clay tablet. (Gordon, Cyrus)

In other words, the translation of *almah* in Isaiah 7:14 as 'virgin' comes from ancient Jewish interpretation, not Gentile, and especially not originating from Christians.

The ancient Jewish interpretation for Isaiah 7:14 came long before Jewish anti-Christ biases, which would like to deny the prophecy of a virgin birth as well as deny the testimony of the birth of Y'hoshua the Anointed One, after the fact. The ancient Jews who wrote the Septuagint were expecting a virgin birth. The last two thousand years of Jews only deny the prophecy of the virgin birth for the sole reason of denying the identity of the Anointed One as Y'hoshua the Son of God. They insist that their expected anointed one will have no share in divinity just so that they can deny Y'hoshua the Anointed One.

They deny the virgin birth and the divinity of the Anointed One so that they can comfort themselves, to rationalize that they were not blinded these last two millennia (Romans 11:25-27). They deny the virgin birth to rationalize that they are not guilty of the blood of the Anointed One. The Truth is that we are all guilty of the blood of the Anointed One. Gentile Romans working together with Jewish priests and a traitor *talmid* (disciple) put the Anointed One on the cross.

In the same spirit of denial, non-messianic Jews also purposely misinterpret Isaiah 53, stating that it references Israel rather than the Anointed One. Jews instead accuse Christians of misinterpretation. Let us examine Isaiah 53 as it appears in the Jews' own English translation of the Hebrew Scriptures (Jewish Publication Society).

Again, I used the same symbols as I did on the Psalm verses in the previous chapter. I also continue to replace the substituted title of "LORD" with the actual name of God. Read for yourself the following correlations, and I dare you to claim in good conscience that Yeshayah (Isaiah) was not prophesying about Y'hoshua (Jesus) the Anointed One, because I certainly cannot:

Isaiah 53

(1) Who can believe what we have heard?

Upon whom has the arm of [YHVH] been revealed?

The Jews and the world at large refuse to believe the message of salvation that comes from the arm of YHVH, blessed be His Name, namely Y'hoshua the Anointed One.[154]

(2) For he has grown, by His favor, like a tree crown,

Like a tree trunk out of arid ground.

He had no form or beauty, that we should look at him:

No charm, that we should find him pleasing.

The Romans whipped Y'hoshua the Anointed One beyond recognition.[155]

(3) He was despised, <shunned by men>,

A man of suffering, familiar with disease.

As one who hid his face from us,

He was despised, we held him of no account.

154 Isaiah 53:1; John 1:10-11; John 7:5; John 12:37-38; 1 Corinthians 1:20-24; Romans 10:16; Romans 11:1-27
155 Isaiah 53:2; Isaiah 52:14; Matthew 27:26; John 19:1-5

The crowd despised, shunned, and held Y'hoshua the Anointed One of no account.[156]

(4) Yet it was our sickness that he was bearing,

Our suffering that he endured.

We accounted him plagued,

Smitten and afflicted by God;

Y'hoshua the Anointed One carried the consequence of our sin.[157]

(5) But he was wounded because of our sins,

Crushed because of our iniquities.

He bore the chastisement that made us whole,

And by his bruises we were healed.

(6) We all went away astray like sheep,

Each going his own way;

The *talmidim* of Y'hoshua the Anointed One scattered and abandoned Him after His arrest, feeling lost and forsaken after His death.[158]

And [YHVH] visited upon him

The guilt of all of us.

(7) He was maltreated, yet he was submissive,

He did not open his mouth;

Like a sheep being led to slaughter,

Like a ewe, dumb before those who shear her,

---

156 Isaiah 53:3; Matthew 26:67-68; Matthew 27:39-44; Mark 15:29-32; Luke 23:35-39; John 1:10-11; 1 Peter 2:21-25

157 Isaiah 53:4; Genesis 2:16-17; Deuteronomy 21:22-23; Acts 5:30; Romans 6:23; Galatians 3:13-14

158 Isaiah 53:6; Matthew 26:31-35, 56, 69-75; Mark 14:27-31, 66-72; Luke 22:31-34, 54-62; 1 Peter 2:21-25

He did not open his mouth.

Y'hoshua the Anointed One willingly submitted Himself to the oppressive judgment of the Sanhedrin and maintained silence against the onslaught of His accusers.[159]

(8) By oppressive judgment he was taken away,

<*Who could describe his abode*>?

For he was cut off from the land of the living

Through the sin of my people, who deserved the punishment.

(9) And his grave was set among the wicked,

Y'hoshua the Anointed One died on an executioner's stake, a method of execution for a death row inmate of ancient days, in-between two guilty thieves.[160]

And with the rich, in his death

Yosef from Ramah (Harimathaia in Greek), a wealthy but secret *talmid* of Y'hoshua the Anointed One and prominent member of the Sanhedrin, made sure to bury Him in a respectable place.[161] Even Nakdimon (Nicodemus), another member of the Sanhedrin and sect of the P'rushim (Pharisees), helped to give the Master a burial fit for royalty (John 19:39).

Though he had done no injustice

And had spoken no falsehood.

Although Y'hoshua was completely innocent according to the standard of the Instruction, of the Law, unblemished and blameless, He endured the unjust penalty for the worst of crimes.[162]

---

159 Isaiah 53:7; Matthew 26:47-56, 63; Matthew 27:12-14; Mark 10:33-34; Mark 14:61; Mark 15:4-5; Luke 18:31-33; Luke 23:9; John 13:21-27; John 19:8-9; Acts 8:30-35; 1 Peter 2:21-25

160 Isaiah 53:9, 12; Matthew 27:38; Mark 15:27-28; Luke 23:33; John 19:18

161 Isaiah 53:9; Matthew 27:57-60; Mark 15:42-46; Luke 23:50-53; John 19:38-42

162 Isaiah 53:9; Matthew 27:3-4, 19, 22-24; Luke 23:15-16; John 19:4-6; 2

(10) But [YHVH] chose to crush him <*by disease*

That, if he made himself an offering for guilt>,

He might see *offspring* and have long life, ("His arm" or "His vindication")

And that through him [YHVH's] purpose might prosper.

(11) Out of his anguish he shall see *it*; ("the arm of the Lord")

He shall enjoy it to the full through his devotion.

"My righteous servant makes the many righteous,

It is their punishment that he bears;"

Y'hoshua the Anointed One resurrected on the third day, demonstrating the vindication of YHVH, blessed be His Name, to an eternal glory.[163]

(12) "Assuredly, I will give him the many as his portion,

He shall receive the multitude as his spoil.

For he exposed himself to death

And was numbered among the sinners,

Whereas he bore the guilt of the many

And made intercession for sinners."

Y'hoshua the Anointed One immediately increased the number of His followers, starting fifty days after His resurrection, ten days after His ascension, and on the appointed time of Shavu'ot (Weeks/Pentecost/fiftieth day) when He sent His Spirit upon all humanity.[164] According to Pew Research Center, "A comprehensive demographic study of more than 200 countries finds that there are 2.18 billion Christians of all ages around the world, representing nearly a third of the estimated global population

---

Corinthians 5:21; 1 Peter 2:21-25; Hebrews 7:26; 1 John 3:5

163 Isaiah 53:11; Matthew 28:1-10; Mark 16:1-13; Luke 24:1-12; John 20:1-19; Acts 4:33; Acts 26:22-23; 1 Corinthians 15:12-20; Romans 1:1-6

164 Isaiah 53:12; Joel 2:28-29; Acts 2:1-41

of 6.9 billion" (Global Christianity). To this day, YHVH, blessed be His Name, adds to His people (1 Corinthians 3:7).

The most prominent overarching theme of Isaiah 53, however, is the fact that the Anointed One carried the sins of humanity upon Himself, willingly volunteering Himself as the required *asham* (guilt offering) for the people, and thereby taking away the sins of the people.[165] A just judge does not acquit a guilty criminal; a just judge does not acquit a rapist, murderer, or child molester. We are all indeed guilty criminals who have violated God Himself by breaking His commandments,[166] whether in will, thought, word, or deed.[167]

Yah, blessed be His Name, is just, and justice requires that punishment be meted out.[168] Our merciful God saved us all from the consequences of our sin by placing the consequent punishment for our sin upon Himself, upon His Anointed One, for which we considered Him plagued.[169] He willingly suffered on our behalf, the innocent taking the punishment so that the guilty could escape punishment, according to the will of God,[170] who loves us, who desires and plans the best for our well-being.[171] The Anointed One's body was wounded, crushed, and bruised in order to heal us, we who are all accursed with the consequence of death.[172] He died as the consequence for sin because he bore our sins in His body.[173] He nailed

---

165 Isaiah 53:4-12; Matthew 1:21; Matthew 26:27-28; Matthew 27:50; John 1:29; 1 Corinthians 15:1-5; Romans 4:23-25; Romans 5:6-8; Romans 6:3-4; 1 Peter 2:21-25; Hebrews 9:27-28; 1 John 3:5

166 Genesis 6:5; Psalm 14:1-3; Psalm 53:1-3; Romans 3:23

167 Genesis 18:25; Psalm 62:12; Psalm 90:8; Proverbs 24:12; Ecclesiastes 3:17; Ecclesiastes 11:9; Ecclesiastes 12:14; Matthew 5:21-30; Matthew 12:36; Matthew 16:27; John 5:28-29; 1 Corinthians 3:12-13; 1 Corinthians 4:5; Romans 2:5-8, 14-16; Romans 14:12; 2 Corinthians 5:10; Ephesians 6:7-8; Colossians 3:25; Revelation 22:12

168 Psalm 9:4-8; Psalm 50:6; Psalm 89:14; Psalm 96:13; Psalm 97:2-6

169 Isaiah 53:4; Genesis 2:16-17; Deuteronomy 21:22-23; Acts 5:30; Romans 6:23; Galatians 3:13-14

170 Isaiah 53:4; Matthew 26:39; Mark 14:35-36; Luke 22:41-44; Acts 2:22-23; Romans 3:23-26; Romans 8:32; 1 Peter 2:21-25; Hebrews 10:23

171 Psalm 40:4-5; Jeremiah 29:11-14; Romans 8:28-30

172 Isaiah 53:5; 1 Samuel 6:3; Psalm 107:20; Proverbs 20:30; Hosea 11:3; Jeremiah 17:14; Isaiah 6:10; Matthew 13:15; 1 Peter 2:21-25

173 Isaiah 53:5; 1 Corinthians 15:3-5; 1 Peter 2:21-25; Hebrews 9:27-28; Hebrews

the consequent punishment to the cross, cancelling the debt, so that we could be made complete, and thus complete only in His Anointed One.[174] Notice the difference. He nailed the consequent punishment for sin, not the Law or the Instruction or even the Sinai Covenant, to the cross.

The First Adam gave the curse of death, through his sin of selfishness, as an inheritance to his earthly children.[175] The Last Adam healed His *talmidim* (disciples) from the curse by giving salvation and eternal life through His selfless love and offering of His life as an *asham* (guilt offering), as an inheritance to His spiritual children (1 Corinthians 15:45-49). Having the unique attribute of being a son of God, having no earthly father, the First Adam's actions affected all of humanity, giving us all the same inheritance. Having the unique attribute of being a son of God, even the only begotten Son of God, the only Word born flesh, having no earthly father, the Last Adam's actions also affected all of humanity, giving the same inheritance to each and every one of us.

The inheritance of the First Adam is the curse of death, a curse that passes through a physical heritage. We are all physical descendants of Adam. We even earn the curse by our own sin, so none can blame Adam for his sin and rebellion as the cause for our own calamity. The inheritance of the Last Adam is the gift of life, the gift of salvation from the previous curse of death, a gift that passes through a spiritual heritage. All *talmidim* of the Anointed One are spiritual descendants of Y'hoshua the Anointed One.[176] We do not earn His salvation; we do not earn a gift, but rather receive His gift with thanksgiving, with the thanksgiving of love and obedience, with the thanksgiving of enduring trust, and with the thanksgiving of a life set-apart for His purpose.

Just as the curse brings forth sin, so does the gift bring forth righteousness. Y'hoshua the Anointed One, the Last Adam, healed us from the curse of death without beginning or end, the curse of hell, which

10:14

174 Isaiah 53:5; Colossians 2:9-15; Hebrews 7:25; Hebrews 10:14

175 Genesis 2:15-17; Genesis 3:2-5; Romans 7:7; Romans 5:12-14

176 John 1:11-13; John 11:49-52; Romans 8:16-17; Romans 9: 8; Philippians 2:14-16; 1 John 3:1-10; 1 John 5:1-3

humanity inherited from the First Adam.[177] Y'hoshua the Anointed One took upon Himself the price for sin, for which the wage is death,[178] and thus the Eternal Father and Immortal King[179] died a physical death to save us mortals from deservedly enduring an eternal spiritual death.[180]

I am not saying that the Anointed One went to hell, the eternal spiritual death. Hell appears to be a place of eternal "fire" reserved for the end of time, also dubbed GeHinnom/Gehenna (Strong's G1067)[181] after the historical events that occurred at the Valley of Hinnom (Strong's H2011).[182] Sh'ol (Underworld), however, is the current place of the after-life, the current spiritual realm, containing both the resting place for the righteous (the Garden of Paradise, Avraham's bosom)[183] and the holding cell for the unrighteous (Tartaros, Strong's G5020, 2 Peter 2:4) until the Day of Judgment.[184] Our Master visited the current Sh'ol, not the future lake of fire, not the spiritual Valley of Hinnom.

The Anointed One, while innocent and fully empowered, neverthe-less submitted Himself to endure abuse in court trials, pain and suffering from scourging, and finally torment and slow death via crucifixion (from which we get the word excruciating). The injustice of punishing the only,

177 Isaiah 53:5; 1 Corinthians 15:45; 1 Peter 2:21-25

178 Genesis 2:16-17; Genesis 3:2-3; Genesis 9:4-6; Genesis 20:7; Proverbs 11:19; Isaiah 3:9; Ezekiel 18:4; Matthew 25:45-46; Romans 1:32; Romans 6:16-21; James 1:15

179 Isaiah 9:6; 1 Timothy 1:17

180 Isaiah 10:18; Matthew 10:28; Romans 5; Ephesians 2:1-18; Hebrews 2:9; Revelation 5:9

181 Matthew 5:22-30; Matthew 10:28; Matthew 23:15-33

182 Joshua 15:8; Joshua 18:16; 2 Kings 23:10; 2 Chronicles 28:3; 2 Chronicles 33:6; Nehemiah 11:30; Jeremiah 7:31-32; Jeremiah 19:2-6; Jeremiah 32:35; Matthew 5:22-30; Matthew 10:28; Matthew 18:9; Matthew 23:15-33; Mark 9:43-47; Luke 12:5; James 3:6; Revelation 19:20; Revelation 20:10-15

183 Genesis 3:24; Ezekiel 31:16-18; Luke 16:19-23; Luke 23:43; 2 Corinthians 12:1-4; Revelation 2:7

184 Genesis 37:35; Genesis 42:38; Genesis 44:29-31; Numbers 16:30-33; Deuteronomy 32:22; 1 Samuel 2:6; 2 Samuel 22:6; 1 Kings 2:6-9; Psalm 6:5; Psalm 9:17; Psalm 16:10; Psalm 18:5; Psalm 30:3; Psalm 31:17; Psalm 49:14-15; Psalm 55:15; Psalm 86:13; Psalm 88:3; Psalm 89:48; Psalm 116:3; Psalm 139:8; Matthew 11:23; Matthew 16:18; Luke 10:15; Luke 16:23; Acts 2:27-31; 2 Peter 2:4; Revelation 1:17-18; Revelation 6:8; Revelation 20:13-14

truly innocent One who is eternal satisfies and meets the demanded justice of eternal punishment for the wicked. We are the wicked ones; even the best of us are guilty of sin.[185] In addition, the life, the soul-spark, the Hebrew *nefesh* (Strong's H5315), is in the blood.[186] He shed His blood, His life, so that we may have life—eternal life—for those who are willing to receive His gift of salvation through the covering of His blood that also cleanses us within our heart and our conscience.

Non-messianic Jews interpret the suffering servant of Isaiah 53 to be themselves, the nation of Yisrael in the sense of the whole ethnic population of Jews. The nation of Yisrael, however, has its own sins. All Jews already carry their own sins, just as we all do. Thus, Jews have no "room" for the sins of the world (Isaiah 26:18) when they have their own sins. Only the One without sin is worthy, is capable, to carry the sins of another. In all honesty and sincerity, Isaiah 53 only makes sense in connection to Y'hoshua the Anointed One as the suffering servant.

---

185 Psalm 14:1-3; Psalm 53:1-3; Romans 3:23
186 Genesis 9:4-5; Leviticus 17:11

CHAPTER NINE

INTERPRETATION

MY CHILDREN, BE aware that there are many interpretations of the Scriptures, many ways of interpretation, but constantly seek Yah, blessed be His Name, for the true interpretation.

Jewish rabbinical leaders and unbelievers claim that the quotes in the Good News and Apostolic Letters from the Instruction and the Prophets were not prophetic or that the early Jewish believers invented their own interpretations, their own esoteric interpretations. Rabbinical leaders, however, are not, as Jews are wont to believe and indeed claim as their ruling standard, the final authority on the written Word of God.

Did you know, for example, that Jews believe that their rabbinical leaders are the only ones with the authority to interpret the written Word of HaShem (The Name)? I heard this shocking information from Nehemia Gordon in 2005, the famous Karaite Jew and scholar on the Dead Sea Scrolls, when referencing his younger years and the instructions from his former rabbi (master). I clarify, in case you do not know, that a Karaite Jew is a Jew who treats the Instruction and the Prophets as authoritative but gives no authority to the Mishnah and the Talmud, which are the works of rabbinical leaders throughout history, the heirs of the sect of the P'rushim (Pharisees).

Nehemia informed his audience that his former rabbi used Bava Metzia 59B to illustrate the folly of challenging rabbinical authority.

> And as my rabbi was reading me this story, he opened up the book of Deuteronomy 30:12 and there it says concerning the Torah, that it is not in heaven. And [these are] the words that the rabbis said to Rabbi Eliezer. And they explained to him that God has no say in interpreting Scripture because the Torah is not in heaven. The Torah is here on earth and the rabbis are the ones with exclusive authority to interpret Scripture. God has no say in it. And my rabbi turned to me as he was telling this story and he said, "You see Nehemia? God Himself can't question the authority of the rabbis. So, who are you to question their interpretation?" (Gordon, Nehemia)

Nehemia thereafter concluded that Rabbinical Judaism was not for him. Nehemia joined the community of Karaites, non-messianic Jews who did not belong to Rabbinical Judaism. The rabbinical mentality simply does not make any sense. How do people think they have more authority than God Himself in any matter? The idea is preposterous.

I include the translation of the actual words from Bava Metzia 59B here for your reference, since I personally wanted to see it for myself:

> This is the "oven of Achnai." What is Achnai? Said Rabbi Yehudah in the name of Shmuel: That they surrounded it with words [of debate] like an Achnai snake, and declared it impure.
>
> It was taught: On that day R. Eliezer answered all the answers on earth and they did not accept it from him. He said, "If the law is like me, the carob tree will prove it"; the carob tree was uprooted from its place one hundred [cubits], some say four hundred [cubits]. They said: "We do not bring proof from a carob tree." . . . He went and said "If the law is like me the water channel will prove it"; the water channel flowed in reverse direction. They said: "We do not bring proof from a water channel." He went and said "If the law is as I say the walls of the House of Study will prove

it"; the walls of the House of Study inclined to fall. R. Yehoshua protested at them, saying to them "If scholars defeat each other in the law, how does it better you?" They did not fall because of the honor of R. Yehoshua and they did not straighten, because of the honor of R. Eliezer, and they still incline and stand . . . [R. Eliezer] went and said, "If the law is like me, from Heaven they will prove it"; a heavenly voice came out and said, "What have you with R. Eliezer, who the law is like him in every place?" R. Yehoshua stood on his feet and said "[The Torah] is not in heaven," (Deuteronomy 30:12). What does "[The Torah] is not in heaven" mean? R. Yirmiyah said: "That the Torah was already given at Sinai. [We] do not pay attention to a heavenly voice, since You already wrote at Sinai in the Torah, 'After the majority to incline,'" (Exodus 23:2). R. Natan met the prophet Elijah and said to him, "What did the Holy One, Blessed be He, do in that hour?" [Elijah] said to [R. Natan]: "[God] smiled and said, 'My sons have defeated Me; My sons have defeated Me.'" (Babylonian Talmud, Baba Metsia 59b)

Now you can see for yourself the source for the rabbinical Jewish belief that their masters have the only authority, not God Almighty, in revealing the true meaning of His written Word.

Rabbinical leaders do not allow supernatural movements of power to sway them (Simmons), which can be both wise and foolish. While I am clearly aware of Deuteronomy 13:1-5, I am also just as clearly aware of Exodus 4. Deuteronomy 13:1-5 does not deny the validity of signs and wonders except for their use to persuade a person away from Yah, blessed be His Name. Signs and wonders in Exodus 4 were perfectly acceptable forms of validity to persuade a person to turn to HaShem (The Name).

Non-messianic Jews trust in men to understand God Most High while we trust the Spirit of God and the Word of God born flesh to understand the Lord. Let us see what HaShem has to say on trusting man.

"It is better to take refuge in YHVH than to trust in man; better to take refuge in YHVH than to trust in princes" (Psalm 118:8-9).

"Trust in YHVH with all your heart and do not rely on your own understanding. In all your ways acknowledge Him, and He will make your paths straight. Do not be wise in your own eyes; fear YHVH and turn away from evil" (Proverbs 3:5-7).

"Thus says YHVH, 'Cursed is the man who trusts in mankind'" (Jeremiah 17:5a).

> Yet we do speak wisdom to those who are mature. But it is not the wisdom of this world or of this world's leaders, who are in the process of passing away. On the contrary, we are communicating a secret wisdom from God which has been hidden until now but which, before history began, God had decreed would bring us glory. Not one of this world's leaders has understood it; because if they had, they would not have crucified the Lord from whom this glory flows; but just as it is written, "No eye has seen, no ear has heard and no one's heart has imagined all the things that God has prepared for those who love him" [Isaiah 64: 4]. It is to us, however, that God has revealed these things through the Spirit; for the Spirit searches all things, even the depths of God. For who knows the thoughts of a person except the person's own spirit inside him? So too no one knows the thoughts of God except the Spirit of God. Now we have not received the spirit of the world but the Spirit of God, so that we might understand the things God has freely given to us. These are the things we speak, not in words taught by human wisdom, but in those taught by the Spirit, by which we explain spiritual things with spiritual things. Now the natural man does not accept the things of the Spirit of God, for they are foolishness to him! Moreover, he cannot understand them, because they are discerned through the Spirit." (1 Corinthians 2:6-14)

Thank the Lord that we have His Spirit dwelling in us, that we have relationship with Him and can approach Him because we have a high priest of the Order of Malki-Tzedek (Melchizedek) in the highest heaven, Y'hoshua the Son of God (Hebrews 4:14-16). We do not need to rely on the words and wisdom of the elders alone, but on God Himself, through both His Word and His Spirit.

One of the greatest dissents that the Jews have against the proclamation of Y'hoshua of Natzeret (Nazereth) being the Anointed One is that "Jesus contradicts the Torah and states that its commandments are no longer applicable" (Simmons). They could not be further from the Truth, but I don't fault them for misunderstanding the Master and His teachings. Mainstream Christianity itself says that "followers of Jesus are not to go back under the regulations of the law" (Ross). I know that statement sounds like it came from the Scriptures, but I will elaborate on that misunderstanding in the concluding chapter.

Non-messianic Jews would then of course follow suit and see Y'hoshua the Anointed One (Jesus the Christ) as a Law-breaking false prophet. They believe that the Anointed One must be Torah-observant and lead the Jews into full Torah observance.[187] I agree. They believe that the Law of God is an eternal law.[188] I agree. They say that the Anointed One will not change an eternal Law.[189] I agree. They say that Y'hoshua thus could not possibly be the Anointed One. Here I must disagree.

Mainstream Christianity supported, for the past seventeen to nineteen hundred years, the same erroneous interpretation as non-messianic Jews that Y'hoshua the Anointed One changed the Law of God. Some Christians are now starting to realize the Truth that Y'hoshua the Anointed One, in fact, followed the commandments so well that the Sanhedrin could find only one accusation against Him amidst the flood of testimonies. Y'hoshua the Anointed One did not change the Law of God. He exemplified the Law of God. The accusation by which non-messianic Jews stood and I previously mentioned was that Y'hoshua the Anointed One committed blasphemy by claiming to be divine, by claiming to be the uniquely and only begotten Son of God, and thereby claiming to be One with God.

The ancient Jewish leaders could not accept the Anointed One's claim of divinity with Yah, blessed be His Name. Y'hoshua, however, was correct

---

187 Deuteronomy 12:32; Deuteronomy 13:1-5 [Deuteronomy 13:1-6]

188 Exodus 12:14-43; Exodus 27:21; Exodus 28:43; Leviticus 3:17; Leviticus 7:36; Leviticus 10:9; Leviticus 16:29-34; Leviticus 17:7; Leviticus 23:14-41; Leviticus 24:3; Numbers 10:8; Numbers 15:15; Numbers 19:10-23; Numbers 35:29; Deuteronomy 29:28

189 Deuteronomy 12:32; Deuteronomy 13:1-5 [Deuteronomy 13:1-6]; Matthew 5:17-18

and accurate in His claim. Thus, the Anointed One completely obeyed and adhered to the commandments of HaShem (The Name). If we are being made into His image,[190] then we too must completely obey and adhere to His commandments, counterculture to Christian beliefs and practices of cherry-picking from His commandments because some are not included in the Good News and the Apostolic Letters.

Further honest study of the Master's teachings displays that He taught the Instruction, the Torah, as the ancient prophets taught it, as God Himself meant for it to be taught. To summarize the *halachic* position of the Master during the time period of His incarnation: He sided with Hillel, the more lenient ancient Jewish elder, in most *halachic* interpretations of the Instruction except in the matter of marriage, in which He sided with Shammai, the stricter elder. The phrase "*halachic* interpretation" comes from the Hebrew word *halacha*, which literally means "the way." *Halacha* is the interpretation of the Scriptures in order to guide one's life, very similar to "hermeneutics."

Practically speaking, it is "the way" in which a Jew should live their lives. It is the instruction that directs their behavior in all aspects of life. Unfortunately, the *halacha* of non-messianic Jewish elders, even if erroneous, is considered binding in Jewish culture. Ancient kings and false prophets typically persecuted the prophets of HaShem (The Name), and they expected the people to follow suit. Thus, the Master prophesied, "Yerushalayim! Yerushalayim! You kill the prophets! You stone those who are sent to you!" (Matthew 23:37a). The Jewish leaders killed Him as they killed the prophets before Him, the completely Torah observant Servant of God.

Christian congregations similarly operate concerning their reaction to unpopular teaching. If someone teaches doctrine that is counter to mainstream acceptance, that person can be excommunicated from some congregations and even be labeled by Christianity at large as an apostate or heretic and/or a cult leader depending on his or her popularity. In the past, they even burned those carriers of unpopular ideas at the stake. They executed people, such as Thomas More and Jan Hus, for words that did not

---

190 Leviticus 11:44-45; Leviticus 19:2; Leviticus 20:7; Romans 8:28-30; 2 Corinthians 3:15-18; 1 Peter 1:13-16

lure people away from God, but for words that drew people to God. They killed people for ideas, not for wrongful deeds.

The Roman congregation considers Protestants as outside what they consider the official congregation of God. Protestants consider the Roman congregation as a cult despite the fact that the Roman congregation does not punish doubt, does not propagate the use of guilt to control its members, does not demand cutting ties with family and friends, does not encourage its members to predominantly socialize with its own members, lacks systematic control over even the minute actions and behaviors of its members, and lacks an us-versus-humanity mentality. Modern mainstream Christianity labels the Hebrew Roots Movement (HRM) as Judaizers and deceivers. The examples of rash condemnation are many, especially when including the history of the last two thousand years.

Current Jewish *halacha* stands upon the *halacha* of past elders, including the ancient Jewish elders after the time of Y'hoshua the Anointed One, meaning after the influx of the bias against Y'hoshua as the Anointed One. Thus, current Jewish *halacha* stands upon anti-Christ biases. Non-messianic Jewish elders claim that their oral tradition was given to Moshe (Moses) at the same time as the Instruction, the Pentateuch, but we have no mention of it in the Prophets.

In addition, the first written record of the Mishnah was AD 200 and the first written record of the Talmud was AD 425 (Halakhah). There is no Scriptural support for the authority of the Mishnah or the Talmud. There is also no Scriptural support for Christian traditions such as, but not limited to, a Sunday Day of Rest or Christmas. There is no Scriptural support for some Christian doctrines such as, but not limited to, the Trinity or rejection of the commandments of Yah, blessed be His Name. Many will claim to have Scriptural support, but when you study the context of their selected verses, you will see that their case rests on shifting sand and not solid rock.

Truly, Y'hoshua the Anointed One is the only *halacha*, the only Way (John 14:6), and He obeyed all the commandments, the whole Instruction, for He is the Instruction in flesh.

CHAPTER TEN

MASHIACH

MY CHILDREN, KNOW both sides of the story because, concerning humanity, there is always two sides to a story, and knowing both sides will help you to discern and defend the Truth.

The main problem that non-messianic Jews have with Y'hoshua the Anointed One (Mashiach in Hebrew, Christos in Greek) is the doctrine of the Trinity, a three-part deity, which in the Jews' eyes, is idolatry. I cannot blame them. The non-Scriptural doctrine of the Trinity is, after all, a culturally pagan Gentile's honest attempt to understand a foreign concept such as HaShem (The Name) at best and a pagan philosophic perversion of the Truth at worst. From beginning to end, the Scriptures have ever only mentioned One God.

Non-messianic Jews also cannot accept Y'hoshua the Anointed One (Jesus the Christ) in His full identity as Yah, blessed be His Name, because they believe that HaShem cannot take physical form.[191] In Exodus, the Lord tells Moshe (Moses) that no one can see His face and live, yet we have examples in Avraham and Ya'akov (Jacob) of those who have seen the face of God and lived.[192]

---

191 Exodus 33:18-20, Deuteronomy 4:14-18
192 Genesis 18:16-33; Genesis 32:24-31

I care not for the commentary of other men when the Scriptures are clear. The Scriptures clearly state that there is a face of God that humanity *cannot* see without their bodies dying (Deuteronomy 4:14-18) . . . and there is a face of the Lord that humanity *can* see without their bodies dying.[193] There are, then, two faces for YHVH, blessed be His Name, which we see in the Scriptures—one that is too powerful for Him to reveal to weak flesh and one that He is able to show us.

Perhaps one 'face' is the full glory of YHVH (Exodus 33:18), blessed be His Name, the full presence of God that resided in the Holiest Place of the Dwelling (Tabernacle).[194] Perhaps the other "face" is the more concealed glory of the Lord[195] with whom Avraham and Ya'akov interacted and later born into the flesh,[196] died on the cross, and resurrected to be the saving strength of His right hand.[197] Perhaps Moshe was requesting to see the full glory of Yah, blessed be His Name. Perhaps HaShem (The Name) blessed Moshe with another "face," a third "face" so to speak, a "face" in-between the full and concealed glory, causing his face to radiate with the glory of God but not destroying his body.[198]

Non-messianic Jews also think that the Lord would never take physical form because they specifically did not see a physical form in the fire that appeared to them on Mt. Chorev.

> Therefore, watch out for yourselves! Since you did not see any form on the day YHVH spoke to you at Chorev from the midst of the fire, do not become corrupt and make yourselves a carved image having the form of any figure, not a representation of male or female, or a representation of any animal on the earth, or a representation of any bird that flies in the air, or the representa-

---

193 Genesis 18:16-33; Genesis 32:24-31
194 Exodus 40:34-35; Leviticus 16:2; 2 Chronicles 7:1-3
195 John 13:3; John 17:5
196 Isaiah 7:14; John 1:14; John 3:13; John 6:33; Colossians 2:9; 1 John 4:2-3
197 Psalm 20:6; Psalm 110:1; Acts 2:33-35; Acts 5:31-39; Acts 7:55-60; Ephesians 1:18-21; Colossians 3:1; Hebrews 1; Hebrews 10:11-13
198 Exodus 33:21-23; Exodus 34:29-35

tion of anything that creeps on the ground, or a representation of any fish in the water below the shoreline. (Deuteronomy 4:15-18)

Moshe, from the fact that the Lord displayed no form in the fire, instructed the people of God never to make a carved image to worship. First, nothing in the verse says that the Lord cannot take physical form.[199] It simply said that He did not take physical form at that particular time. Secondly, Moshe stated the reason that the Lord did not take physical form at that given time was to drive home the point that they were to never create a carved image of Yah, blessed be His Name.

I now bring to your attention the bronze serpent that Moshe made according to the command of the Holy One of Yisrael (Numbers 21:9). Didn't the Almighty command them to never carve an image? Obviously HaShem's command to never carve an image specifically concerned idolatry (2 Kings 18:4) and that carving an image for a purpose other than idolatry did not violate His Instruction. His Instruction also did not forbid the Creator Himself from taking physical form.

Non-messianic Jewish elders interpret the prophecies in the Scriptures to say that He must be a descendant of David from his father's side.[200] I see the logic behind such a conclusion, especially in light of the prophecies, but I also know that human understanding is lacking and that our thoughts and ways are not His thoughts and His Way. As much as non-messianic Jewish elders would like to insist that the Anointed One must be Jewish from the father's side, even a direct descendant from David, their own culture says that their Jewish identity is received from the mother, not the father. "Jewishness is not in our DNA. It is in our soul. The reason it is passed down through the maternal line is not just because it is easier to identify who your mother is. It is because the soul identity is more directly shaped by the mother than the father" (Moss). As I stated previously, Y'hoshua the Anointed One came from the tribe

---

199 Genesis 3:8; Genesis 18:16-33; Genesis 32:24-31; Daniel 7:9-10, 13-14; Exodus 3:1-6; Joshua 5:13-15; Exodus 20:24; Deuteronomy 12:5-28; Judges 6:11-21; Judges 13:17-19; Genesis 19:24-25; Psalm 110:1; Zechariah 3; Zechariah 12:8
200 Isaiah 11:1-9; Jeremiah 23:5-6, 30:7-10, 33:14-16; Ezekiel 34:11-31, 37:21-28; Hosea 3:4-5

of Y'hudah (Judah) from the line of King David, not only from Yosef his adopted father, but also through Miryam (Mary) his earthly mother.[201] Also, one can conclude that upon Yosef's passing, Y'hoshua the Anointed One received the double portion inheritance of the physically descended firstborn although He was not the biological child of Yosef (Matthew 13:55).

I hear the opposing argument from non-messianic Jews that Y'hoshua the Anointed One is not God. In fact, they believe that Y'hoshua the Anointed One was not the Anointed One because He did not fulfill the only messianic prophecies that non-messianic Jews recognize today, mainly:

1. Building the third Temple[202]
2. Gathering all Jews back to the land of Yisrael[203]
3. Bringing world peace[204]
4. Bringing universal knowledge to all people that Yah, blessed be His Name, is the only God[205]

Truly, the only verse in the Scriptures that states the Anointed One will build the Temple is Zechariah 6:12-13.

The Jews recognize four types of explaining or interpreting the written Word of Yah, blessed be His Name: *p'shat* (simple), *remez* (hint), *d'rash* (to examine), and *sod* (secret). *P'shat* is the literal, straightforward, or simple interpretation. *Remez* goes deeper into the "spirit of the letter."[206] *D'rash* is a contextual symbolic interpretation that is not explicit in the text, typi-

---

201 Genesis 49:10; 2 Samuel 7:12-13; Isaiah 9:7; Matthew 1:6-18; Luke 1:32-33; Luke 3:23-33; Romans 1:3; Hebrews 7:14

202 Isaiah 56:6-8; Jeremiah 33:15-18; Ezekiel 43-46; Daniel 9:27; Daniel 11:31; Daniel 12:11; Zechariah 6:11-14; Zechariah 14:16

203 Deuteronomy 30:1-5; Isaiah 11:11-12; Hosea 1:8-11 [Hosea 1:8-9; Hosea 2:1-2]; Jeremiah 29:13-14; Jeremiah 31:38-40; Ezekiel 20:41-42; Ezekiel 37:11-25; Zechariah 10:8-10

204 Isaiah 2:4; Isaiah 32:15-18; Isaiah 60:15-18; Micah 4:3-4; Hosea 2:18 [Hosea 2:20]; Jeremiah 28:9

205 Isaiah 2:2-3; Micah 4:1-2; Zephaniah 3:9; Zechariah 8:23; Zechariah 14:9

206 Romans 2:29; 2 Corinthians 3:4-6

cally requiring cross-references. *Sod* is the hidden or secret meaning. Jews define *sod* as esoteric, meaning intended for or likely to be understood by only a small number of people who have specialized knowledge.

I puzzle at the Jews' willingness to accept the *d'rash* and *sod* of other men, even the witchcraft of Kabbalah with its astrology[207] and "magical and theurgic assumptions" (Tirosh-Samuelson), but squawk at the idea of accepting the *d'rash* and *sod* of the Anointed One Himself.[208] We have the Anointed One's own *sod* that His body was the Temple, [209] which HaShem (The Name) raised on the third day.[210] This teaching came from One who was fanatical about the physical Temple in Yerushalayim and its set-apartness.[211] Y'hoshua the Anointed One clearly stated that His body was the Temple, fulfilling most of Zechariah 6:12-13.[212]

Furthermore, all the other verses[213] the Jews use to support their belief that the Anointed One will build the third Temple only state that the third Temple will be standing when the Anointed One arrives. I also believe the third Temple will be standing when the Anointed One returns,[214] but I hold all beliefs concerning future events tentatively since I do not want to be caught in the same position as the ancient Jews who denied Him the first time.

The ancient Jews had, and present Jews have, such strong ideas of

---

207 Deuteronomy 4:19; Deuteronomy 18:10-14; Isaiah 47:13-14

208 Psalm 22; Jonah 1:17; Isaiah 53; Hosea 6:2; Matthew 12:38-42; Matthew 16:1-4, 21; Matthew 17:22-23; Matthew 20:18-19; Matthew 28:1-6; Luke 9:21-22; Luke 11:29-32; Luke 13:31-35; Luke 18:31-34; Luke 24; Acts 10:38-43; 1 Corinthians 15:1-11

209 Matthew 12:6; Matthew 27:39-41; Mark 14:57-59; Mark 15:29-30; John 2:13-22

210 Psalm 22; Jonah 1:17; Isaiah 53; Hosea 6:2; Matthew 12:38-42; Matthew 16:1-4, 21; Matthew 17:22-23; Matthew 20:18-19; Matthew 28:1-6; Luke 9:21-22; Luke 11:29-32; Luke 13:31-35; Luke 18:31-34; Luke 24; Acts 10:38-43; 1 Corinthians 15:1-11

211 Matthew 21:12-13; Matthew 23:16-35; Mark 11:15-17; Luke 19:45-46; John 2:13-17

212 Isaiah 11:1; Jeremiah 23:5; Jeremiah 33:15; Matthew 1:1-17; John 15:1-17; Matthew 19:28; Matthew 25:31

213 Isaiah 56:6-8; Jeremiah 33:15-18; Ezekiel 43-46; Daniel 9:27; Daniel 11:31; Daniel 12:11; Zechariah 14:16

214 Matthew 24:15-21; 2 Thessalonians 2:1-4; John 5:43; Revelation 11:1-2

future events that they rejected the signs so obviously presented to them. To be fair, I see Christians as having the same problem, loyal to their premillennial, postmillennial, or amillennial views, even to a fault. I do not want to deceive myself in the same fashion with preconceived notions, lest I fall prey to the anti-Christs and beasts of the sea and the earth who precede the Anointed One.[215]

As I said, most of the referenced verses say that the third Temple will already be standing upon the arrival of the Anointed One. A person should then wonder as to who builds the third Temple. If an anti-Christ or the "beast of the sea" or the "beast of the earth" builds the Temple, I truly pity the Jews who follow him/them and his/their deception. Perhaps the fact that the anti-Christ and the beasts will be without the Instruction of God will protect some Jews, at least the orthodox, from such deceit.

Jews also look for the gathering of all Jews into Yisrael as a necessary fulfillment to recognize the Anointed One. I also wholeheartedly agree with them.[216] Even more than the Jews (Y'hudah—Judah), I believe the Anointed One will also gather His scattered *talmidim* (disciples) from among the Gentiles, whom I believe to be the popularly called "Ten Lost Tribes" (Efrayim—Ephraim), into Yisrael.[217] I believe the Anointed One will accomplish this gathering at His return.

Non-messianic Jews, however, have a problem with this reasoning. Firstly, they have a problem with the Anointed One. Secondly, they have a problem of welcoming Gentiles into their elitist uniqueness and sole claim to relationship with Yah, blessed be His Name. Sha'ul (Saul/Paulos/Paul) already refuted this reasoning through utilizing the Instruction and the Prophets.[218] Salvation is based on trusting HaShem (The Name), not birthright or membership to any group,[219] Jewish or Christian. God is the hope for all peoples and all nations.

---

215 Matthew 24:21-31; Mark 13:21-23; Revelation 13
216 Matthew 23: 37; Matthew 24: 29-31; Luke 21: 24; John 11: 50-52; Acts 1: 6-7
217 Hosea 1 [Hosea 1; Hosea 2: 1-2]; Ezekiel 37
218 Genesis 15: 5-6; Genesis 17: 5; Romans 4: 7-18; 2 Samuel 22: 50; Psalm 18: 49; Deuteronomy 32: 43; Psalm 117: 1; Isaiah 11: 10; Isaiah 52: 15; Romans 15: 7-12
219 Ezekiel 18; Romans 1:16; Romans 2:9-10; Romans 10:12-13; Galatians 3:28; Colossians 3:9-11

Jews also expect the Anointed One to bring world peace,[220] and I agree with them. Some verses, however, address peace only in reference to Yisrael,[221] while other verses address worldwide peace.[222] In addition, Jeremiah 28:9 states that "The prophet who prophesies of peace, when the word of that prophet is fulfilled, then that prophet will be recognized, that YHVH did truly send him."

I can understand the Jewish rejection of Y'hoshua the Anointed One based on this sole verse. The Master prophesied peace, and as we can all see, war still plagues the earth. He said that the Kingdom of YHVH, blessed be His Name, was at hand, and yet we have the Holocaust, Stalin, Pol Pot, and many other examples of war (Isaiah 8:19-20). Nevertheless, the Master not only prophesied peace but also offered peace. He may not have brought peace to the world as we understand or expect, but He gifted us with the first fruits of peace in our spirits and in our hearts. He may not have brought peace to the physical borders of Yisrael and Yerushalayim, but He offered it to His spiritual Kingdom, to spiritual Yisrael, His *talmidim* who follow and obey Him in spirit/sincerity and in Truth.[223] When He stated that the Kingdom of Yah, blessed be His Name, was at hand, He meant it; He also said that His Kingdom had not yet reached its completion.[224]

The Kingdom is in the hearts of those who obey HaShem (The Name) because a Kingdom entails a ruler and citizens who obey. Thus, Y'hoshua the Anointed One said that the Kingdom was open to children. Note that the children of ancient days knew obedience better than the kids of modern entitlement. Such children understood and applied obedience. Children obeyed their parents because they trusted their parents, even when they did not understand.

The Kingdom is at hand because it is in the hearts of those who

220 Isaiah 2:4; Isaiah 32:15-18; Isaiah 60:15-18; Micah 4:3-4; Hosea 2:18 [Hosea 2:20]; Jeremiah 28:9

221 Isaiah 32:15-18; Isaiah 60:15-18

222 Isaiah 2:4; Micah 4:3-4; Hosea 2:18 [Hosea 2:20]

223 Luke 2:14; John 14:27; John 16:33; Acts 10:36-38; Romans 14:17; Ephesians 2:11-22

224 John 21:20-23; Acts 1:6-11

obey Him. It will be fully realized on the earth upon the Anointed One's return. In similar fashion, the peace that Y'hoshua the Anointed One offered and offers is currently available in the hearts of those who follow Him, and it will be fully realized on the earth upon His return. The true *talmid* (disciple) of the Anointed One has peace in the midst of tragedy, in the midst of crisis, persecution, loss, and chaos. I am not saying that a *talmid* may not grieve, panic, fear, mourn, or have confusion, but such reactions will not perpetuate in their life nor consume or control them. A true *talmid* remembers upon whom his/her life, both earthly and eternally, depends, and trusts His will to its fruition, thereby overcoming the previously mentioned reactions. A true *talmid* remembers that he/she is a citizen of His Kingdom, an eternal Kingdom, and in time overcomes reactions to this temporal world.

Jews expect the Anointed One to bring universal knowledge of the God of Avraham, Yitzchak (Isaac), and Ya'akov (Jacob) to all the nations. I don't know if non-messianic Jews are aware, but the main driving purpose of the *talmidim* of the Anointed One, since the inception of the Second Temple Judaism sect of Christianity, is to bring the knowledge of God and the Good News of His salvation to all nations. His *talmidim* received this purpose directly from the Anointed One, who told us:

> All authority has been given to Me in heaven and on earth. Therefore, go and make people from all nations into *talmidim*, immersing them in the Name of the Father, the Son, and the Holy Spirit, teaching them to obey everything that I have commanded you. And remember! I am with you always, until the end of the age. (Matthew 28:18b-20)

What started with 500 *talmidim*, is now an assembly, albeit bickering and divided, of 2.18 billion, which is almost a third of the world's population. "While the Gospel has gone to every political country in the world, when Jesus commanded His followers to 'make disciples of all the nations' in Matthew 28:18-20, He was not referring to political nations such as Canada, Kenya, Russia, etc" (Has Everyone Heard). The efforts of the Jews are not what spread knowledge of the God of Avraham,

Yitzchak, and Ya'akov to the world. The world knows about God and His commandments because of the *talmidim* of the Anointed One, servants, workers, and citizens of the Kingdom of God.

Nevertheless, I did not say that the mission was complete.

So how many of the approximately 16,300 ethnic groups are considered unreached i.e. less than 2% Christ-follower and less than 5% Professing Christian? The latest estimates suggest that approximately 6,550 people groups are considered unreached. That means over 40% of the world's people groups have no indigenous community of believing Christians able to evangelize the rest of their people group. Over 42% of the world's population live in these over 6,550 people groups. (Has Everyone Heard)

Furthermore, "Operation World presents data suggesting that after peaking in the mid-1990s the growth rate of both Christianity in general and Evangelicals . . . has slowed significantly" (Has Everyone Heard). If the mid-1990s is the peak for spreading the Good News throughout the world, I wonder if we have reached the fullness of the Gentiles (Romans 11:11-31). As I previously stated, Messianic Judaism only started making its noticeable waves on the scene in the 1990s and turn of the millennium. While the work is not yet complete, non-messianic Jews still fail to realize that the Anointed One worked and is working through His people to bring universal knowledge of HaShem (The Name).

I previously mentioned the Jewish problem of welcoming Gentiles into their elitist uniqueness and sole claim to relationship with Yah, blessed be His Name. They had this problem from the beginning (Acts 13:42-46), and with good reason, considering past follies of intermixing with Gentiles leading to idolatry.[225] As with many Christian movements throughout the years, the Jews began with good intentions, separating themselves from foreign nations and their idolatry, but continued to an extreme of folly, isolating themselves and their relationship with the Creator from all others . . . in direct rebellion to the commandment of

225 Numbers 25; 1 Kings 11:1-13; Ezekiel 16:15-34; Ezra 9:1

the Holy One of Yisrael.[226] I see the same pattern in movements within Christianity, starting from good intentions and morphing over time to an unintended extreme, which then becomes folly.

Non-messianic Jews also have prerequisites for the announcement of the Anointed One. Firstly, they believe a person can only be the Anointed One if the announcement of his identity comes to the entire ethnicity of Jews, meaning God speaking to the entire people, i.e., the personal eyewitness of every man, woman, and child, just as HaShem (The Name) did on Mount Sinai.[227] If non-messianic Jews truly adhered to this tenet of "national revelation" and if they adhered to consistency in their beliefs and practices, then they would have to deny all the writings of the Prophets and maintain only the Instruction, the Pentateuch, as their sole religious text.

I say this because Yah, blessed be His Name, did not speak to every man, woman, and child at one given time when He sent His prophets to chastise them and warn them of the oncoming punishment and consequences for their sin. Obviously then, according to their own doctrine, they must reject the Prophets and all the prophecies concerning the Anointed One. History shows that Yisrael rejected the prophets and suffered calamity, just as they rejected Y'hoshua the Anointed One and His apostles. The Master said, "Rejoice and be glad because your reward is great in the heavens; [Yisrael] persecuted the prophets before you in the same way" (Matthew 5:12). He also said:

> Woe to you, Torah-teachers and P'rushim! You build tombs for the prophets and decorate the graves of the *tzadikim*, and you say, "If we had been in the days of our fathers, we would not have been partakers with them in killing the prophets." In this you testify against yourselves that you are worthy descendants of those who murdered the prophets. Go ahead then, finish what your fathers started! You snakes! Sons of snakes! How will you escape being condemned to Gei-Hinnom? Therefore, behold, I

---

226 Leviticus 17:8-9
227 Exodus 19:7-11; Exodus 20:18-21 [15-18]; Deuteronomy 5:3

am sending you prophets and sages and Torah-teachers; some of them you will kill, indeed, you will have them executed on stakes as criminals, and some you will scourge in your synagogues and persecute from city to city. And so, on you will fall the guilt for all the righteous blood shed on earth, from the blood of righteous Hevel to the blood of Zecharyah Ben-Berekhyah, whom you murdered between the Temple and the altar. Truly I say to you, all these things will come upon this generation! Yerushalayim! Yerushalyaim! You kill the prophets! You stone those who are sent to you! How often I wanted to gather your children together, just as a hen gathers her chicks under her wings, but you refused! (Matthew 23:29-37)

Non-messianic Jewish scholars will accept the Prophets despite the absence of "national revelation." Nevertheless, they deny Y'hoshua the Anointed One while at the same time using "national revelation" as one excuse for their disbelief. Well, they are only using the same excuses that their ancestors used to ignore and then execute the same prophets that they now claim to honor.

Secondly, non-messianic Jews say that a person can only be announced as the Anointed One if the majority of all Jews lived in the physical borders of ancient Yisrael, using the Isaiah Targum as their defense (Simmons). Let us examine this Targum version of Isaiah 11:1-2:

11.1 And a *king* shall come forth from the *sons* of Jesse, and *the Messiah* shall *be exalted* from *the sons of* his *sons*. 11.2 And *a* spirit *before* the LORD shall rest upon him, a spirit of wisdom and understanding, a spirit of counsel and might, a spirit of knowledge and the fear of the LORD. 11.3 And the LORD shall *bring him near to* his fear. And he shall not judge by the sight of his eyes, and he shall not reprove by the hearing of his ears; 11.4 but in *truth* he will judge the poor, and reprove with *faithfulness* for the needy of the *people*; and he shall strike *the sinners of* the land with the *command* of his mouth, and with *the speaking* of his lips the wicked shall *die*. (Cathcart)

Non-messianic Jewish elders will spout Christian twisting of the Scriptures, but how did they come to the conclusion of "national revelation" and majority population for the announcement of the Anointed One by this Targum translation of Isaiah? If they truly believed the majority of Jews needed to reside in the land of Yisrael before the Anointed One appeared, they would not have been seeking for Eliyah (Elijah) at the end of each Passover for the past two thousand years. The majority of Jews do not currently reside in the borders of Israel, so why look for Eliyah? Their actions do not align with their beliefs, and actions are the true proof of one's beliefs (James 2:18-26).

Considering the previously mentioned Targum translation of Isaiah 11:1 – 2, I ask that you review all that Y'hoshua the Anointed One already accomplished while He walked this earth and then review Revelation 19:11-21, especially the last verse. "The rest were killed with the sword that goes out of the mouth of Him who is sitting on the horse, and all the birds gorged themselves on their flesh." Yeshayah appears to be speaking about Y'hoshua the Anointed One.

Rabbinical Jews will uphold the *sod* (esoteric interpretation) of their ancient "sages" and yet denounce the *sod* of the apostles and authors of the Apostolic Scriptures. If you compare the *sod* from these two groups, the Rabbinical "sages" versus the apostles, I am sure you will agree with me that the *sod* of the apostles more closely follows logic and understanding over the *sod* of Rabbinical Jewish "sages." Remove all bias, and I find more logic and sense in the *sod* of the apostles. These two invented requirements of "national revelation" and majority population in Yisrael strike me as the greatest absurdity.

Most Jews also believe, and have believed throughout the ages, that there can only be one appearance of the Anointed One, not two appearances. Yet some Jews also historically believed in two future prophesied anointed ones, distinct from the usual and past anointed ones.

No scroll found by the Dead Sea contains any conclusive evidence of a New Testament text, and neither is there any clear reference to Jesus Christ, John the Baptist, or any early Christian by name . . . the authors of the Scrolls were waiting for two messiahs rather than one. The authors of the Scrolls expected one priestly and another kingly messiah, qualities that are in large part combined into the description of Jesus in the New Testament writings. Nevertheless, the commonalities between the scrolls and early Christian ideas show that there were clear Jewish precursors to the thought and ideas of what later became the Jesus movement. (Schofield)

Another version of the two anointed ones states that someone will "wage war against Messiah b. Joseph, and slay him. His corpse . . . will be hidden . . . until Messiah b. David comes and resurrects him" (Singer, Vol. 8). The first set of future prophesied anointed ones, according to ancient Jewish belief, is the Anointed One of Aharon and the Anointed One of Yisrael, and the second set being Anointed One son of Yosef and Anointed One son of David.

Some groups of Jews can accept two anointed ones that appear close to the same time, but one after the other and in specific order. Hear it from their own mouth, from a portion of their Babylonian Talmud, Sukkah 52a:

Two Messiahs

"Our rabbis taught: The Holy One, blessed be he, will say to Messiah ben David (May he reveal himself speedily in our day!), 'Ask of me anything and I will give it to you,' as it is said, 'I will tell of the decree [of the Lord],' etc. 'This day I have begotten you. Ask of me and I will give you the nations for your inheritance' (Ps. 2). But when he will see that Messiah ben Joseph is slain, he will say to him, 'Lord of the universe, I ask of you only life.'"

Here Messiah ben Joseph appears in the same scene as the Messiah from David. Therefore, the two figures are not part of rival eschatological schemas, but part of the same drama. As in the previous passage, Messiah ben Joseph has been slain by unnamed foes. But here we learn that this event takes place before Messiah ben David receives authority over the nations. This suggests that a sequence of eschatological events is envisaged, an idea implicit in some biblical texts. (Mitchell, pp. 83-84)

I do not understand why the idea that a single Anointed One who appears at two completely different times should be so difficult to grasp, considering this pre-existing Jewish belief of two anointed ones.

I have shown you the reasons for why the Jews do not accept Y'hoshua the Anointed One as the Anointed One. First, they restrict YHVH, blessed be His Name, in that they do not believe that the Lord is capable of taking physical form. I explained how He did take physical form even in the Instruction, even before the eyes of Avraham and Ya'akov (Jacob).

Second, they are looking for a descendant of David through the father's side. I explained how the ancient Jews treated Y'hoshua as the physical firstborn of Yosef the carpenter, a descendant of David, and that even Miryam (Mary) physically descended from the line of David.

Third, they expect the Anointed One to build the Temple. I explained how the Anointed One already raised the Temple of His body after three days in Sh'ol (Sheol/Underworld) and that the Scriptures mainly referenced the Temple as already being built when He arrives.

Fourth, they invented the extra prerequisites of national revelation and majority population in order to recognize the Anointed One. I explained how these requirements did not align with any worthwhile logic or honest interpretation of the Scriptures and was frankly not consistent with their own beliefs and actions.

Fifth, they are only expecting and looking for the fulfillment of the kingly prophecies of the in-gathering of His people, world peace, and world enlightenment, while ignoring the priestly prophecies of service, self-sacrifice, and giving His life through death as the ultimate sacrifice. He came first, not as a priest of the Order of Aharon, but as a priest of the Order of Malki-Tzedek (Melchizedek). [228]

I explained how even the ancient Jews were aware of the priestly prophecies and how Y'hoshua the Anointed One fulfilled them, as explained by the esoteric interpretations of the author of the letter to

---

228 Psalm 2:7; Psalm 110:4; Hebrews 5:5-6

the Hebrews. Even the Talmud recognized the prophecies of a kingly Anointed One in addition to a priestly Anointed One. I explained how He will fulfill the kingly prophecies at His return, His second appearance, and that there is only one Anointed One who appears twice rather than two anointed ones who each appear once.

CRITICISM

MY CHILDREN, STAND strong in your allegiance to Yah, blessed be His Name, to His Word born flesh and the Seven Spirits of God; stand strong against the numerous lies and seductive deceptions that fill the world.

You will find assault from atheists, Muslims, Jews, and even from within the various folds of Christianity, both cultic and mainstream. Atheists will swing the incomplete battle axe of science even though they have only scraped the surface of knowledge, and it will break upon contact with the fullness of reality that HaShem (The Name) created. Science observes the world, but HaShem created it. Science is limited, constantly changing, and still growing into its maturity. Atheists pose the presumption of how the world began as if it were fact, quick to reject others' ideas, yet they were not present at the beginning. They find some scientific markers from their observations, make an assumption, couch it in technical terms of education, and pander it to the benighted masses. Science, by far, is not the gateway to all knowledge. Yet atheists place all their trust and their faith in it as if it were the path to enlightenment (though they strive to deny the word "faith"). It is a limited tool, not an omniscient crystal ball. You will find arrogance at the core of most atheists, at least in my experience (to be fair, you will find the same folly of arrogance in

Christians). They raise themselves as their own idols. Some Agnostics, recognizing the folly of arrogance, hide behind an illusion of their own created external third-party idol, which they define and still thereby control. Others will simply rest in languid self-proclaimed ignorance.

Atheists and agnostics have long claimed the Scriptures were inaccurate.

[The] late British philosopher and avowed agnostic wrote this in his *History of Western Philosophy*: "The early history of the Israelites cannot be confirmed from any source outside of the Old Testament, and it is impossible to know at what point it ceases to be purely legendary." [He] dismisses the Bible as unreliable legend in just a few sentences. Even though printed in 1945, his book is still widely read by university students and is considered one of the best books of its kind . . .

The scholars' main attack on Bible history in the early 20th century was that no secular records existed to provide evidence of the Flood, the Exodus, or the lives of David and Solomon. Many claimed that Moses could never have written the first five books of the Bible, since writing had not been invented at that time. But when the curious, energetic men and women dug up the past, these commonly held ideas were proved to be without foundation. (Leap)

The wonderful rise of the new field of archaeology attested over time to the geography and events to which the Scriptures declared.

The conclusion of [archaeological] evidence was summed up by Nelson Glueck that "no archaeological discovery has ever controverted a biblical reference. Scores of archaeological findings have been made which confirm in clear outline or exact detail historical statements in the Bible." Millar Burroughs notes that "more than one archaeologist has found his respect for the Bible increased by the experience of excavation in Palestine." (Geisler)

Nevertheless, we need nothing to supplement our trust in Yah, blessed be His Name. He is simply who He is. Our relationship with Him and life experiences with Him according to His Word is the only proof we need that His Word is true. We have to know it for ourselves. If we can know it for ourselves, then nothing external can convince us for or against it.

We should not need proof of the past works of the Lord. He is God, God of all creation. He has no responsibility to prove Himself to each and every generation time and time again. Archaeology is still science and science is still only a limited tool.

> In many ways it is unrealistic to expect much of the archaeological enterprise to relate specifically to the events or people of the Bible . . .
>
> A major methodological understanding in any enterprise is to recognize the limited range of questions that the discipline might answer. Archaeology does not provide answers to all the questions that we might conceivably ask. The questions we pose to archaeology must respect the data base providing the answers.
>
> When we consider the full range of human existence and experience, only a fraction of that will be preserved in any way since much of it decays and is removed from the scene. Of those that are preserved, written works are a significantly smaller range of representation. Artifacts and materials directly related to the Bible and its record are minuscule in proportion to the variety and volume of the archaeological record.
>
> It is true that archaeology has discovered some remarkable finds that mesh well with the biblical texts—references to David, Ahab, Jehu, Jeremiah, Hezekiah, and others—but these are few in relation to the mass of material connected with everyday life . . .
>
> Sadly, there is often a tendency to seek a premature correspondence of archaeological finds with the Bible . . . It is disconcerting and seriously hurts the cause of the believer to make claims that are unsubstantiated and which many times require retraction. The effect to the skeptical searcher will likely be further skepticism

than faith . . . If and when we find evidence from archaeology that meshes with the Bible, our faith may be corroborated, but it should not rest primarily upon that basis. (Manor)

We should simply trust His Word, but not blindly and ignorantly. He gave us minds and the ability to discern and understand. We should trust His Word because relationship with Him according to His written Word proves it through our life experiences with Him. We should thereafter strive to understand His written Word upon the foundation of our trust.

In other words, we should not discount scientists who claimed the earth was round when religious leaders claimed the earth was flat. Weigh information provided by both sides with the realization that science is limited in scope and finite human minds are limited in understanding the written Word of God. His Spirit teaches us, but we are still flawed, and the Lord has decided that some matters should remain hidden from our knowledge.[229] Weigh all information from all sides according to the commandments of right living and relationship with HaShem (The Name). Judge for yourself if it changes your relationship with Him or if it changes your behavior with other people. If it does not, then the information should be filed under trivial possibilities and mysteries, and proceed with your life.

Just on the much-argued topic of creation and evolution you will find warring tribes within Christianity of young earth creationists, old earth creationists, intelligent design, and theistic evolutionists, etc. Knowing the specifics of whether God created Adam from dust, or through an extended process of dust to one-celled organism, to animals, to Neanderthal really doesn't affect your relationship with Him or your interaction with others.

The spirit of a person still comes from Yah, blessed be His Name. Knowing the specifics of whether God meant seven literal twenty-four-hour periods or seven ages of unknown time doesn't really affect your relationship with Him or your interaction with others. The curse of death

---

229 Deuteronomy 29:29; Proverbs 25:2; Daniel 12:4-9; John 20:30; John 21:25; Revelation 10:4

upon Adam because of his sin still affects all of humanity and acknowledges the need for salvation from death.

I personally believe in a combination of both. I believe that the Lord created the world in six epochs, resting on the seventh. I also believe that God created Adam and Chavah (Eve) directly from the dust as He said, and not from apes. I believe dinosaurs, leviathans, and behemoths walked the earth beside humanity.[230] Either way, I really don't care (but Mama does). Changing my understanding of the beginning or the end does not change my trust in Him. My understanding may change, but His Word remains steadfast. I may grow in knowledge and understanding, but the Creator knows everything. Scientists and theologians cannot really prove their theories of the beginning. Neither of them were eyewitnesses. Each group uses their tools to the best of their ability, both the consumers of science and the adherents to the written Word of God, respectively.

The tools of science are faulty, as are the interpretations and understandings of theologians. Trust neither. Trust the Lord (Proverbs 3:5), who set eternity in our hearts (Ecclesiastes 3:11). Should we really concern ourselves with concrete ideas of the beginning and the end, or focus more on grasping His principles of right heart and right living?[231] I encourage you to seek out the revelation of mysteries from Yah, blessed be His Name, but prioritize your questions according to their significance as they affect your relationship with Him and others. While knowledge is helpful, relationships are what matter (1 Corinthians 13:1-3). If you take a stance against the Scriptures, you will be proven wrong.

The compilation called the Bible or the Scriptures proved doubting atheistic historians to be erroneous over the course of time.

Modern archaeology has challenged the world of education to admit that the Bible is factual. Solid, documented evidence outside the Bible record confirms events and persons that were at one time considered to be suspect or plain false. . .

One of the most ridiculous claims of the critics has been that

---

230 Job 40:15; Job 41:1
231 1 Timothy 1:3-5; Titus 3:4-11

the Babylonian captivity did not take place. This is on a par with those who believe the Holocaust of World War II did not happen. The Bible gives specific details about the captivity of Judah by the armies of Babylon early in the 6th century B.C. (II Kings 24-25). Scholars have said it's all just another Jewish myth. However, between 1935 and 1938, important discoveries were made 30 miles southwest of Jerusalem at a site thought to be ancient Lachish. Lachish was one of the cities recorded in the Bible as being besieged by the king of Babylon at the same time as the siege of Jerusalem (Jeremiah 34:7).

Twenty-one pottery fragments inscribed in the ancient Hebrew script were unearthed in the latest pre-exilic levels of the site. Called the *Lachish Ostraca*, they were written during the very time of the Babylonian siege. Some of them are exchanges between the city's military commander and an outlying observation post, vividly picturing the final days of Judah's desperate struggle against Babylon! Since the 1930s, there has been more unearthing of Babylonian historical texts describing the conquest of Jerusalem by Nebuchadnezzar. The historical fact of the Babylonian captivity is firmly established. (Leap)

We should be able to see the proof of His work in our lives by aligning our lives to His written Word and seeing the resulting consequences according to His Word. I am saying to apply His Word to your life and strengthen your trust in Him by seeing His Instruction and His Word bear the results that He says it will bear when we implement them. Notice that He does not promise a life of luxury and easy street, but rather a life of difficulty and persecution.[232] He also offers the only worthwhile and lasting purpose and fulfillment.[233]

---

232 Numbers 13-14; 1 Samuel 30:6; Matthew 5:1-12; 2 Corinthians 6:1-10; Revelation 2:10

233 Genesis 1:26; Exodus 9:16; Psalm 138:8; Psalm 139:1-16; Proverbs 19:21; Ecclesiastes 12:13-14; James 1:18; 2 Thessalonians 1:11-12; Galatians 1:15-17; 1 Corinthians 1:26-31; 1 Corinthians 3:11-15; Romans 8:28; Ephesians 1:11-21; Ephesians 4:1-6; Philippians 2:12-13; 2 Timothy 1:8-10; 2 Peter 1:10-11

Be careful. I am not saying to test Him.[234] He said to test Him in only one thing, and that is tithing and offerings (Malachi 3:8-12). Even the famous author of *Rich Dad, Poor Dad*, whom I perceive to be fully unbelieving and secular, implements tithing as his mentor taught him because he experiences its blessing.

The written Word of God and our experience of relationship with Him should be the basis for our trust. We should be able to see the proof of the Lord through our relationship with Him. We should be able to trust Him because He has proven to us through relationship that He is trustworthy according to His Way, and not by our finite and misguided ways. We should be able to trust Him because He proved and continues to prove that He keeps His Word (Jeremiah 1:12). The bottom-line is: He desires relationship. I thank the Lord, however, for giving us the secular outlet of archaeology with which to shut up the blasphemies of atheists.

It had been fashionable in some circles for many years to ridicule Isaiah 20:1 for its allusion to "Sargon king of Assyria." Excavations of Nineveh had seemingly revealed all the kings of Assyria, but there was no Sargon. The Bible must have gotten it wrong. However, in 1843, Paul Emile Botta found a virgin site northeast of Nineveh, later excavated by the University of Chicago with details published in the 1930s. Sargon had built his own capital there in 717 B.C. His son, however, moved the capital back to Nineveh, so the site was lost as was Sargon's name. Now Sargon is one of the best known Assyrian monarchs…

Discoveries of other biblical names have confirmed biblical reliability, including King Jehoiachin's presence in Babylon, Sanballat as governor of Samaria along with some of Nehemiah's adversaries such as Tobiah the Ammonite, and Geshem the Arab (Nehemia 2:19). Other discoveries confirm well-known biblical

---

234 Exodus 17:2-7; Numbers 14:22-24; Deuteronomy 6:16; Psalm 78; Psalm 95:9; Psalm 106:13-15; Malachi 3:13-18; Matthew 4:5-7; Luke 4:9-12; Acts 5:1-9; Acts 15:3-11; Numbers 21:4-9; 1 Corinthians 10:9; Psalm 95; Hebrews 3:7-11

individuals such as Balaam, David, Ahab, Jehu, Hezekiah, Menahem, and others.

Until Hugo Winckler discovered the Hittite Empire in 1906, many unbelievers doubted the Bible's insistence that the Hittites were part of the land of Canaan (Genesis 10:15; Joshua 1:4). Now they are so well documented that scores of volumes has been necessary to build a Hittite dictionary based on the tablets left in their civilization…

Another example is the disputed list of sites along the route of exodus in Numbers 33. But Charles Krahmalkov noted three ancient Egyptian maps of the road from Arabah to the Plains of Moab, with the earliest of the three maps inscribed on the walls of Karnak in the reign of Thutmosis III (c. 1504 – 1450 B.C.). According to this list, the route from south to north follows precisely the way the Israelites listed in Numbers 33 with four stations especially noted: Iyyim, Dibon, Abel, and Jordan.

Discovered by Grenfeld in Egypt in 1920, the "John Rylands Papyrus" yielded the oldest known fragment of a NT manuscript. This small scrap from John's Gospel (Jn 18:31-33, 37-38) was dated by papyrologists to 125 A.D., but since it was so far south into Egypt, it successfully put an end to the then-popular attempt to late-date John's Gospel to the second century rather than to the traditional first century date of A.D. 85-90.

The Dead Sea Scrolls, found in 1948 in caves at Qumran, near the northwest end of the Dead Sea, gave us some 800 manuscripts of every book (in part or the whole) of the OT except for Esther. Prior to that, the earliest Hebrew texts dated to around A.D. 1000, but the scrolls at Qumran are generally more than one thousand years older! These Hebrew texts illustrate that a thousand years of copying had provided us with an amazingly pure text, with one of the best examples being the book of Isaiah where only three words had slight modifications . . .

Space precludes discussion of the many archaeological cor-
roborations, such as the Pontius Pilate Inscription, the Pool of
Siloam excavated in 2004, and the amazing Ketef Hinnom Amulets discovered in 1979 (with inscriptions of Nm 6:24-26 and
Dt 7:9 perfectly matching the biblical Hebrew text—amazing
since these seventh to sixth century B.C. amulets contain OT
texts skeptics argued could not have been written until the 400s
B.C.). (Kaiser)

Archaeology will not prove the Bible for us, but it is a complement
to our understanding of His written Word through cultural background,
historical and geographical context, and interlinking information between
the discoveries of archaeology and testimony of HaShem (The Name).
The fact of the matter is, when historians doubted the accuracy of the
written Word of God, archaeology proved them wrong time and time
again. "And He answered them, 'I tell you that if they become silent, the
stones will cry out!'" (Luke 19:40). I rejoice to see the Lord vindicate
Himself in the face of idol and self-worshipers even though He has no
requirement or responsibility to do so.

Those who desire their own ways will always reject the Creator and
His Word.[235] No amount of evidence will ever change their heart because
the matter at hand is not evidence.[236] Nature itself gives evidence to the
Creator.[237] Rather, the matter at hand is one's heart.[238] The true question
is, will you humble yourself before God or invest arrogance into yourself?
Do you simply want to do things your way and damn what anyone else
has to say?

Evidence is not the issue. If ever beliefs were wrong, such as the earth
being flat, the problem was with human interpretation, and not His writ-

---

235 Deuteronomy 8:2-3; Deuteronomy 32:15; Proverbs 3:34; James 4:6-10; 1 Peter
5:5; Proverbs 11:2; Proverbs 16:18; Proverbs 18:12; Proverbs 29:23; Isaiah 2:11-12;
Isaiah 66:2; Matthew 23:12; Luke 14:11; Luke 18:10-14; Romans 8:6-8

236 Deuteronomy 1:26-33; Luke 16:31

237 Job 12:7-12; Psalm 19:1-6; Jeremiah 5:21-31; Romans 1:20

238 Deuteronomy 13:1-3; Proverbs 3-4; Proverbs 23:26; Psalm 51:10; Psalm 73:26;
Matthew 6:19-21, 25-33; Philippians 4:7

ten Word. The *talmidim* (disciples) of the Anointed One had no business persecuting people for holding different beliefs. Such was never instructed or encouraged by the Master, especially in an earthly kingdom not His own. Excommunication (1 Corinthians 5:1-6), sure, but we *talmidim* should not employ persecution, and especially not execution, not unless we had His direct instruction through the Urim veTumim (Lights and Wholeness) [239] and were under His direct government presided by His Anointed One. Speaking of which, the Urim veTumim have been lost for millennia. Human interpretation can be flawed, but God's written Word is complete and accurate.

Atheists claim they desire evidence, but I heard from an atheist's own mouth, "I'll believe in your God when Jesus appears before me at night, glowing in radiant light, and I can touch and feel Him and the holes in His hands or wrists . . . and at the same time He turns every car in the world upside down and then levitates them."

Those words are not the words of a person who desires evidence of God for the purpose of bowing down in submission and humbly following Him. Those are the words of arrogance that desires self-will over the eternal and loving will of Yah, blessed be His Name. I know that even if such things as he required occurred, the man with whom I spoke would still not submit to the will of the Anointed One (Luke 16:19-31). I repeat myself: you will find the same folly of arrogance in Christians. I fear for the safety of anyone filled with arrogance.

C. S. Lewis stated that Y'hoshua the Anointed One (Jesus the Christ) can only logically be who He claimed to be, or else He must be a false prophet or crazy. Some will try to poke holes into C. S. Lewis' reasoning, but these critics' attempts are far-fetched endeavors at logic, fancy fortune cookie ways of saying "maybe he was wrong" or "not necessarily." They play mental gymnastics with amazing stretches to try and distort a quite simple and logically sound statement.

The critics complain that C. S. Lewis based his statements on a premise that the Scriptural accounts of Y'hoshua the Anointed One are actually

---

239 Exodus 28:30; Leviticus 8:8; Numbers 27:21; Deuteronomy 33:8-9; 1 Samuel 28:6; Ezra 2:63; Nehemiah 7:65

true. The critics propose that perhaps Y'hoshua the Anointed One was simply a legend. Legends are not real. We have enough historical evidence to prove that a man stirred the Jews, stirred the local Roman authority, and gathered *talmidim*, many of whom witnessed and confirmed His resurrection. His earthly life occurred during the time of recorded history, not in the antediluvian ages of pre-history.

How can people take such critics seriously?

Other critics claim that C. S. Lewis used fallacious logic in that he used a false trilemma. These critics then contrive other possibilities outside of the three stated by Lewis, but further examination of their proposals shows that the additional alternatives can be easily boiled back down to the three options originally offered by Lewis. These critics only postulate additional categories to Lewis' three in order to create more "politically correct" verbiage and thus more appealingly paint deniers of the divinity of Y'hoshua the Anointed One.

I say call a spade by what it is, a spade. These critics don't want to appear in stark light as deniers of the Anointed One, as those who would call the historically proven Anointed One a false prophet or a madman. They prefer to be like Wormtongue in Tolkien's *The Lord of the Rings*, dripping sweet sounding words that are truly lies. They would rather say the Anointed One was "a good teacher who was just a little deluded." No, my dear. That's just a fancy and misleading way of saying false prophet. At least non-messianic Jews can be straightforward.

My conclusion, after hearing many sides of the debate, is that C. S. Lewis is correct. Y'hoshua the Anointed One is either who He says He is or a false prophet or crazy. All the attempts to say "not necessarily" that I have read and heard are simply vain exercises in semantics and ambiguity. The stark honest fact: the Jews see Y'hoshua the Anointed One as a false prophet and atheists see Him as crazy. Let no one tell you Y'hoshua the Anointed One was a good teacher or a prophet unless they bow down to Him as the Son of God, the Word of God born flesh.

Atheists are not the only group of scoffers that you will face. I know a Christian textual critic who rejected the Anointed One and became a Muslim because of (1) the overwhelming doubts raised from textual criticism, (2) his inability to understand the Scriptures, (3) the unsatisfactory yet popular answers from Christian elders and leaders of "you just need to have faith," and (4) the seeming straightforwardness of the Quran (or Koran).

First, Christians are confident enough in the infallibility of the written Word of God that they are able to offer it for scrutiny; Muslims, on the other hand, will not allow the Quran to face the same rigid standards.

Second, if you do not seek the in-dwelling and supernatural instruction and decryption of His Spirit, you will fail to understand the encrypted Word of God.[240] His instruction on right living is clear enough, but you need His Spirit to know and understand Him through His written Word. You need to have a relationship with God. Theology will not finish your race.

Third, too many Christian leaders and pastors are content to rest on formal education in schools of thought rather than investing blood and sweat effort to wrestle with HaShem (The Name) and His written Word in relationship with Him; they are content with the clichéd answers that they receive from peers or in school, but which do not satisfy the seeker of Truth. Thus you, my children, need to find your own answers directly from Yah, blessed be His Name (Colossians 2:1-3). Don't seek your answers from elders and leaders. Once you get your answers through meditation upon His written Word with His Spirit, then and only then compare the answers you receive with the wisdom of elders. The wisdom of elders is still valuable.

Fourth, straightforwardness is not necessarily always the right way.[241] If the ideas are easy to accept and no wrestling is involved,[242] you are probably reading the work of mankind, not God.[243]

I witnessed Christian methodologies that promised success and bless-

---

240 John 14:26; 1 Corinthians 2

241 Deuteronomy 29:4; Isaiah 6:9-10; Isaiah 29:10, 13-14; Jeremiah 5:21; Matthew 11:25; Luke 10:21; Matthew 13:10-17; Mark 4:11-12; Luke 8:10; John 12:39-41; Acts 28:24-27; Romans 11:7-8; Ephesians 3:8-10; Colossians 1:25-27

242 Luke 18:31-34; Luke 19:41-44; 1 Corinthians 2:6-10

243 1 Corinthians 2:11-16; Romans 11:33-36

ings if you followed their "Word of Wisdom," "49 Commands of Christ," or "Divine Principle." There is no simple equation, no magic formula for success and blessing. Do not accept pre-packaged theology. A relationship with the Lord and sincere meditation on His written Word will always involve wrestling, for the finite mind needs to wrestle in order to glimpse the infinite Way of Yah, blessed be His Name.

You will also experience the assault of non-messianic Jews. They are joining the fray of open debate due to the unabashed and fairly effective sharing of the Good News from Messianics toward non-messianic Jews. Their main points are:

1. The Passover Lamb is not a foreshadow of Y'hoshua the Anointed One (Jesus the Christ), but instead a symbol of Egyptian idols.

2. Isaiah 53 describes Yisrael, not Y'hoshua.

3. The apostles twisted verses from the Instruction and the Prophets in order to use them as prophecies pointing to the Anointed One.

4. Jeremiah 22:18-30 invalidates the lineage of the Anointed One in Mattityahu's (Matthew's) account.

5. Y'hoshua was shy and vague about announcing His position as Anointed One, very unlike God, whom the Scriptures portrayed as being bold.

6. The Messianic Age has not yet arrived since predator and prey aren't chillin' together and not everyone knows the commands of God.[244]

7. The Instruction and the Prophets do not require us to trust an anointed one when he appears.

8. God tells us not to follow anyone who tries to persuade us against His Instruction and commandments.

9. Y'hoshua was not anointed with the special anointing oil.

10. The end-times king will offer a sin-offering for himself and

---

244 Isaiah 11:6-7; Jeremiah 31:33

Yisrael,[245] which means he can't be sinless. Christians say Y'hoshua is sinless, so He therefore cannot be the end-times king.

11. The Good News is confusing. Is a person supposed to trust Y'hoshua the Anointed One[246] or obey the commandments of God in order to enter into the salvation of God (Mathew 19:16-17)?

Some non-messianic Jews claim that the Passover Lamb is a symbol of Egyptian idolatry. If that is the case, why did the Israelites cover their home with it? Why cover the doorpost of one's home with a symbol of Egyptian idolatry? The doorpost is the entrance to a person's home. It symbolizes one's household, the metaphorical face of one's household. Isn't that the reason for the Lord's command in Deuteronomy 6:4-9 and 11:13-21? Haven't Jews been affixing the *k'laf* with the Deuteronomy verses written upon it since the Second Temple Period, and possibly even since Yisrael's occupation of Kena'an? It makes no sense to cover the entrance to one's home with the blood of Egyptian idolatry unless someone wanted to advertise himself or herself as an Egyptian idolater. The covering of blood, itself a symbol of life, makes more sense in light of Y'hoshua the Anointed One being the aim to which the blood on the doorpost points. Y'hoshua is the Passover Lamb.

Furthermore, if you compare the *d'rash* (using scattered verses to reach a comparative meaning) or *sod* (secret or esoteric meaning) of the apostles with the *d'rash* and *sod* of rabbinical leaders, you will find more sense with the apostles. At least I do. I read the *d'rash* and *sod* of rabbinical leaders and I cannot help but be flabbergasted at the "stretchiness" of their reasoning. I already explained Isaiah 53. I already provided the testimony from Nehemia the Karaite concerning his former rabbi. Jews are smart people, too. How can so many of them buy into rabbinical reasoning?

I can only conclude that the phenomenon is a temporary supernatural blindness (Romans 11:25-27). I believe we are in that day and age where such temporary supernatural blindness has reached its expiration date.

---

245 Leviticus 4:13-21; Ezekiel 45:17-25
246 John 20:31; 1 John 3:23

The blindness is melting off the eyes of Jews and many are coming to see that Y'hoshua is the Anointed One. At the same time, more Gentile Christians are realizing that the Anointed One did not remove a single *yud* or stroke from the Instruction (Matthew 5:18-19). As with the rest of humanity, the majority will always follow the desires of their own heart and their own will, disregarding the will of God. The remnant are the ones to seek Him. The few walk the narrow path. The many walk toward destruction from their own pride and lust, from their greed and their fear.

Non-messianic Jews say that Jeremiah 22:18-30 invalidates Y'hoshua's (Jesus') lineage, according to Mattityahu's (Matthew's) account. Well, if that was the case, then Jews should simply disregard even looking for an Anointed One following David's lineage. According to Yeremyah (Jeremiah), quoting the Lord Himself, "none will sit on David's throne or rule again in Y'hudah" (Jeremiah 22:30c).

Wow. It seems no Anointed One will be coming to rule over Yisrael and lift Yisrael above the nations. That is . . . unless the Lord meant to revoke the Jeremiah 22 curse on Y'hoyakim (Jehoiakim) and Y'hoyakhin (Jehoiachin). Y'hoyakim was to have no one mourn him at his funeral and have a "donkey's burial." Y'hoyakhin would be as if childless, he and his child and baby mama dying as foreigners in a foreign land, and none of his offspring would succeed. Yet, Y'hoyakhin fathered Sh'alti'el (Shealtiel) and Sh'alti'el fathered Z'rubavel (Zerubbabel).

Quoting the Lord Himself, "I will take you, Z'rubavel, my servant, the son of Sh'alti'el, and wear you like a signet ring; for I have chosen you" (Hagai 2:23).

It appears that the curse only hit Y'hoyakim, Y'hoyakhin, and the next generation, Sh'alti'el, but stopped with Z'rubavel. You see, the mercy of God is greater than His wrath. While His wrath might last to the third or fourth generation, His loving-kindness lasts for a thousand generations.

Non-messianic Jews sarcastically mock Y'hoshua the Anointed One for being shy and vague about His identity. They say, if He is God, then He should be bold like God. Well, He announced Himself clearly in John 8:56-59 and John 10:27-39. The reaction of the Jewish leaders? Kill Him. Non-messianic Jews scornfully respond that He had nothing to fear if He was God. Except that His initial mission was not to rule, but to sacrifice, much like the Yosef anointed one that some in Second Temple Judaism interpreted from the prophecies.

Since He did not come to rule for His first appointment with mankind, He had to keep His presence on the downlow. He used logic to confound His accusers, not to refute His own claim (John 10:34-38). He also used supernatural means to escape those who wanted to kill Him.[247] The time was not right (John 11:8-57). He still needed to complete His first mission the way He planned from the foundation of the world.[248] He still needed to make His sacrifice at the right time, knowing that the Jews would reject Him, so that He could bring the Gentiles into the fold.

Jews weren't known for opening their special covenants with the One True God to the public. Many of the Jews were like Yonah (Jonah) the prophet. Gentiles didn't deserve to have a close intimate relationship with Yah, blessed be His Name. Thankfully, the Lord wants relationship with everyone. When the right time arrived, He boldly made His claim at His trial with no argument or supernatural escape.[249]

Non-messianic Jews claim that Y'hoshua could not be the Anointed One because He did not bring about the Messianic Age. We are not yet in the Messianic Age because wolf and lamb are not lying down together and not everyone knows the Instruction of God.[250] The people in Jeremiah 31 who will all know HaShem (The Name) refers to those in covenant with the Lord, not every living person on the earth.

Interestingly, Yeshayah says, "On that day the Lord will raise His hand again, a second time, to reclaim the remnant of His people who remain from Ashur, Egypt, Patros, Cush, 'Eilam, Shin'ar, Hamat, and from the islands of the sea" (Isaiah 11:11). I repeat myself. Y'hoshua the Anointed One only completed the prophecies of the first appointments, which are the prophecies of the self-sacrificing priest and prophet, the Yosef anointed one recognized by Second Temple Judaism, foreshadowed

247 John 8:59; John 10:39
248 Ephesians 1:3-6; 1 Peter 1:18-20; Rev 13:1-8
249 Isaiah 55; Zechariah 9:9; Daniel 7:13; Luke 19:35-40; Mark 14:60-65
250 Isaiah 11:6-9; Jeremiah 31:33-34

in the spring appointed times. There will come a time when "the Lord will raise His hand again, a second time."

Y'hoshua's second coming, foreshadowed by the autumn appointed times, will address the prophecies that concern His kingship, the Messianic Age, and what Christians refer to as the Millennial Kingdom. His first arrival was on a donkey, in humility.[251] His second arrival will be on the clouds, in glory.[252] There is no other satisfactory explanation for merging both Zechariah 9:9 and Daniel 7:13.

Non-messianic Jews say that the Instructions and the Prophets do not direct us to trust a particular anointed person. They say that God tells us not to follow anyone who tries to persuade us against the Instruction and commands of HaShem (The Name). Furthermore, they say that no one ever anointed Y'hoshua the Anointed One with any anointing oil as commanded by the Lord (Exodus 30:22-33).

First of all, God *does* tell us to trust and obey an anointed who comes in His Name (Deuteronomy 18:15-19). "Whoever doesn't listen to My words, which he will speak in My name, will have to account for himself" (Deuteronomy 18:19). The rest, however, is completely true. God tells us not to follow anyone who tries to persuade us against His Instruction and commands, even when they perform miracles (Deuteronomy 13). Christians are the ones who say the commandments of Moshe have been done away with. Y'hoshua the Anointed One encourages us to obey the Instruction and commands of HaShem (Matthew 5:17-20). Finally, no one anointed either Y'hoshua or Moshe with the anointing oil, and the Lord promised to send a prophet like Moshe (Deuteronomy 18:18).

Non-messianic Jews say the Anointed One cannot be sinless because the Anointed One will make sin offerings (Ezekiel 45:17-25). Therefore, Christians have the wrong conclusion concerning the sinless Anointed One who is God. The prince in Ezekiel 45 who makes a sin offering at the Temple, however, does not need to have sinned in order to bring a sin offering (Leviticus 4:13-21). If the prince is innocent but the assembly sinned, then the prince must still make the sin offering for the assembly.

---

251 Zechariah 9:9; Luke 19:35-40
252 Daniel 7:13; Mark 14:60-65

He is bringing the sin offering for himself and the assembly even if he is innocent.

Non-messianic Jews say the Good News is confusing. Is a person supposed to either trust that Y'hoshua is the Anointed One[253] or obey the commandments of God in order to enter into the salvation of God (Mathew 19:16-17)? The answer is yes.

It's not confusing at all. You see, it's not an either-or situation.

The Instruction says, "He believed in YHVH, and He reckoned it to Him as righteousness" (Genesis 15:6).

The Prophets say, "Look at the proud, he is inwardly not upright; but the righteous will attain life through trusting faithfulness" (Habakkuk 2:4).

The Instruction says, "You are to observe My laws and rulings; if a person does them, he will have life through them" (Leviticus 18:5).

"'In short, he lives according to My laws and observes My rulings, so as to act faithfully. Such a person is righteous, and he will certainly live,' says the Lord YHVH" (Ezekiel 18:9).

Y'hoshua the Anointed One said something similar. "Why do you call Me, 'Lord! Lord!' but not do what I say?" (Luke 6:46).

Entering into the salvation of HaShem (The Name) is to trust Y'hoshua the Anointed One, and because of trusting Him, to obey His exposition of the Instruction of Yah, blessed be His Name. I will address the full picture of the Good News in my next book. For now, you can't go wrong with trusting and obeying Him.

Jewish elders and leaders claim sole authority over accurate translation of the Hebrew written Scriptures, but they are not the only ones who know and understand ancient Hebrew. They also arrogantly believe that their rabbinical leaders have the sole authority to interpret the Scriptures, even above the Lord Himself. Jews are certainly able to provide cultural insight, but Jewish elders and leaders are not the fount of all Scriptural understanding, as our Master clearly displayed.[254] Non-messianic Jews lack the indwelling of His Spirit, who is the true teacher of His written

253 John 20:31; 1 John 3:23
254 Matthew 22:22, 34, 46; Mark 3:4; Luke 14:3-4; Luke 20:20-26

Word.[255] Non-messianic Jewish interpretation via *p'shat* (the plain meaning of the text) can be taken at face value. However, take only the *remez* (symbolic meaning in context), *d'rash* (using scattered verses to reach a comparative meaning), and *sod* (secret or esoteric meaning) of the apostles in the inspired Good News and Apostolic Letters[256] and ignore the anti-Christ biased attempts of uninspired individuals.

There are many other groups, each with their own views concerning Y'hoshua the Anointed One, scattered throughout the world. Muslims invent their own Isa (Jesus) to suit their desires. Hindus are polytheists, meaning they believe in and follow any number from many available powers, powers they believe can become flesh at will, and they believe Y'hoshua the Anointed One was just one such divinely incarnate individual amongst many others. Buddhists view Jesus practically as one of their own, as a Zen teacher, except for the fact that I think they skim over His role as the Lion of Y'hudah (Revelation 5:4-5) and the image of our Jealous God[257] with His justice[258] and righteous will. They instead focus solely on His mercy and compassion.

As C. S. Lewis stated, He can only be who He says He is, a demon possessed false prophet, or crazy. Muslims try to re-invent history just as they attempt to deny the reality of the Holocaust (Ali) while Hinduism and Buddhism attempt to re-invent the identity of the Anointed One by denying Yah, blessed be His Name.

Other major religions of the world include the following: Zoroastrianism with one hundred thousand followers dating back as old as Judaism and Hinduism from around 2000 BC, Confucianism with six million followers dating back from around 500 BC, Taoism with three million followers dating back from around 500 BC, Jainism with five million followers dating back from around 400 BC and stemming from Hinduism,

---

255 John 14:26; 1 Corinthians 2:6-10; 1 John 2:26-27

256 2 Timothy 3:16-17; 2 Peter 3:14-16

257 Exodus 20:5-6; Exodus 34:13-15; Deuteronomy 4:24; Deuteronomy 5:9-10; Deuteronomy 6:14-15; Nahum 1:2; 2 Corinthians 4:3-4; Colossians 1:15

258 Leviticus 19:15; Deuteronomy 16:18; Psalm 9:4; Psalm 37:6; Psalm 72:2; Psalm 89:14; Psalm 97:2; Psalm 119:7, 62, 75, 106, 160, 164; Proverbs 1:1-6; Hosea 2:19-20; Zephaniah 2:3; Revelation 19:11-21

Shinto with 2.7 million followers dating back from around AD 500, Sikhism with twenty-five million followers dating around AD 1500 and also stemming from Hinduism, and Baha'i with five million followers dating around AD 1800 and stemming from Islam.

The two most prominent strings seem to be Judaism with fourteen million followers and Hinduism with one billion followers. Judaism birthed Christianity with 2.2 billion followers and Islam with 1.6 billion followers, which in turn birthed Baha'i. Hinduism birthed Buddhism with 500 million followers, Jainism, and Sikhism. Zoroastrianism is one of the oldest three religions and still survives today. Confucianism, Taoism, and Shinto appear to be isolated to the East and are mainly concerned with worldly government. Add to these numbers approximately 400 million followers of folk religions and 1.1 billion non-affiliated people and you reach 6.86 billion people populating the world. I only mention these broad numbers to give you an idea of the present state of this world.

I do not know how they all react to Y'hoshua the Anointed One, but I hope you respect individuals from all possible walks of life. There is enough of a reputation of self-righteousness and disdain and hypocrisy linked with Christians to fill Sh'ol (Sheol/Underworld) without you adding to it. Remain true to your trust in Yah, blessed be His Name, share His Good News of salvation to those whom you sense are seeking Truth and whom you have grown to love, [259] and at the same time respect your neighbor. [260]

I myself hear my fill of contempt from atheists and Muslims and Jews against Y'hoshua, the Anointed One of HaShem (The Name) and the only unique begotten Son of God. I have weighed them all with a desire to seek the Truth and have found their arguments against my Master lacking. Such arguments are weak in the face of the proven dependability of the Scriptures, testimonies of those who hear the Word of God and witness His power over the span of thousands of years, some even predicting future events centuries and millennia in advance . . . that came to

---

259 Leviticus 19:18; Matthew 5:43-48; Matthew 22:35-40; Mark 12:28-34; Luke 10:25-28; James 2:8; Galatians 5:14; Romans 13:7-10

260 Romans 13:7; 1 Peter 2:17

pass. Such arguments are weak in the face of current testimonies about the work of the Lord in the lives of His *talmidim* (disciples) today. Most importantly, such arguments are weak in the face of my own relationship with Him.

On a few occasions, I have heard beguiling persuasions from people I could almost swear were demon possessed; their words confused even my mind. These suspicious individuals shared something in common. Their eyes were bloodshot but they weren't high on marijuana. All I could do on such occasions was cling to my trust in God and His Anointed One, relinquishing all claims to doctrine and intellectual understanding, meanwhile asking HaShem to guard my mind and erase my memory of their words upon the conversation's end, which He did. Be careful with whom you engage in conversation. The lies and deception of the Enemy wait to devour you at every turn (1 Peter 5:8). I am not advising you to avoid conversations. I am exhorting you to be prayerful in your conversations.

The Master also warns us not to cast the precious Truth of His Good News of His salvation to those who will not appreciate it (Matthew 7:6). Avoid and do not waste your time with vain arguments[261] for in so doing you court anger and sin.[262] Instead, only engage those who are truly seeking, and share the Good News of His salvation with those who honestly and sincerely desire Truth, Life, God.

Beware of Christian cults. They may take the form of large isolated organizations led by charismatic madmen or even widespread movements, such as the oppressive and legalistic shepherding movement. Some cults continue to this day. They are defined by the following characteristics:

1. Dictatorial: Restricts the freedom to analyze for yourself or to question

2. Elitist: Displays self-righteousness by claiming to be the only group discovering or maintaining the "truth" and the only group

---

Romans 16:17-20; 1 Timothy 1:3-5; 1 Timothy 6:20-21; Titus 3:9-11; 2 Timothy 2:15-19

262 Leviticus 19:16; Zechariah 8:16; Psalm 4:4; Ephesians 4:25-27

that has the authority to credit others with faithfulness to the "truth"

3. Cowardly: Avoids publicly addressing the challenges and scrutiny brought by leaders and elders of other congregations

4. Controlling: Employs emotional manipulation to effect control over members via twisting of the Scriptures, threats of losing salvation, or resorting to guilt at the supposed disappointment of God

5. Isolated: Minimizes contact with people outside the group with some perverted instruction on purity and remaining undefiled; pushes for a polarized us-versus-them mentality, even and especially against others within the Body of the Anointed One

6. Arrogant: Claims special revelation or special authority converging on one individual at the ultimate head of the organization

7. Legalistic: Indirectly and subtly insists that dependence on their teachings and methods is a condition for salvation, usually based on a perversion of the Scriptures

8. Restricted: Contrives an additional mediator, either directly through the leaders of the group or indirectly through the instruction of the group, as necessary in order to have relationship with God, thereby effectively making the group's leadership, instead of the Anointed One, the gatekeepers to God

9. Formularized: Asserts rigid uniformity to their direction, which must be identical for all members, as the only way a person can enter into or maintain an undefiled relationship with God; i.e. a relationship with God can happen only one way and can only continue in one way, but specifically only by their way

10. Speculative: Encourages unquestioning commitment to its leadership (whether alive or dead) and their teachings, which are typically bogus, to the point of discouraging studying the teachings of others

11. Passive aggressive: Imbeds the practice of unmerciful shunning and disdainfully avoiding those who question the teachings of the group as the social norm through a perversion of ex-communication

12. Abusive: Domineeringly forces women and children into duties warped with the absence of compassion, justice, and mercy, thereby creating the ideal environment for sexual exploitation

13. Superficial: Perverts modesty through dictatorial uniformity for all members according to misinterpretations of the Scriptures or culturally invented standards not specified in the Scriptures

A cult does not need to have an overflowing amount of every above-mentioned quality in order to be a cult, and there is no quick method of concluding whether or not some group is cultic. Just know that the more of these warning signs you find, the more dangerous the group is to your relationship with the Lord and the more likely that the group is a cult.

By comparison, the Body of mature *talmidim* should instead (1) encourage newer *talmidim* to obey the written Word of God as the *talmid* grows and learns and is convicted, (2) humbly approach knowledge, and carefully welcome and weigh the thoughts and interpretations of others, (3) be confident, but not unreasonable or forceful, in explaining their doctrines and beliefs to others, (4) practice freedom in seeking a personal relationship with HaShem (The Name), (5) fellowship with *talmidim* from all walks of life and backgrounds, (6) be accountable to other mature *talmidim* and implement restraints with safeguards from corruption when in positions of authority, as well as the humility and transparency to admit error or misuse or abuse in order to ease healing for the victim(s), (7) abstain from making requirements to salvation not explicitly revealed in the Scriptures, (8) encourage others to seek their own direct relationship with the Lord, (9) allow for HaShem to move as He wills upon whom He wills however He wills, (10) not restrict themselves to only one side of a statement but be able to practice discernment through studying multiple sides of a matter, (11) practice compassion, justice, and mercy, (12) uphold the cause of the helpless, the weak, the vulnerable, and the lonely,

(13) and apply modesty for themselves while understanding that modesty changes definition from culture to culture and group to group.

You will find criticism and even persecution and condemnation from mainstream Christianity if you maintain my teachings. Some will even label you cultic, because "deviation from any of the doctrinal essentials as defined by the Bible would qualify a group as being a cult." Mainstream Christianity insists on a salvation by grace through faith alone as well as adherence to the doctrine of the Trinity. "Though the Trinity is not explicitly defined in Scripture and stated to be a necessity, it is a logically necessary doctrine since it properly describes the true nature of God" (Slick). I find the phrase "as defined by the Bible" humorous considering that Slick admitted that the doctrine of the Trinity was "not explicitly defined in Scripture and [not] stated to be a necessity." Concerning Slick's doctrine of faith alone, I quote the Scriptures, "You see that a person is declared righteous because of works and not by faith alone" (James 2:24). I stress the importance of the verse. A search in the entirety of the Scriptures for the presence of both the words "faith" and "alone" in the same verse . . . will result in only one verse: James 2:24.

I gave you the verses in the Scriptures that led me to my beliefs. Nevertheless, do not seek to make me the final arbiter of your relationship with HaShem (The Name). Also, allow no one else to dictate the parameters, appearance, and essence of your relationship with Him. I encourage you to be like the Bereans (Acts 17:10-12), to seek the Scriptures yourselves, seek the indwelling and instruction of His Spirit yourselves (1 John 2:27), and find the answers to any questions you may have directly from Yah, blessed be His Name. Only you and no one else will be held accountable for your thoughts, your words, and your actions.

Furthermore, I re-emphasize the dangers that inherently await you in the Hebrew Roots Movement (HRM). The HRM brings great insight into the Scriptures by opening the door of cultural understanding, but there is also a great trend of deniers of the Anointed One among Christians who journey through the movement (Hebrews 10:28-31). Once again, I warn you against the present-day anti-Christ spirit that persists among non-messianic Jews. I warn you against the occult philosophy of

Kabbalah. Be careful with the possible fancifulness of Gematria. Be sure that the insight you seek in the HRM concerns the ancient roots of two thousand years ago and earlier, rather than the current anti-Christ biases. Seek insight and not supernaturally imposed blindness and darkness, the resulting curse for rebellion.

You will find traps and attacks from all sides, ranging from atheists, to global religions, even to within the group that calls themselves Christians. At least among Christians you will find a remnant of *talmidim*. As if the innate selfish desires of your flesh, the seductive ways of this world, and the deception of the Enemy were not enough, you face the opposition of humanity.

Life is a battle and every day is spiritual warfare. Equip yourself for combat with daily conference/communion with HaShem, meditation on His written Word, fasting to control your flesh and strengthen your spirit, and fellowship with other *talmidim* for refreshment and morale. Equip yourself with gathering Truth from His instruction, protecting your heart by living according to His righteous commands, living according to the responsibility of having the Good News of His salvation, trusting the Way of the Lord and not the ways of the world to keep you on the path of life, understanding His salvation and knowing your covenant in His salvation, and mastering the dual edged offensive power of His written Word (Ephesians 6:14-18). Our battle is against Enemy spirits, not people; be aware that people are influenced by, and sometimes even the pawns of, spirits or the Spirit of God, whom they voluntarily or ignorantly choose to follow (Ephesians 6:12). Pray unceasingly. Beware of the seasons of comfort and always ask for His help. You are meant to endure more than you can handle. When you falter, circumstances force you to lean on Him. The *talmid* always lives best under persecution and suffering.

CHAPTER TWELVE

CONCLUSION

MY CHILDREN, IF you desire any Truth, the meaning and purpose of Life, a more abundant Life, seek Him. You will find that relative truth will not satisfy you in the long run. Do not simply invent your own master, your own idol, based on what you think is right and wrong, what you think should and should not be. Do not be arrogant so as to set yourself up as an idol. You have no answers to give that originate from you and solve the mysteries of life. Do not be foolish so as to create your own idol whom you can control by giving it characteristics that allow you to act and behave however you wish. Such an idol will obviously approve of all your decisions; you created it. You cannot save yourself from death. You have no power over life. Creating an idol for yourself is only a sham to deceive yourself. I guarantee it. My children, I beg you . . . seek God, know YHVH, blessed be His Name, as He revealed Himself.

Seek the Truth. Seek Life. Seek HaShem (The Name). You can know Him through His Word-born-flesh who explains His written Word, through the mediation of His Spirit, through relationship with Him. You can know His character through His commandments, Word, works, and the example of His Anointed One because He stands by His Word. He does not cross the boundaries of His set-apartness from the sin and death infesting the world. He does not cross the boundaries of His righteousness. He remains righteous and set-apart and loyal.

My children, obey all of His *applicable* commandments and know the heart, the significance, and the essence of all of His commandments. For example, the commandments concerning the priesthood do not apply to you, but they can still teach you. Treat traditions as ancillary help, discretionary suggestions, and always secondary to His commandments. Traditions are not necessarily evil, but they are man-made, and thus many are flawed on some level, even flawed to misleading and corruptive proportions. Traditions can help in your worship and your methods, but by no means make them "written in stone" or inflexible. His commandments should be the ones "written in stone" and intimately written upon your hearts.

Therefore, do not fear to say His Name, but rather boldly call on Him as He commands us.[263] Set His Name apart with the appropriate honorific. Say Yah, who is great and exceedingly praiseworthy. Call upon His earthly Name, Y'hoshua, with the same due respect, for demons truly fear it.[264] Say the Name Y'hoshua the Anointed One (Jesus the Christ), our Lord and Shield of Salvation and Right Hand of God, and trust Him. The Name of the Anointed One means "Yah is salvation." He has introduced Himself and given His Name to us. We grow in our relationship with the Creator who makes Himself known to us. How? He progressively reveals Himself to us throughout our life, through the instruction of His Spirit concerning His written Word, so that He, the progenitor of Life, through His living Word, Y'hoshua His Anointed One, can live in us.

Unless you humble your heart before Him, unless He opens your eyes and awakens your heart to understand the Instruction and the Prophets (Luke 16:19-31), unless you have a relationship with YHVH, blessed be His Name, through Y'hoshua the Anointed One . . . you will not know the One True God, the Creator of all that is seen and unseen, the

---

263 Exodus 3:15; Exodus 9:16; Exodus 20:24; Numbers 6:27; Deuteronomy 6:13; Deuteronomy 10:20; Jeremiah 4:1-2; John 14:13-14; John 15:16; John 16:23-27; Hebrews 4:16

264 Acts 19:1-17

One who loves you more than anyone else. "Word" (Greek—Logos, Aramaic—Memra), "Instruction" (Torah), and "Wisdom" all play their roles accordingly, even together at the creation of the world.[265] They, along with the Seven Spirits of God, are all God, the only One True God, YHVH, blessed be His Name. Do not use the enigmatic vastness and mystery of the identity of God as an excuse not to strive to know Him.

I understand the confusion, the questions, and the complexity of trying to comprehend His identity. The Western mind always seeks to understand, and understanding is a good thing. Contriving and forcing an understanding, even if comprehension is incomplete, however, is debilitating, not beneficial. The ancient Greeks forced their stories to explain the constellations, just as Gentile Christians forced the doctrine of the Trinity to explain the mystery of the identity of Yah, blessed be His Name.

Do not allow the desire for understanding to be a trap, such as the person caught in a mental puzzle that is not meant to be solved at that time. Do not be a monkey who perceives something shiny in a jar and attempts to possess it but finds he is trapped and immobilized by it. Do not be a monkey who is unable to remove his clenched fist from the narrow neck of the jar, trapped by his greed.

Rather than seeking to snatch understanding because of the selfish desires of your own heart,[266] passionately strive and wait for HaShem to break the jar in His time and reveal the gem of understanding so that you can fully admire it and thereafter rightly possess it. Know that some answers can be reached in a day, some require a lifetime, and some may have to wait until you righteously cross into the next life, into your eternal life. Be content with what the Lord reveals and what He conceals.[267] Shun the arrogance that demands an answer right now, but rather humble yourself to the wisdom of Yah, blessed be His Name.[268]

My children, do not be fooled with lies and deception, but rather

---

265 Genesis 1:1-5; Proverbs 8:22-31; John 1:1-5; Colossians 1:15-17

266 Genesis 1:16-17; Genesis 3:2-13; Matthew 11:12-24; Luke 16

267 Deuteronomy 29:29; Daniel 2:22; Proverbs 25:2; Matthew 11:25-27; Luke 10:21-22; Matthew 16:17

268 Genesis 11:1-9; Isaiah 55:8-9; John 14:6; Matthew 24:36; Mark 13:32; Acts 1:7-8

consume His written Word, seek Him for the answers, for the Truth. That is the crux of my heart and my life—the Truth. I have always desired the Truth, even as young as twelve years old when I asked a Roman priest to explain the Fallen (N'filim/Nephilim) (Genesis 6:4-5). I still seek it. To believe in the existence of absolute truth, you must believe in the existence of a higher power, a Creator of the world, the source for Truth, the Truth Himself.

You cannot have absolute morality without the Power who creates the world with its physical, spiritual, and moral laws. Atheists try to argue for the case of absolute morality without God, but their arguments are built on sinking sand. Any true and honest thinker who analyzes the case for absolute morality will conclude that a higher power is necessary for the existence of universal and absolute morality. Otherwise, morality simply becomes relative and vulnerable to a shifting definition by what-ever majority is in authority. . .and therefore ceases to have any inherent significance because of inconsistency.

If God is good, atheists will argue, "then how can so much evil infest the world?" God is love. Love involves choice. He loves us, and He desires that we love Him. Thus, He gives us choice. Some choose to rebel against and reject Him. Since He is the only good, in His absence is wickedness. The evil in the world is the direct result of people turning away from God, from the only One who is good. The fact that atheists recognize evil means they must recognize good. If they can recognize good, it begs the question, "How can they know the quality of 'good?'" They can only know what is good because the Lord wrote His Instruction of right and wrong, of good and evil, upon their hearts,[269] which anyone can choose to burn away and cauterize to the point of callousness and insensitivity through transgression and rebellion.[270]

You will find everything else outside His written Word, all other written documents, all other religious texts, all Christian theologies and other religious commentary, even my words, to be diluted Truth at best and twisting of the Truth at worst. Discern between Truth and tradi-

---

269 Joel 2:28-29; Acts 2:17-18; Romans 1:20; Romans 2:14-16
270 Jeremiah 7; Jeremiah 11:1-17; Romans 1:21-32

tion, knowing that Truth is necessary while tradition is optional, and sometimes misleading, even dangerous. When you open the Scriptures, ask Him to fill you with His Spirit and teach you with a heart that truly desires to know Him, to know the Truth.[271] This instruction is important, so I will repeat myself. When you open the Scriptures, ask Him to fill you with His Spirit and teach you.

Every gap or perversion of the Truth leaves you vulnerable to deception. Truth is the first armor of God (Ephesians 6:10-18). Truth holds together all other aspects of your relationship with Yah, blessed be His Name. Make sure you know the Truth, as close to absolute truth as you can, and you will find it in the accurate context of the Instruction, the Prophets, the Good News, and the Apostolic Letters, through the teaching of His Spirit.

Since we will never attain complete understanding of the Truth, completely accurate doctrine on this side of life,[272] keep your eye on the prize—the crown of finishing this life in love for and service to our King, Y'hoshua the Anointed One, His Word born flesh, God in flesh. He will do, and has already done, what we cannot, what we fail to accomplish. Our part is to give our best effort with all our strength and resources.[273] He is Yah, blessed be His Name, in flesh, and our mediator and our key to relationship with the full glory of the Lord. Corny but true: do your best and let God do the rest.

I empathize with the frustrations that may arise from lacking knowledge, information, or understanding. Again, HaShem (The Name) is beyond our complete understanding on this side of life; I am content to know Him as He reveals Himself without needing to restrict Him into the triangle symbol (Trinity) of Christians and their theology or even the tree symbol (S'firot) of Jews and their Kabbalah. He is too vast to be captured

---

271 Exodus 33:17-23; Exodus 34:5-9, 29; Proverbs 8:17; Jeremiah 33:3; John 14:16-27; James 1:5-8

272 Proverbs 3:5-12; Isaiah 55:8-9; 1 Corinthians 13:9-13

273 Deuteronomy 6:5; Matthew 22:37; Mark 12:30; Luke 10:27

and bound into a symbol, except for One of His own making, which is His Word born flesh.[274]

Doctrinal fanatics from all walks do not care how flawed their understanding might be, how ill-equipped they might be in their deduction, reasoning, logic, or conclusions. All they want to hear is that they are right, and they are quick to denounce opposing viewpoints as heresy in order to avoid wrestling in their spirit and in their heart. They do not struggle with the Scriptures like the Bereans (Acts 17:10-12). Do not concern yourself with them. Speaking with brick walls is useless; and you will find no iron in them with which to sharpen yourself. How can you recognize these "brick walls?" Hint: They will speak over you and will not allow you to state your case. Avoid blindly stubborn people, proud of their own interpretations.

I cannot read the prophecies in Zechariah, trust them as the Word of God, be aware of the writings of the Good News and the Apostolic Letters, and be so blasé about the claims of Christianity. I also cannot read the exhortation of the Master in Matthew 5:17-20 and disdain the dedicated obedience of the Jews to the commandments of HaShem. I understand that Christians parade the Anointed One as a Law-breaking (Law-less) false prophet (Deuteronomy 13:1-5), but the Scriptures testify to the Truth (Matthew 7:21-23) despite Christians representing Him poorly, or even misrepresenting Him altogether.

I may disagree and be cautious of others' doctrines, beliefs, and views, but I also do not claim to have all the answers. My doctrines change throughout the years as I grow in knowledge of the written Word of God. It does not change like the fickle wind (Ephesians 4:14) with the relative trends of humanity and religions. It changes as my relationship with Him deepens throughout years of experience and living and walking, Him and me, together.

All influence that changes my doctrine must come from the Scriptures, not commentary, theologian opinion, pagan philosophy, or even the limitations of science. If a person comes to me with a case for change, they

---

274 Genesis 1:26-27; Genesis 9:6; Leviticus 26:1; Deuteronomy 4:23; 2 Corinthians 4:3-4; Colossians 1:15

must be able to show me from the Scriptures and convincingly defend their case. As the years progress, I find fewer and fewer instances in which a person can defend such cases for change. Each forthcoming change in my beliefs increases the difficulty of the next change, because as I grow, my beliefs become even more fortified by His written Word. Meditations, study, and discussions strengthened my understanding.

I kept focus on the Instruction, the Prophets, the Good News, and the Apostolic Letters, while avoiding commentaries in order to minimize biases for the first twelve years of my diligent research, study, and meditation. Only in the last six years have I started to include the occasional commentary into my study. I sense that I now have a solid grasp of the Scriptures and will not be so easily deceived by the many differing opinions, printed and online. The point is—keep your focus on the Scriptures and not commentaries. If you think commentaries suffice because they quote from the Scriptures, consider that they often use verses out of context.

My children, stay true to your orthodoxy, or lack thereof. If you desire orthodoxy, if you desire the most Scripturally accurate method and form of worshiping Yah, blessed be His Name, turn to the first century practices, turn to the apostles, turn to our Hebrew roots, and understand the Scriptures. I encourage you to accept no tradition but the tradition of the twelve apostles. Take to the ancient paths (Jeremiah 6:16).

Traditions change over time, and Christianity has been known to adopt pagan methods in its journey and development. Pagan influence served its purpose in the past to draw in the Gentiles, but now is the time to heed the warnings of the Master through Y'hochanan (John) (Revelation 2-3). We had two thousand years of the age of ancients, two thousand years of the age of Yisrael (Israel) and Y'hudah (Judah), and two thousand years of the age of Gentiles. We are now drawing close to the seventh millennia, to the return of the Anointed One, having the same urgency that the apostles and elders felt in that first century after His resurrection.[275] He did not come then, and He may not come soon for us, yet I believe His return is imminently close.

---

275 James 5:8; 1 Corinthians 7:29-31; Romans 13:11-14; 1 Peter 4:7; 1 John 2:18

The time is drawing near to bring the two sticks of Y'hudah (Judah) and Efrayim (Ephraim) together (Ezekiel 37). I believe Y'hudah represents the Jews and Efrayim symbolizes the Gentiles. HaShem (The Name) scattered the northern kingdom of Yisrael to the four corners of the world, feeding the bloodline of His people to the Gentiles so that, not only spiritually, but also physically, He can call a people who are not His people . . . His people.[276] Even your mother has a 9% trace of Jewish heritage (southern kingdom of Y'hudah). I wonder how much Israelite bloodline (northern kingdom of Yisrael) she may have. You will find that God works both physically and spiritually. His written Word has at least two layers, one for physical application and one for spiritual application.

We are coming full circle and everyone is either submitting to the commandments of God Almighty and His Anointed One or rejecting Him and His Way (John 14:6). The separation of the wheat and tares, between wheat and chaff, has begun.[277] While some traditions may be harmless, I have an innate desire for the original way, the ancient paths (Jeremiah 6:16-19). Seek the Truth. Accept no example and standard except for the Master Himself, and He obeyed the commandments of God.

You will hear the claim from some unbelievers that the Christian sect started simply from the conspiracy of the apostles. I tell you, poor shepherds and fishermen are not ones to start conspiracies, but rather those in power, such as court officials, religious leaders, and political authorities who tried to shut down the testimony of shepherds and fishermen, but failed in their striving against Yah, blessed be His Name.[278]

Striving against HaShem is a lost cause. God is the ultimate power. His plan pre-dates any conspiracy of even the highest authorities and dominions of humanity to include Babylon, the Illuminati, Big Brother, the New World Order, and their equivalents, even to include the Enemy and his evil spirits in the spiritual realm.

The Lord displayed His plan in unbreakable encrypted code through forty authors of sixty-six books via allegories, stories, songs, poetry, prose,

---

276 Hosea 1:9-10; Hosea 2:23; Romans 9:23-26

277 Deuteronomy 29:14-21; Matthew 3:12; Luke 3:17; Matthew 13:24-30

278 Psalm 2:1-3; Nahum 1:9; Acts 4:23-31

etc. These authors came from backgrounds such as prophets, military generals, priests, kings, shepherds, farmers, prime ministers, cupbearers, tax collectors, doctors, rabbinical scholars, and fishermen. They lived in scattered locations from Asia to Africa to Europe. They came from different walks of life and spanned 1600 years of time; yet, their writing cohesively binds together, more so than any other written work in history. The complicated tapestry of God Almighty's written Word confounds the wise yet can be simple even to guileless children.[279]

I have seen *talmidim* (disciples) fall away from trusting the Lord because their trust did not have deep roots into their heart and spirit,[280] but rather frolicked only as philosophical and theological ideas in their mind. I have seen *talmidim* fall away because they traded their first love for HaShem (The Name) in exchange for the distractions of this world.[281] I witnessed *talmidim* fall away from trusting God Almighty because they instead trusted doctrine, which crumbled in discussions with trained debaters and wily seducers. I have seen them fall away because they trusted elders, who committed heinous acts and were capable of hypocrisy and falling away, instead of trusting Him. They fell away because they trusted their own feelings and emotions, which were obviously fickle, over trusting Him. I have seen *talmidim* fall away because they entered into the Hebrew Roots Movement (HRM) and, instead of seeking the roots, they sought the anti-Christ and/or Kabbalah biases of modern day non-messianic Jews. I have seen drugs, chemicals, witchcraft, and muddying philosophy cloud the minds, hearts, and wills of dedicated, even anointed, *talmidim*, causing them to stray from Him.

Beware the lies of the Enemy, the evil inclination of your own flesh nature, the distractions of this material world, and the tests that will surely oppress you and gravely hurt you, that will strive to infect you with bitterness against the Lord. Fight against bitterness and protect your

---

279 Deuteronomy 29:4; Isaiah 6:9-10; Isaiah 29:10, 13-14; Jeremiah 5:21; Matthew 11:25; Luke 10:21; Matthew 13:10-17; Mark 4:11-12; Luke 8:10; John 12:39-41; Acts 28:24-27; Romans 11:7-8

280 Matthew 13:20-21; Mark 4:16-17; Luke 8:13

281 Matthew 13:22; Mark 4:18-19; Luke 8:14

allegiance to Yah, blessed be His Name. Be wary of wealth, authority, and fame, for they easily corrupt. Be wary of the misleading convolution of Kabbalah, rabbinical philosophy, and some mainstream Christian theology. Beware of the material distractions of this world that will steal your passion for God[282] and of stagnancy that results from comfort and sometimes tradition.[283] Vehemently reject and shun all deceptive forms and subtle lingering traditions of paganism and idolatry.[284] Beware of disdaining any of the commandments of God Most High[285] and beware of self-righteousness.[286] We are in a spiritual battle, which can include our spirit versus our flesh[287] or our spirit versus evil spirits.[288]

Spiritual warfare against this world is a daily affair, so daily nurture your relationship with Him to place you in the best position for warfare. He is your strength, your stable rock foundation, your fortress, your shield, your alerting trumpet blast, your secure height, and your combat trainer.[289] Be still and know that HE IS . . . I AM.[290] Make Him the first and the last of your day,[291] engaging Him at the first of your waking in the

---

282 Deuteronomy 32:15; Daniel 4; Matthew 13:22; Mark 4:18-19; Luke 8:14; Matthew 6:31-33; Luke 12:29-31; Revelation 3:15

283 Deuteronomy 32:15; Isaiah 29:13-14; Luke 21:1-4; 1 Timothy 6:17-19; Revelation 3:2

284 Deuteronomy 12:30; Judges 2:11-22; Revelation 2:19-28

285 Genesis 22:18; Genesis 26:4; Joshua 22:5; Matthew 5:17-20; 1 John 5:3; Revelation 2:14

286 Deuteronomy 9:4-6; Job 42:7-9; Matthew 7:3-5; Luke 18:9-14; Romans 14:10-13; Revelation 2:5

287 Genesis 4:3-16; Proverbs 1-7; Proverbs 27:20; James 4:1-6; Galatians 5:16-25; Galatians 6:7-9; Romans 7:18-25; Romans 8:5-14; Romans 12:1-2; Romans 13:13-14; 1 John 2:15-17

288 Genesis 3; Daniel 10:5-21; Matthew 4:1-11; Mark 1:12-13; Luke 4:1-13; Matthew 8:28-34; Mark 5:1-20; Luke 8:26-37; Matthew 17:17-21; Mark 9:14-27; Luke 9:38-42; Luke 4:33-36; Acts 19:13-16; James 4:7; 1 Corinthians 11:2-16; 2 Corinthians 10:3-4; Ephesians 6:10-18; Jude 1:8-9

289 Exodus 23:20-28; 2 Samuel 22:2-3; Psalm 9:9-10; Psalm 18:1-3; Psalm 59; Psalm 62:1-8; Psalm 144:1-2; Luke 1:67-75; 1 John 5:18

290 Exodus 3:13-15; Deuteronomy 32:39; Psalm 46; Isaiah 43:10-13; Isaiah 51:12; Jeremiah 29:22-23; John 8:18-28, 58; John 13:19; John 18:5-6; Revelation 2:23

291 Isaiah 44:6; Isaiah 41:4; Isaiah 48:12; Revelation 1:17; Numbers 28:1-8; Job 1:5; Psalm 5:3; Psalm 57:8; 2 Chronicles 29:20; Isaiah 33:2; Matthew 14:23; Luke 6:12; Mark 1:35

morning and at the beginning of the next day as the sun sets. Ask Him for help when the sun rises and confess your disobedience and renew your dedication to obedience at sunset. Get your bearings before and after the daily battle so that you are not taken unaware and ambushed. It doesn't need to be anything formal or prolonged, but as in anything else in life, better preparation leads to better results.

Prayer, or simply conversation with HaShem, can take many shapes. Sometimes it can take the form of a simple conversation, and sometimes it can be a formal plea. Good books from better teachers than I already exist that teach you how to pray, such as *How to Pray* by Reuben Archer Torrey, *How to Pray* by Clive Staples Lewis, *The Essentials of Prayer* by Edward McKendree Bounds, and *Praying God's Word* by Beth Moore. Nevertheless, these standing instructions may tend more to the formal side of the spectrum and neglect the informal side. Nanay told me that daily prayer was the most important responsibility of life. Her exhortation started my relationship with Yah, blessed be His Name. My prayers in those early years of my relationship with Him were not built on formal structures or knowledge of the Scriptures, which can be daunting to obtain and take many years to achieve. Simple conversations with Him are all you need, at least for now in the beginning.

Relationship with God should never be postponed by such requirements as knowledge. Knowledge takes time, and we continue to grow in our knowledge of God throughout the years. The growth, in fact, should never cease. We should be growing in our knowledge of God Almighty until our last breath. There is no measurable amount of knowledge required before starting a relationship with God Most High.

Start your relationship with Him through conversation, through prayer. In order to have any relationship, whether with God or a person, communication is fundamental. We speak to Him in prayer and, at the very least, He speaks to us through His written Word. "Sometimes people say, 'Why pray if Christ is sovereign?' To which I answer: 'Why pray if he is not sovereign?'" (Piper). The point of prayer is relationship, and relationship moves the heart of the One who has all the power (Genesis 18:16-33), the power to make it so (Romans 4:16-17).

Although beneficial and effective, you do not need structure in prayer, especially in the beginning. Simply have a conversation with Him and implement structure as you grow; even as you grow, refrain from always using structure and guard against dulling the passion of your prayers. Praise Him for who He is, as much as you know who He is: God, Creator, Savior, Redeemer, Life, Truth, Comforter, etc. Thank Him for the life He gives you, for each day He gives you. Thank Him for the family He gives you when they irritate you, for the legs He gives you when you're tired of walking, for the clothes He gives you when you're cold, for sustaining you throughout the years when you're hungry, etc. Confess to Him all the ways in which you fall short of the Standard of wholeness and complete righteousness. Plead for His forgiveness through the sacrifice of the Anointed One on the cross (and remember to forgive those who wrong you). Ask Him to teach you, to guide you, to open your eyes to the Truth, to give you wisdom, to draw near to you, to work in your life and in your heart, to help you, to search your heart for all sin and impurity, etc. Open your heart and share your heartaches, your bitterness, your disappointments, your hopes, your dreams, your desires, etc.

Take into account that the Lord first welcomes children into His Kingdom. He welcomes the illiterate servant before the learned master, typically because humility accompanies the servant while self-righteousness courts the scholar. He welcomes the weak, the disadvantaged, and the underdog. In the beginning, there is no right or wrong way to pray. Over time, He will teach you righteousness and the Way. Right now, He desires relationship with you.

My children, do not strive for loyalty to any group of mankind, do not strive for inappropriate loyalty to any individual, but rather strive only for loyalty to the Lord, to the guidance of His Spirit and His Word, both written and in flesh.[292] I understand the necessity of government within religious groups. I understand the necessity of decisions to maintain order and identity. I understand the necessity to defend against teachings and teachers who lead others away from God, against figurative snakes and

---

292 Psalm 40:4; Psalm 118:8-9; Psalm 146; Proverbs 3:5-6; Isaiah 31:1; Micah 7:2-10; Jeremiah 17:5-10

wolves in sheep's clothing. I also recognize the unpopularity of the ancient prophets and the apostles and the loyalty of the Bereans to the Scriptures (Acts 17:11-12).

Anyone can be wrong. Does that mean trust no one? Even the wise can become misguided and have the wrong interpretation of the Scriptures.[293] Nevertheless, give considerable weight to the wisdom and the leadership of the elders, but always keep Yah, blessed be His Name, your first love, your first priority, and your final authority.[294] As God Himself said, "Do not trust in princes or in mortals, for he hath no salvation" (Psalm 146:3). "It is better to take refuge in [YHVH] than to trust in human beings" (Psalm 118:8) (CJB). "Trust in YHVH with all your heart and do not rely on your own understanding" (Proverbs 3:5). Be like the Bereans who eagerly received knowledge and immediately tested it against the Word of God (Acts 17:11-12).

Place your relationship with Him above the wisdom, direction, and leadership of elders. Test your relationship with Him, test the direction you receive from Him according to His written Word in order to verify that you are truly hearing the Lord and not another spirit. Ask Him to fill you with His Spirit and teach you before you open the Scriptures and meditate upon His written Word for guidance. Listen to the wisdom of the elders and weigh it according to the Scriptures. Discern and judge for yourself the Truth according to the Scriptures in its full context. I caution you never to flippantly disregard the wisdom of the elders. If ever you go against the wisdom of elders, be sure that you have searched their words and seriously weighed it against the written Word of God. Definitely do not, by any means, blindly obey any person.

Although you, my children, all have the heritage of Y'hudah, beware of the ones who do not follow the Anointed One. I say beware of the Jews who are anti-Anointed One, anti-Christ, because they entertain dangerous spirits. Beware of the ones who delve into Kabbalah. I do not wish you to be infected with the same pollution and witchcraft. In many non-

293 Deuteronomy 32:15; Isaiah 29:14; Isaiah 44:25-26; Jeremiah 8:8-9; Jeremiah 51:57; Matthew 11:25
294 Genesis 27:18-29; 1 Samuel 24; Acts 5:29; Revelation 2:4

messianic Jews, you will find an anti-Christ spirit despite their claims of looking forward to His appearance. I say this to impart this message: be careful of their words and their teachings because they will try to separate you from HaShem by persuading you to turn away from His Anointed One as revealed in Y'hoshua. Non-messianic Jews believe, concerning Christians, that "biblical verses, upon which their Christian belief was based, were—when examined in the original Hebrew—were mistranslations and taken out of context . . ." (Shapiro). They believe, concerning *talmidim* of Y'hoshua the Anointed One, that "the main motivating factor [is] the fear of burning in Hell forever" (Shapiro). They could not be further from the Truth.

I do not know how those who were previously Christians could have believed this lie. Perhaps their parents unintentionally raised them with such inaccuracies. Perhaps Christian teachers and preachers unintentionally misled their congregations. They completely misunderstood the Good News of HaShem through His Anointed One. The main motivating factor for *talmidim* of the Anointed One should be and is the love of Yah, blessed be His Name. His love sent His Word born flesh to pay the price of covering us. That covering is the protection of His complete blood so that we may approach HaShem by our spirit and worship Him in spirit. We worship Him in spirit because He is a spirit, not tangible. He is set-apart from this physical world. He even took away His physical Temple to make the point. He loves us first and we choose to return His love. The love of God is our "main motivating factor."

In other non-messianic Jews you will find a deep love for the Lord as proved by sincere devotion to Him and a spirit of love for all, absent of the arrogance of being in privileged status. They do not follow Y'hoshua the Anointed One, but they also do not foam in the mouth at the mention of His Name. If both characteristics of faithfulness and love simultaneously appear in a Jewish individual, then give them special attention as due to a stubbornly misled older sibling who has lost the Way, but still a sibling.[295]

---

295 Exodus 20:5-6; Exodus 34:6-7; Numbers 14:18; Deuteronomy 5:9-10; Deuteronomy 23:7-8; Obadiah 1:11-15; Matthew 23:37-39; Luke 13:34-35; Luke 15:25-30; Romans 11:13-16

Do not treat them with disdain as Christian history sadly displays. Do not treat them as hypocritical "swine."[296] Some non-messianic Jews who truly seek Yah, blessed be His Name, breed no secret or seething hostility against Y'hoshua the Anointed One, and can still be examples to you in your walk with HaShem (The Name). Encourage a Jew *not* to forsake the Sinai Covenant if he or she turns to follow the Anointed One. Encourage such a Jew to build the New Covenant upon the foundation of the Sinai Covenant.[297]

Do your best and give your full effort to emulate the complete Instruction born flesh in Y'hoshua the Anointed One and share the Good News of His salvation, first by deeds of love and then by words. Yet do so *not* from disdain that stems from a position of privilege, but from the humility that is unfortunately uncommon amongst Christians. At the same time, remember that Jews are and always will be His people just as Christians are and always will be His people. Do not force your ways or understanding upon them. Rest assured that God takes care of His own.

Do not for one moment hold Jews in contempt because they do not trust the salvation of God through His Anointed One . . . because they are still His people and He is still coming back for them. Gentile *talmidim* (disciples) of the Anointed One are the ones newly grafted into His people and thus are now His people. We have no inheritance apart from Yisrael. Every promise He ever gave through the prophets is to Yisrael, and we are added beneficiaries because we are grafted to Yisrael. If you encounter some who are arrogant, simply go in humility. Brush their insults from your shoulders and the "dust" from your "sandals" (Matthew 10:14).

While you may have the bloodline of Y'hudah, take note that Jews will consider you as a Gentile for all intents and purposes. Samarians/Samaritans had the blood of Yisrael also, but they were considered Gentiles because they did not live within the boundaries of the Sinai Covenant.

---

296 Leviticus 11:7-8; Leviticus 15:31; Matthew 7:6; Luke 10:25-37; John 18:28; Revelation 21:27

297 Galatians 3:17; Revelation 2:13-16

In addition, the modern State of Israel will refuse you citizenship because you follow Y'hoshua the Anointed One.

I call us Gentiles grafted into Yisrael, and not Jews, because you and I were not raised in the Sinai Covenant, and thus even Jews would consider us Gentiles despite our Jewish bloodline. Your grandfather, my dad, Aharon Shalomsohn, was a full Romanian Jew, even if he was only a Passover/Yom Kippur Jew, the equivalent of an Easter/Christmas Christian. The Nazis bombed his ship as he tried to flee Romania via the Mediterranean Sea. The State of Israel's Law of Return will accept an atheist whose grandfather was fully Jewish, but they will not accept you if you are a *talmid* of Y'hoshua the Anointed One. Such is the blind rebellion that Jews have against His Word born flesh.

My advice is to let the Lord deal with His stiff-necked people, both Jews and Christians. There are most certainly stiff-necked Christians who insist that the Anointed One abolished the Law (Matthew 5:17-19), although they will be sly enough to couch it in more palatable phrases. For example, mainstream Christians believe, "Now that Christ has fulfilled the law, followers of Jesus are not to go back under the regulations of the law as if Jesus accomplished nothing" (Ross). They will argue that the Anointed One did not destroy the Instruction, but instead He fulfilled it with the conclusion that we are no longer to "go back under the regulations" of the Instruction. In other words, He completed the Instruction with the conclusion that "the Instruction is no longer valid." That reasoning is asinine. How do you complete something and it all of a sudden loses all its value? The Instruction of God is not a video game that you shelf or trade-in once completed.

Should we now commit adultery because the Anointed One fulfilled the Instruction? Do you see how unreasonable that line of thought becomes? Some Christians will then debate that the authority of the apostles upholds that commandment of loyalty in marriage. Well, the apostles upheld the entirety of the Instruction.[298]

Mainstream Christianity misunderstands the point of Sha'ul's letter to

---

298 Acts 18:21 (KJV); Acts 21:20-26; Acts 24:14; Acts 25:8; Romans 2:13, 25-27; Romans 3:31; Romans 7:12

the Galatians. I would need to write another book in order to explain the point of Sha'ul's letter, but someone else already did an exemplary job of it. Read D. Thomas Lancaster's *The Holy Epistle to the Galatians: Sermons on a Messianic Jewish Approach*. I quote him heavily in my next book. In short, now that the Anointed One completed the covenantal plan, His *talmidim* are not to go back under the regulations of being a Jew under the Sinai Covenant for the purpose of salvation—as if the Anointed One accomplished nothing on the cross.

Y'hoshua the Anointed One did not destroy the Instruction, but rather there is now no need to become Jewish and put yourself under the regulations of rabbinical judgments and the correlating punishments by the authority of the Sinai Covenant in order to enter into the New Covenant with God. You do not have to become a Jew in order to enter into covenant with Yah, blessed be His Name. Y'hoshua the Anointed One fulfilled the Instruction so that Gentiles can now enter into relationship with HaShem. That fulfillment in no way invalidates the Instruction.

If the Anointed One fulfilled the Instruction, and He did, and He is our example, how much more should we "go back under the regulations" of God and emulate the complete "Law" in flesh, the Word born flesh? Do not worry yourself with the fate of arrogantly unrepentant mainstream Christianity. After all, salvation is not based on meticulous obedience to the Instruction but a heart that loves and seeks and trusts the Lord. You concern yourself with your own relationship with the Lord and encourage the Body of *talmidim* to love Him as He convicts them.

You will find Instruction-breaking, Law-breaking, Christians who love HaShem and strive to obey the commandments that, to their understanding, apply to them. Beware of their foundationally flawed doctrines, but most certainly love them like fellow siblings who lack deeper understanding. Take note that they may even have a greater level of commitment to HaShem than you, and that speaks to their credit. Relationship with God is neither about academic knowledge nor the number of commandments that you obey, but a heart of worship and a life of action, a life of love.[299]

---

299 Deuteronomy 32:1-43; Isaiah 29:13-24; Matthew 19:16-30; Mark 10:17-31; Luke 18:18-30

We are all on the same journey of knowing the Creator of the world, the God of Avraham, Yitzchak (Isaac), and Ya'akov (Jacob). We should love all and, in addition, fellowship on some level with all who serve the One True God, YHVH, blessed be His Name.

You will find anti-Christ Jews who love the Lord and eagerly look forward to the coming of the Anointed One as they understand Him. Beware of their foundationally flawed doctrines, but most certainly love them like older siblings who lack the revelation from His Spirit. Take note that they may even have a greater level of commitment to the Lord than you, and that speaks to their credit. Relationship with God is neither about historical knowledge nor the perception of privilege, but a heart of worship and a life of action, a life of love. We are all on the same journey of knowing the Creator of the world, the Alpha and the Omega, the Beginning and the End. We should love all and move the Jew to jealousy by our relationship with our Father and our obedience to His commandments (Romans 11:13-14).

Non-messianic Jews are not the only ones who may have relationship with HaShem outside the formal binding to His New Covenant. Sha'ul (Saul/Paulos/Paul) said:

> For when Gentiles who do not have the Torah, do instinctively what the Torah requires, then these, even though they don't have the Torah, for themselves are Torah! For their lives show that the conduct the Torah dictates is written in their hearts, their conscience also witnessing with them, while their thoughts bring accusation or even make defense among themselves in the Day of Judgment when, according to the Good News as I proclaim it, God, through the Messiah Yeshua, passes judgment on people's inmost secrets. (Romans 2:14-16)

Thus, I believe that when people who do not have the Anointed One, live instinctively as the Anointed One, their lives show that the Anointed One lives in them. There are those who are seeking Him and have not yet found Him, either because they live under an oppressive government or are surrounded by false representatives of the Anointed One. They are living the best relationship they can with Him while in ignorance of His written Word and His Anointed One, yet they are seeking knowledge of and intimacy and covenant relationship with Him. There are also others who turn away from Y'hoshua the Anointed One after knowing Him in their own attempt to find a different path to HaShem (The Name). The Scriptures clearly judge them:

> Anyone who has set aside the Torah of Moshe is put to death without mercy on the word of two or three witnesses. How much severer punishment do you think the one will be considered worthy who trampled underfoot the Son of God, and treated as common the blood of the covenant by which he was set apart, and also insulted the Spirit, giver of God's *chesed* [loving-kindness]. (Hebrews 10:28-29)

Y'hoshua, who is worthy of praise, is more than just the Jewish Anointed One . . . He is the Way, the Truth, and the Life (John 14:6).

My children, all intimate relationship involves struggle. Marriages and friendships that endured through several decades will testify to this fact. Growing to know the other is a struggle. Humbling oneself to the needs and desires of the other is a struggle. Love is a struggle because love encourages us to sacrifice ourselves for the gain and well-being of another, which grates against the selfish and self-centered inclinations of our sin nature, our flesh. Relationship with the Lord is a struggle because of our sin nature, not because of God.

I guarantee that you will encounter difficult times in your relationship with Yah, blessed be His Name. The trust of some will waver in the midst of tests. Do not be one of those who waver because life becomes difficult or because the elder or congregation disappoints or betrays you. Do not give up the greatest and hardest relationship because you lose someone dear to you. Do not lose trust because you have unanswered questions or because you may not understand. Do not lose heart because you feel alone. Do not give up the good fight because you want to die, persecution endangers and harms your life, or for any other reason. Shun the rocky soil.[300] Instead grow deep roots into the Lord through relationship with Him that is nurtured in daily prayer, meditation, fasting, fellowship, service, purpose . . . and focus and endurance.

My children, continue the struggle to draw near to the Lord even if you do not hear His voice. Anjezë Gonxhe Bojaxhiu, more widely known as Mother Teresa of Calcutta, did not hear from God for sixty years, yet she maintained faithfulness, enduring trust, in Him. Questions and doubt may arise—endure anyway. Challenges in your life and in your walk with God will come—persist anyway.

If you stand firm, persecution will come, but please never give up, never quit. He might take your mother and me, you might lose dear ones, but do not allow bitterness to corrupt your heart. Seek Him for comfort, for purpose, and for answers. Even if you do not receive a response, sustain in your walk with the Lord. No matter how difficult the Way, the struggle, the fight, the race, may be . . . persevere. Trust Him. Trust Him for salvation and Life. I so desire to enjoy eternity with you.

Obey His commandments and do good (Ecclesiastes 12:13). Never quit as you strive and struggle in your relationship with HaShem (The Name) with all your strength, energy, and resources. Keep Him your first love, your first focus, your first priority—always. Hate sin and the indulgence of the flesh, but never forget humility by ever thinking you are greater than others, greater than whatever group suffers the label of sinners.[301]

Do not seek persecution and pain and tests for their sake, but also do not fear them when they come. Know that persecution and pain will come if you stand with His Anointed One (Revelation 2:9-10), but He will be there to help you every step of the way (2 Corinthians 12:7-10). He will be with you even if the test means the death of your body.[302]

Maintain confession of your allegiance to the Anointed One and relationship with the Lord via the New Covenant, even upon the threat and event of execution and physical death. Maintain and nurture the follow-

---

300 Matthew 13:3-23; Mark 4:2-20; Luke 8:4-15
301 Romans 11:30-32; Revelation 2:2-6
302 Matthew 10:28; Acts 7:55-60; Hebrews 11:35-38

ing, all for God: love, loyalty, service, and endurance in your covenantal relationship.

Seek fanatic passion for righteous deeds of love gleaned from the Truth, and hold action above chasing theology and philosophy.[303] Seek and display the power and miracles that come from relationship with the Lord, which surpasses human cultures and ways, from God-given talents to gifts of His Spirit . . . from having respectful authority over Enemy spirits to love, trust, hope, long-suffering, boldness, and peace that transcends human understanding, summed up in—a changed heart.[304]

You can only know Him through relationship, not through doctrine. Doctrine might, and the Scriptures definitely will, teach you *about* Him, but you can only *know* Him through direct relationship. I knew Him and began my relationship with Him when I was six years old, after Nanay instructed me that the most important act of life was to daily pray to Him.

Throughout the years, I asked Him for help, and He obliged me. He helped me find dire things that I lost and thereby protected me from further instances of physical abuse. He gifted me with good weather despite stormy threats of cloudy mornings. He opened previously closed opportunities to enjoy time with Nanay and family, and even kept me safe in over twenty car accidents—three of which completely devastated the vehicle beyond repair.

He was my companion when no one else knew how alone I felt. At twelve years old, I rode my bicycle to Mass, the Roman service, with a 102-degree fever because I loved worshiping Him. I even attended the six o'clock Mass daily when I was in junior high school. I still love worshiping, albeit in different methods, the One who loves me most and cares most for my life.

When I was 18 or 19, and could not find Him in the midst of my congregation, I concluded that He did not abide in Christianity or Juda-

---

303 Deuteronomy 32:15-18; Hosea 6:7-9; Micah 3; Jeremiah 5:20-31; Ezekiel 22:23-31; Luke 14:1-6; James 2:14-24; Revelation 3:1-4

304 Genesis 42:18–Genesis 45:1-15; Psalm 51:10; Jeremiah 24:7; Ezekiel 11:19; 2 Corinthians 5:17; Romans 12:2; Revelation 3:8-11

ism. I sought Him in Buddhism, Hinduism, and Islam, but still could not find Him. He pointed me to His written Word despite my skepticism, and I found the greatest manual and treasure map of Truth. I warn you; it is encrypted. The decryption key is neither the convoluted philosophies of humanity nor the theologies of Jews and Christians. While scholarly work on culture and history has its rightful place, the decryption key is His Spirit.

Our relationship with Him should always be growing and maturing. Evaluate your relationship with Him every three to five years. If you have not grown in wisdom or righteousness, be *very* concerned. If you have not worked in your purpose, consider your spiritual health as ill. Stagnancy should raise alarm bells and give you a surge of adrenaline. You should have a sense of urgency to daily immerse yourself in hours of the Scriptures, prayer, and fasting. You will have low and high tides in activity and meditation throughout your life. Seasons are normal, but never let the low tides go too long. A year is too long. Be passionate in your relationship with God Almighty.[305]

Among other things, selfishly speaking, relationship with the Lord guarantees our reunion. He is life, and eternal life guarantees our reunification. "For we will surely die and are like water spilled on the ground which cannot be gathered up again. Yet God does not take away life, but plans ways so that the outcast is not cast out from Him" (2 Samuel 14:14). If we live according to His Way, we abide in Him.[306] If we are in Him, who is the Life, then we will continue to live.[307] If we continue to live, we will see each other again.

Nothing in this world compares to, is as beautiful, as difficult, as fulfilling, as purposeful, and as rewarding as nurturing a relationship with Yah, blessed be His Name. Nothing else in this world will offer you life in

---

305 Deuteronomy 6:4-5; Joshua 22:5; Matthew 22:35-40; Mark 12:28-34; Luke 10:25-28; John 14:15; Revelation 3:15-18

306 Deuteronomy 7:7-11; Deuteronomy 33:26-29; Psalm 15; Psalm 37:27-34; John 3:36; John 14:15; John 15:10; 1 Thessalonians 4:1-12; Romans 8:12-17; 1 John 3:24

307 Leviticus 18:4-5; Deuteronomy 4:1-2; Deuteronomy 5:31-33; Deuteronomy 8:1-2; Deuteronomy 30:6-20; Job 19:25-27; Psalm 49:1-15; Isaiah 26:19; Daniel 12:1-3; Matthew 22:29-32; 1 Thessalonians 4:13-18; Romans 14:7-9; 2 Corinthians 4:13-14

eternity. Only a relationship with HaShem (The Name) offers you eternal life. He revealed that relationship with Him is through His living and complete Word, His Word born flesh, His Anointed One, Y'hoshua, who is worthy of praise. Relationship with Him is the New Covenant. My children, if you faithfully endure in Him, we will all be re-united in His time. Know God by knowing His clearest revelation of Himself to humanity through His Word born flesh, Y'hoshua the Anointed One. Know HaShem through His written Word as taught through His Spirit.

Forgive me for all the ways in which I fall short. Forgive me of my mistakes, my weaknesses, and my selfishness. Please free yourself from any possible bitterness you may hold against me, and especially from any bitterness that you may hold toward the Lord if He takes me before you are ready. . .and before I am ready to let go of you.

This life is only temporary. It is not our Home. Our only Home is with Him. Yes, I will miss you dearly, but probably not as much as you will miss me simply because I will be engulfed in His presence; I am sure time does not pass in the same way in the spiritual realm as it does in the physical. Nevertheless, my heart will always be yearning for you until we reunite. Fight the good fight, my children. I am cheering for you to finish the race, right there along with Yah, blessed be His Name.

Should He take me soon, I look forward with excitement to seeing you again my sweet beloved children. . .in His time and as He wills.

I love you . . . period.

GLOSSARY

Angel/Apostle

- *Mal'ak* – sent-one (Strong's H4397)
- *Apostolos* – sent-one (Strong's G652)

Christ

- *Mashiyach* – Anointed One (Strong's H4899)
- *Christos* – Anointed One (Strong's G5547)

Church

- *Kahal* – assembly (H6951)
- *Ekklesia* – assembly (G1577)

Disciple

- *Talmid* – scholar, disciple, taught (Strong's H8527)
- *Matheiteis* – learner, student, disciple (Strong's G3101)

Gospel

- *Basar* (v) – to announce good news (Strong's H1319)
- *Euangelizo* (v) – to announce good news (Strong's G2097)
- *Besorah* (n) – gospel, good news (Strong's H1309)
- *Euangelion* (n) – gospel, good news (Strong's G2098)

Grace

- *Chanan* (v) – to be gracious, to give grace/mercy (Strong's H2603)

- *Chein* (n) – favor, grace, favorable (Strong's H2580)
- *Chesed* (n) – loving-kindness (Strong's H2617)
- *Charis* (n) – grace, mercy (Strong's G5485)

Faith

- *Emunah* – faith – firmness, fidelity, steadfastness (Strong's H530)
- *Aman* – to believe – to trust (H539)
- *Pistis* – faith – belief, fidelity, faithfulness (Strong's G4102)
- *Pisteuo* – to believe – to trust (G4100)

Hosanna

- *Hoshana*
- *Yasha* – to save, be saved, be delivered (H3467)
- *Na* – I/we pray, now, please (Strong's H4994)
- *Hosana* – please save us now (Strong's G5614)

Law

- *Torah* – Instruction (Strong's H8451)
- *Nomos* – Law (Strong's G3551)

New Moon

- *Chodesh* – New Moon (Strong's H2320)
- *Neomenia* – New Moon (Strong's G3561)

Pharisees

- *P'rushim* – Pharisees – Separated Ones (not in Scripture until New Testament)
- *Pharisaios* – Pharisees – Separated Ones (Strong's G5330)

Master

- *Rav* – great/many, implies great one, leader, master (Strong's H7229)
- *Rabi* – great one (Strong's G4461)

Peace

- *Shalom* – peace (Strong's H7965)
- *Eirene* – peace (Strong's G1515)

Pentecost

- *Shavu'ot* – Weeks – 7 weeks (Strong's H7620)
- *Pentakosta* – Pentecost – 50th day (Strong's G4005)

Righteousness

- *Tsadak* – to be righteous, to declare as righteous, to justify (Strong's H6663)
- *Dikaiosis* – judgment in reference to what is just, being declared righteous, justification (Strong's G1347)
- *Dikaioo* – to make/declare as righteous, to justify (Strong's G1344)
- *Tsedek* – technically means straightness, but translated as righteousness (Strong's H6664)
- *Tsedakah* – that which is right (Strong's H6666)
- *Dikaioma* – what has been established by the Law, being declared righteous, justification (Strong's G1345)
- *Dikaiosynei* – virtuous and the condition acceptable to God (Strong's G1343)

Sabbath

- *Shabbat* – Rest (Strong's H7676)
- *Sabbaton* – Sabbath – Rest (Strong's G4521)

Sadducees

- *Tzadikim* – Sadducees – Righteous Ones – of Tzadok, student of Antigonus of Sokho (Strong's H6662)
- *Saddoukaios* – Sadducees – Righteous Ones (Strong's G4523)

Sin

- *Chata'ath* (n), *Chata* (v) – sin, miss the Way (Strong's H2403, H2398)

- *Hamartia* (n), *Hamartano* (v) – sin, miss the Mark (Strong's G266, G264)

WORKS CITED

Ali, Ayaan Hirsi. "Why They Deny the Holocaust," *Los Angeles Times*, 16 December 2006. Available at https://www.latimes.com/news/la-oe-ali16dec16-story.html

Anderson, Karla O. *Did God Forsake Jesus on the Cross?* Xulon Press, 2013.

Bard, Mitchell G. "The Written Law – Torah." *Jewish Virtual Library*. N.P. 1988. Web. 13 August 2015. https://www.jewishvirtuallibrary.org/jsource/Judaism/The_Written_Law.html

Barry, A. S. with J. D. "Enoch, Books of." In J. D. Barry, D. Bomar, D. R. Brown, R. Klippenstein, D. Mangum, C. Sinclair Wolcott, . . . W. Widder (Eds.), *The Lexham Bible Dictionary*. Bellingham, WA: Lexham Press. 2012, 2013, 2014, 2015.

Barry, John D. "Psalms as Seasons." *Bible Study Magazine*. 28 May 2015.

"Bava Metzia 59b." *Sefaria*. N.P. Web. 20 August 2015. http://www.sefaria.org/Bava_Metzia.59b?lang=en&layout=block&sidebarLang=all

Ben Ya'ocov, Yehoiakin-Barukh. *Book of the Shining Path*. New York: NY, Page Publishing, 2014.

Bergsma, John S. "The Jubilee from Leviticus to Qumran: A History of Interpretation." *Vetus Testamentum Supplements Series*. Vol. 115. Leiden: Brill Academic Publishers, Inc., 2006. 277-290.

Block, D. I. Pentateuch. In C. Brand, C. Draper, A. England, S. Bond, E. R. Clendenen, & T. C. Butler (Eds.), *Holman Illustrated Bible*

Dictionary (p. 1265). Nashville, TN: Holman Bible Publishers. 2003.

Botkin, Daniel. "Linguistic Superstition and the Sacred Name Only Movement." *The Simple Truth*. N.P. 20 November 2015. http://www.thesimpletruth.net/booklet/sno.html

Cathcart, K., Maher, M., & McNamara, M. (Eds.). *The Aramaic Bible: The Isaiah Targum*. (B. D. Chilton, Trans.) (Vol. 11, Is 11: 1-4). Collegeville, MN: The Liturgical Press. 1990.

Chapman, Gary. *The 5 Love Languages*. Chicago: Northfield, 2015.

"Communion." *Merriam-Webster*. Merriam-Webster, 2015. Web. 31 August 2015. http://www.merriam-webster.com/dictionary/communion

Copan, Victor A. "Μαθητής and Μιμητής: Exploring an Entangled Relationship." *Bulletin for Biblical Research*, Vol. 17 (2007): 320.

Cross, F.L., & Livingstone, E. A. (Eds.). *In The Oxford Dictionary of the Christian Church* (3rd ed. Rev., p. 1652-1653). Oxford; New York: Oxford University Press. 2005.

Deffinbaugh, Robert L. "Discipleship: Its Definitions and Dangers (Matthew 23:1-12)." *Bible.org*. 1 June 2004. Bible.org. 5 November 2015. https://bible.org/seriespage/15-discipleship-its-definitions-and-dangers-matthew-231-12

Dempster, S. "From Many Texts to One: The Formation of the Hebrew Bible." In P. M. M. Daviau, J. W. Wevers, and M. Weigl (Eds.), *The World of the Aramaeans I: Biblical Studies in Honour of Paul-Eugène Dion* (Vol. 324, p. 22). Sheffield: Sheffield Academic Press. 2001.

Duffield, Guy P., and Nathaniel M. Van Cleave. *Foundations of Pentecostal Theology*. Los Angeles, CA: L.I.F.E. Bible College, 1983.

Ellens, J. H. *Sophia in Rabbinic Hermeneutics and the Curious Christian Corollary*. (J. Krasovec, Ed.) (Vol. 289, p. 537). Sheffield: Sheffield Academic Press. 1998.

Elwell, Walter A., and Barry J. Beitzel. *Baker Encyclopedia of the Bible* 1988: 531 – 536.

Elwell, W. A., & Elwell, W. A. In *Evangelical dictionary of Biblical Theology* (electronic ed.). Grand Rapids: Baker Book House. 1996.

Estes, D. "Logos." In J. D. Barry, L. Wentz, D. Mangum, C. Sinclair-Wolcott, R. Klippenstein, D. Bomar, . . . D. R. Brown (Eds.), *The Lexham Bible Dictionary*. Bellingham, WA: Lexham Press. 2012, 2013, 2014.

"Etymological Origin of the Week Days." *Aula Hispanica*. N.P. Web. 6 May 2016. http://www.aulahispanica.com/node/187

Fortescue, Adrian. "Liturgy." *The Catholic Encyclopedia*. Vol. 9. New York: Robert Appleton Company, 1910. 16 September 2015. http://www.newadvent.org/cathen/09306a.htm

Geisler, Norman L. *Baker Encyclopedia of Christian Apologetics 1999: 95*. Baker Reference Library.

"Global Christianity – A Report on the Size and Distribution of the World's Christian Population." *Pew Research Center*. The Pew Charitable Trusts, 18 December 2011. Web. 27 August 2015. http://www.pewforum.org/2011/12/19/global-christianity-exec/

Gordon, Cyrus H. "Almah in Isaiah 7:14." *Journal of the American Academy of Religion* (Vol. 21, Issue 2, p. 106). Oxford University Press. April 1953.

Gordon, Nehemia. "The Hebrew Yeshua vs. the Greek Jesus." *YouTube*. Hilkiah Press, 2005. Web. 20 August 2015. https://www.youtube.com/watch?v=tddCNY6U77Y

Gritsch, E.W. "Was Luther Anti-Semitic?" *Christian History Magazine-Issue 39: Martin Luther: The Later Years*. 1993.

"Halakhah: The Laws of Jewish Life." *My Jewish Learning*. N.P. Web. 16 September 2015. http://www.myjewishlearning.com/article/halakhah-the-laws-of-jewish-life/#

Harper, Douglas. "Church." *Online Etymology Dictionary*. N.P. Web. 12 August 2015. http://www.etymonline.com/index.php?term=church

Harper, Douglas. "Communion." *Online Etymology Dictionary*. N.P. Web. 31 August 2015. http://www.etymonline.com/index.php?term=communion

"Has Everyone Heard." *Joshua Project*. Frontier Ventures. Web. 3 May 2016. https://joshuaproject.net/resources/articles/has_everyone_heard

Hiehle, J. A., & Whitcomb, K. A. "Enoch, First Book of." In J. D. Barry, D. Bomar, D. R. Brown, R. Klippenstein, D. Mangum, C. Sinclair Wolcott, . . . W. Widder (Eds.), *The Lexham Bible Dictionary*. Bellingham, WA: Lexham Press. 2012, 2013, 2014, 2015.

Ignatius of Antioch. "The Epistle of Ignatius to the Magnesians." In A. Roberts, J. Donaldson, & A. C. Coxe (Eds.), *The Apostolic Fathers with Justin Martyr and Irenaeus* (Vol. 1, pp. 62-63). Buffalo, NY: Christian Literature Company. 1885.

Jewish Publication Society. *Tanakh: The Holy Scriptures*. Philadelphia: Jewish Publication Society, 1985.

Kaiser Jr., Walter C. "How Has Archaeology Corroborated the Bible?" *The Apologetics Study Bible: Real Questions, Straight Answers, Stronger Faith*. Ed. Ted Cabal et al. Nashville, TN: Holman Bible Publishers, 2007. 1148-1149.

Keener, C. S. *The Gospel of John: A Commentary & 2* (Vol. 1, p. 351-380). Grand Rapids, MI: Baker Academic. 2012.

Keener, Craig S. *The Gospel of Matthew: A Socio-Rhetorical Commentary*. Grand Rapids, MI; Cambridge, U.K.: Wm. B. Eerdmans Publishing Co., 2009.

"Ketuvim (Writings)." *My Jewish Learning*. N.P. Web. 9 August 2015. http://www.myjewishlearning.com/article/ketuvim-writings/

Kimmel, Dan. "My D'var Torah." *Soc.culture.jewish.moderated*. Narkive. com, 5 August 2006. Web. 13 August 2015. http://soc.culture. jewish.moderated.narkive.com/xWUxxl5t/my-d-var-torah

Kittel, G., Bromiley, G. W., & Friedrich, G. (Eds.). *Theological Dictionary of the New Testament* (electronic ed., Vol. 4, p. 135). Grand Rapids, MI: Eerdmans. 1964.

Klippenstein, Rachel. "Names of God in the Old Testament." Ed. John D. Barry et al. *The Lexham Bible Dictionary*. 2012, 2013, 2014, 2015: n. pag.

Kohler, Kaufmann. "MEMRA." *JewishEncyclopedia.com*. N.P. Web. 30 July 2015. http://www.jewishencyclopedia.com/ articles/10618-memra

Lea, T. D., & Black, D. A. *The New Testament: It's Background and*

Message (2nd ed., p. 516). Nashville, TN: Broadman & Holman Publishers. 2003.

Leap, Dennis. "Archaeology Proves Bible History Accurate." *The Trumpet.com*, Vol. 16, No. 10. Philadelphia Church of God, December 2005. Web. 16 November 2015.

Lewis, C. S. "Mere Christianity." *The Complete C. S. Lewis Signature Classics*. New York: HarperCollins, 2002. 36.

Manning, David. "'That Is Best, Which Was First': Christian Primitivism and the Reformation Church of England, 1548 – 1722." *Reformation & Renaissance Review*. Spec. issue of *The Church of England as "Primitive Christianity Restored?"* 13.2 (2011): 153-193. Web. 18 August 2015.

Manor, Dale. "The Bible and Archaeology." *Old Testament Introduction*. Ed. Terry Briley, Paul Kissling, and Mark Mangano. Joplin, MO: College Press Pub., 2005. 78-80. Print. The College Press NIV Commentary.

Mish, F. C. "Preface." *Merriam-Webster's Collegiate Dictionary*. (Eleventh ed.). Springfield, MA: Merriam-Webster, Inc. 2003.

Mitchell, David C. "Rabbi Dosa and the Rabbis Differ: Messiah Ben Joseph in the Babylonian Talmud." *Review of Rabbinic Judaism Series*. Ed. Alan Avery-Peck. Vol. 8. Leiden: Brill Academic Publishers, Inc., 2005. 79-84.

Moss, Aron. "Why Is Jewishness Passed Down Through the Mother?" *Chabad.org*. Chabad Lubavitch Media Center. Web. 16 September 2015. http://www.chabad.org/theJewishWoman/article_cdo/aid/968282/jewish/Why-Is-Jewishness-Passed-Down-Through-the-Mother.htm

Murphy, F.J. *Early Judaism: The Exile to the Time of Jesus*. Grand Rapids, MI: Baker Academic. 2010.

The Navigators. "How to Spend Extended Time in Prayer." *Navigators.org*. The Navigators. 14 March 2006. Web. 28 October 2015. http://www.navigators.org/About-Us/Stories/Navigator%20Stories/March%202006/How%20to%20Spend%20Extended%20Time%20in%20Prayer

Nelte, Frank W. "The Timing of the Barley Harves in Israel." *Franknelte. net.* N.P. 9 November 2015. http://www.franknelte.net/article. php?article_id=43

Odor, J. A. "Enoch, Third Book of." In J. D. Barry, D. Bomar, D. R. Brown, R. Klippenstein, D. Mangum, C. Sinclair Wolcott, . . . W. Widder (Eds.), *The Lexham Bible Dictionary.* Bellingham, WA: Lexham Press. 2012, 2013, 2014, 2015.

"Orthodoxy." *Merriam-Webster.* Merriam-Webster, 2015. Web. 11 August, 2015. http://www.merriam-webster.com/dictionary/ orthodoxy

"Parthenos." *Dictionary.com.* Harper Collins, 2015. Web. 20 August, 2015. http://content.dictionary.com/

Piper, John. "All Authority in Heaven and Earth." *Desiring God.* 8 October 2015. Web. 31 May 2016. http://www.desiringgod.org/ messages/all-authority-in-heaven-and-earth

Powell, D. *Holman QuickSource Guide to Christian Apologetics* (p. 185). Nashville, TN: Holman Reference. 2006.

Ray, Steve. "Should Catholics Go to Non-Denominational Bible Studies?" *Catholic Answers Magazine.* Volume 18, Number 1. Catholic Answers: January 2007. Web. 3 May 2016. http://www.catholic.com/magazine/articles/ should-catholics-go-to-non-denominational-bible-studies

Rich, Tracey R. "The Name of G-d." *Judaism 101.* N.P. Web. 21 July, 2015. http://www.jewfaq.org/name.htm

Roberts, R. D. "Pentecost." In J. D. Barry, D. Bomar, D. R. Brown, R. Klippenstein, D. Mangum, C. Sinclair Wolcott, . . . W. Widder (Eds.), *The Lexham Bible Dictionary.* Bellingham, WA: Lexham Press. 2012, 2013, 2014, 2015.

Rose, Or N. "Heaven and Hell in Jewish Tradition." *MyJewishLearning.* 70FacesMedia.org. Web. 28 April 2016. http://www.myjewishlearn- ing.com/article/heaven-and-hell-in-jewish-tradition/

Ross, A. P. *Holiness to the Lord: A Guide to the Exposition of the Book of Leviticus* (p. 64). Grand Rapids, MI: Baker Academic. 2002.

Schofield, A. "Dead Sea Scrolls, Biblical." In J. D. Barry, D. Bomar, D.

R. Brown, R. Klippenstein, D. Mangum, C. Sinclair Wolcot, . . .
W. Widder (Eds.), *The Lexham Bible Dictionary*. Bellingham, WA:
Lexham Press. 2012, 2013, 2014, 2015.

Shapiro, Debbie. "From Jesus to Judaism." *Aish.com*. N.P. 22 May 2010.
Web. 18 November 2015. http://www.aish.com/sp/so/93663419.
html

Simmons, Shraga. "Why Jews Don't Believe in Jesus." *Aish.com*. N.P.
6 March, 2004. Web. 28 July, 2015. <http://www.aish.com/
jw/s/48892792.html>.

Singer, I. (Ed.). In *The Jewish Encyclopedia: A Descriptive Record of the
History, Religion, Literature, and Customs of the Jewish People from the
Earliest Times to the Present Day*, 12 Volumes (Vol. 5, p. 589). New
York; London: Funk & Wagnalls. 1901-1906.

Singer, I. (Ed.). In *The Jewish Encyclopedia: A Descriptive Record of the
History, Religion, Literature, and Customs of the Jewish People from the
Earliest Times to the Present Day*, 12 Volumes (Vol. 8, p. 511-519).
New York; London: Funk & Wagnalls. 1901-1906.

Singer, I. (Ed.). In *The Jewish Encyclopedia: A Descriptive Record of the
History, Religion, Literature, and Customs of the Jewish People from the
Earliest Times to the Present Day*, 12 Volumes (Vol. 9, p. 405). New
York; London: Funk & Wagnalls. 1901-1906.

Singer, I. (Ed.). *In The Jewish Encyclopedia: A Descriptive Record of the
History, Religion, Literature, and Customs of the Jewish People from the
Earliest Times to the Present Day*, 12 Volumes (Vol. 10, p. 604). New
York; London: Funk & Wagnalls. 1901-1906.

Slick, Matt. "What Are Some Signs and Practices of a Cult?" *Christian
Apologetics & Research Ministry*. N.P. 24 November 2015. https://
carm.org/signs-practices-of-a-cult

Slick, Matt. "Why Do Bibles Use 'LORD' Instead of
YHWH or Jehovah?" *Christian Apologetics & Research
Ministry*. N.P. Web. 21 July 2015. https://carm.org/
why-do-bibles-use-lord-instead-yhwh-or-jehovah

Soanes, C., & Stevenson, A. (Eds.). (2004). *Concise Oxford English
dictionary* (11th ed.). Oxford: Oxford University Press.

SparkNotes Editors. "SparkNotes on The Kaballah." *SparkNotes.com.* SparkNotes LLC, 2005. Web. 9 September 2015. http://www. sparknotes.com/philosophy/kabbalah/section1.rhtml

"Statistics." *Jewish Israel.* Ning, 2016. Web. 28 April 2016. http:// jewishisrael.ning.com/page/statistics-1

Stone, Barton W. *An Address to the Christian Churches in Kentucky, Tenessee, & Ohio on Several Important Doctrines of Religion.* Lexington, KY: I. T. Cavins, 1821. 31-32.

Stuart, D. "Review of Parallelism in Early Biblical Poetry, by Stephen A. Geller." *Journal of Biblical Literature*, 100, 272. 1981.

Tarán, Leonardo. *Speusippus of Athens.* Leiden: E. J. Brill, 1981.

Thornhill, A. C. "Enoch, Second Book of." In J. D. Barry, D. Bomar, D. R. Brown, R. Klippenstein, D. Mangum, C. Sinclair Wolcott, . . . W. Widder (Eds.), *The Lexham Bible Dictionary.* Bellingham, WA: Lexham Press. 2012, 2013, 2014, 2015.

Tirosh-Samuelson, H. "Review of Textual Reasonings: Jewish Philosophy and Text Study at the End of the Twentieth-Century Edited by Ochs, Peter and Nancy Levene." *Review of Biblical Literature: 2004.* 2004.

"Torah – Definition." *Torah Resources International.* Shoreshim Publishing, Inc. Web. 13 August 2015. http://www. torahresourcesinternational.info/definition.php

Wallace, Daniel B. "Dr. Wallace: Earliest Manuscript of the New Testament Discovered?" *Dallas Theological Seminary (DTS) – Teach Truth. Love Well.* N.P. Web. 6 August 2015 http://www.dts.edu/ read/wallace-new-testament-manscript-first-century/

Webber, R. *The Sacred Actions of Christian Worship* (Vol. 6, p. 251). Nashville, TN: Star Song Pub. Group. 1994.

Webber, R. *The Services of the Christian Year* (Vol. 5, pp. 5-42). Nashville, TN: Star Song Pub. Group. 1994.

Wilson, Clifford A. Interview with Carl Wieland. "Archaeology Confirms Creation and the Bible." *Creation.* September 1992: 46-50.

Witthoff, D. (Ed.). In *The Lexham Cultural Ontology Glossary.* Bellingham, WA: Lexham Press. 2014.

Young, Brad H. *Meet the Rabbis: Rabbinic Thought and the Teachings of Jesus.* Peabody, MA: Hendrickson Publishers, 2007.

Zecher, H. "The Bible Translation that Rocked the World." *Christian History Magazine-Issue 34: Martin Luther: The Reformer's Early Years.* 1992.

ABOUT THE AUTHOR

R. H. Ben-Shalom is a Filipino Ashkenazi Jew, raised Roman Catholic. Parental upbringing brought him to the throne of the divine, but child abuse pushed him into the arms of God. Needing to find the answers for himself when religious leaders could not answer his childhood questions of the Nephilim, he researched the major religions and concluded the truth was somewhere else; it was in the Bible.

He now seeks answers to new questions through ancient religious texts, meditation, cultural and historical insights, and scholarly works, while refining his understanding through dialogue with respected elders.

Surviving his grandparents, parents, and six siblings, the impermanence of earthly life became very real. Ben-Shalom felt the need to pass a legacy of his understanding and testimony down to his children concerning the greatest import of life: God.

He lives in Texas with his family.

CAN YOU HELP?

Thank you for reading my book!

I very much appreciate all your constructive feedback,
and I love hearing what you have to say.

I need your input to make my future books better.

Please leave an honest review on Amazon to
let me know what you thought of the book.

Thank you so much!

R. H. Ben-Shalom

INDEX

Eusebius Sophronius Hieronymus (Jerome), 46, 61

Evangelicals, 71, 142

evolution and creation, balancing views on, 152–53

F

First Enoch, 79–81, 82

First Fruits of Zion group, 73

Fortescue, Adrian, 59–60

G

Geisler, Norman L., 150

Geller, Stephen A., 39

Gematria, warning against, 84, 173

Glueck, Nelson, 109, 150

Gordon, Cyrus H., 117

Gordon, Nehemia, 126–27

grace (loving-kindness), 8, 39–41, 63, 66, 94, 106, 172

Great Ejection, 69, 70, 74

Great Schism, 68, 69, 70

Gregory of Nazianzus, 45, 57, 61

Gregory the Great, 46, 61

Grenfeld, Francis W., 156

H

halachic debates, 36

HaOlam Haba (World to Come), 89

HaShem, 134

    commandments of, Gentiles ignoring, 190

    commandments of, Gentiles sincerely obeying, 163, 190

    commandments of, Gentiles striving to obey like Jews, 73

    daily conference/communion with, 173

    Elohim, using term in reference to, 19

    Enoch texts, not viewed as inspired by, 80

    gift of food, giving blessing to HaShem for, 61

    identity of, not Scripturally linked with doctrine of Trinity, 34, 36

    as infinite, 43

    liturgy, worship of HaShem through, 65

S'firot, as symbolized by, 44, 178
Kaiser, Walter C., Jr., 157
Karaite Jews, 126–27, 162
Keener, John, 78–80
Ketuvim (Writings), 100
Kimmel, Dan, 104
Kittel, Gerhard, 85
Klippenstein, Rachel, 29
Knox, John, 46, 57, 62
Kohler, Kaufmann, 84
korbanot (offerings), 92–96
Krahmalkov, Charles, 156

L

Lachish Ostraca pottery fragments, 154
Lancaster, D. Thomas, 190
Law of Return policy, 189
Lea, Thomas D., 66
Leap, Dennis, 150, 154
Lewis, Clive Staples, 47, 90, 158–59, 167, 184
liturgy, 54, 58–59, 62–63, 64–66
Lord of the Rings (Tolkien), 159
loyalty, maintaining right relationship with, 185–86
Luke, Gospel of, 35–36, 58, 99, 107–8
Luther, Martin, 26–27, 46, 62, 63, 66
Lutherans, 61, 62, 64, 65, 73

M

Maimonides (Moshe ben Maimon), 17, 18, 35, 55
mainstream Christianity, cautions regarding, 172, 189–90
Malki-Tzedek (Melchizedek), 88, 91–92, 95–96, 111–13, 129, 147
Manning, David, 69
Manor, Dale, 152
Mark, Gospel of, 107–8
Matthew, Gospel of, 6, 107–8, 179
    authority of Jesus, highlighting, 20
    gift of food, blessing HaShem for, 61

nomos (law), 77–78, 85
non-denominational congregations, 53
non-messianic Jews, advice on treating, 187–88
non-messianic Jews, concerns with theology, 143–45, 161–67

O

Odor, Judith A., 81
Old Testament, 7, 10, 30, 81, 150. *See also* Instruction and the Prophets
On the Jews and Their Lies (Luther), 27
Onkelos, 84–85
Orthodox Jewish Bible (OJB), 7, 82
orthodoxy
 of the apostles, 75, 180
 defining, 56–57
 Gentile Christian orthodoxy, 53–54, 74
 Orthodox Jews, 139
 "orthodoxy of the faith" argument, 58, 62–63
 Proto-Orthodox Christianity, 21
 topic, categorizing orthodoxy by, 66
 See also Eastern Orthodox faith
Osey HaTorah (Essenes), 19, 22

P

paganism
 Christmas, pagan roots of, 72
 doctrine of the Trinity, influence on, 36, 134
 Gentile Christianity, pagan influence on, 35, 67, 180
 lingering traditions of, advice to beware, 66, 183
 pagan philosophy, disregarding, 43, 179
Passover Lamb, 161, 162
Patrick, Simon, 68
Paul, Apostle. *See* Sha'ul, Apostle
Pentateuch (Five Scrolls), 76–77
Pentecost, 19, 121
Pentecostals, 51, 62, 70
Pharisees (Separated Ones). *See* P'rushim
Philippos, Apostle, 98

written Word of God, four ways to interpret, 137–38, 162

Wycliffe, John, 46, 57, 62, 63

Y

Ya'akov (Jacob), 28, 94–95, 134–35, 147

Yechezkel (Ezekiel), 81

Yehoshua, Avram, 73

Yeshayah (Isaiah), 16, 38, 39, 81, 111, 145, 164
  Isaiah 7:14, clarifying, 115–17
  Isaiah 53, examination of, 118–22, 125, 161, 162

Y'hochanan (John, Apostle), 23, 38, 79, 114, 180

Y'hochanan the Immerser (John the Baptist), 35, 88, 94, 96, 145

Y'hoshua the Anointed One (Jesus the Christ), 9, 20, 130
  anointment of, 87–88
  David, as descended from, 136–37, 147
  as the firstborn, 106–7
  halachic stance, 131, 132
  historical evidence of existence, 158–59
  Isaiah 53 as prophesizing on, 118–21
  as the Last Adam, 88, 89, 123–24
  Malki-Tzedek, link with, 111–13, 129
  non-messianic Jewish rejection of, 140, 147
  Psalms, prophecies in text as linked to, 100, 104–5
  return of as drawing near, 180
  as the Son of God, 88–90, 110
  virgin birth, 88, 114, 115–17

Y'hudah the betrayer (Judas, Apostle), 11, 117

Yitzchak (Isaac), 5, 94

Young's Literal Translation (YLT), 7

Z

Zealots, sect of, 19, 22, 89

Zecher, Henry, 26

Zohar, Books of, 73, 74, 83

Zoroastrianism, 108, 167, 168

Made in the USA
Columbia, SC
28 June 2021